CHARLES BRANDON
The King's Man

SARAH BRYSON

For Peter and Ellie
xx

Charles Brandon
The King's Man

M
MadeGlobal Publishing

For more information on
MadeGlobal Publishing, visit our website:
www.madeglobal.com

Cover image: detail from an etching of the wedding portrait of Charles Brandon and Mary Tudor from *Henry VIII*. Coloured by T. Ridgway.

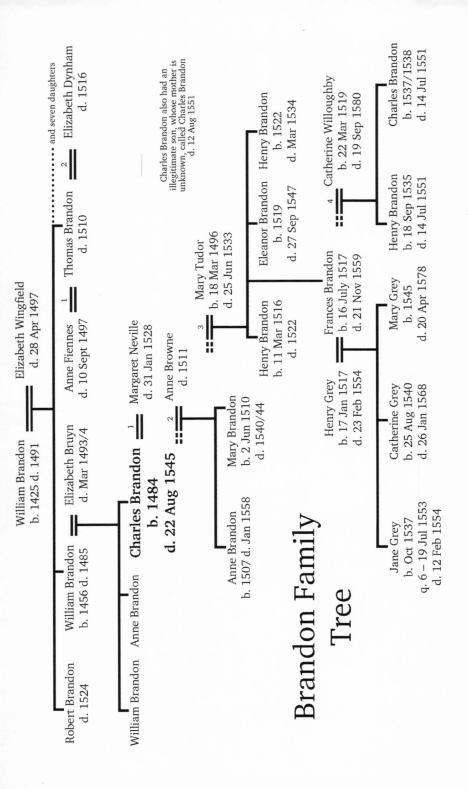

Brandon Family Tree

William Brandon
b. 1425 d. 1491
═══ Elizabeth Wingfield
d. 28 Apr 1497

Anne Fiennes
d. 10 Sept 1497
═══¹ Thomas Brandon
d. 1510
═══² Elizabeth Dynham
d. 1516

········ and seven daughters

Robert Brandon
d. 1524

William Brandon
b. 1456 d. 1485
═══ Elizabeth Bruyn
d. Mar 1493/4

William Brandon   Anne Brandon

Charles Brandon
b. 1484
d. 22 Aug 1545
═══¹ Margaret Neville
d. 31 Jan 1528

═══² Anne Browne
d. 1511

Anne Brandon
b. 1507 d. Jan 1558

Mary Brandon
b. 2 Jun 1510
d. 1540/44

═══³ Mary Tudor
b. 18 Mar 1496
d. 25 Jun 1533

Henry Brandon
b. 11 Mar 1516
d. 1522

Eleanor Brandon
b. 1519
d. 27 Sep 1547

Henry Brandon
b. 1522
d. Mar 1534

═══⁴ Catherine Willoughby
b. 22 Mar 1519
d. 19 Sep 1580

Henry Brandon
b. 18 Sep 1535
d. 14 Jul 1551

Charles Brandon
b. 1537/1538
d. 14 Jul 1551

Frances Brandon
b. 16 July 1517
d. 21 Nov 1559
═══ Henry Grey
b. 17 Jan 1517
d. 23 Feb 1554

Jane Grey
b. Oct 1537
q. 6 – 19 Jul 1553
d. 12 Feb 1554

Catherine Grey
b. 25 Aug 1540
d. 26 Jan 1568

Mary Grey
b. 1545
d. 20 Apr 1578

Charles Brandon also had an
illegitimate son, whose mother is
unknown, called Charles Brandon
d. 12 Aug 1551

Contents

Foreword

In my early twenties I fell in love with Tudor history, specifically the reign of Henry VIII. You can be guaranteed that there will always be a book by my bedside table having something to do with Henry VIII or the events of his reign. Through reading about the second Tudor king I came across a fascinating man who went by the name of Charles Brandon. I discovered that Brandon was a man who was born into humble beginnings yet rose through the ranks to become not just a duke and one of the leading magnates in Lincolnshire, but also, and perhaps more importantly, one of Henry VIII's most beloved friends.

Who was this man? How did this friendship with Henry VIII form? How did he achieve such great prominence in so short a period of time? I had to know more. Luckily for us in modern times there is a large number of letters written by Charles Brandon, or letters written about Brandon during his life, that still survive today. My first challenge was to get my hands on these letters. I wanted to examine them, to look deeper to gain a greater understanding of not just what this man did but who he was. I needed to find out what he thought, what he felt, what his desires and dreams were. I wanted to gain an understanding of Brandon the man and not just the courtier who is mentioned from time to time in books about the life of Henry VIII. Once I started researching Brandon's life I simply could not stop, I was hooked and thus this book was born.

I want to take a moment to thank some people who have helped me along my journey, from my very first ideas about researching Brandon's life right through to the final, published product. First and foremost I must thank my husband Peter for his never-ending love and support, and for putting up with the countless hours I have spent lost in books or research papers. (And also I must apologise for the multiple times that he tripped over my huge pile of research books that I continuously left scattered all over the floor.) To my beautiful daughter Ellie, for all her cuddles and kisses, which were invaluable while I was writing.

I must thank my mum for passing on to me her love and passion for reading, research and history.

I would also like to give a very big thank you to Claire and Tim Ridgway for having faith in me and for putting up with my constant questions. I thank them for all their help tracking down letters and references that seemed near impossible to find. Their ongoing encouragement and support is the main reason I was able to finish this book and to them I will be forever grateful.

To my amazing best friends I must thank you for postponing coffee dates so I could focus on my writing, and for always being willing to listen while I happily discuss Brandon's life.

Heartfelt thanks go to Dr Steven Gunn and Dr Josephine Wilkinson for all their advice, support and encouragement, as well as to my amazing online Tudor friends, who are far too many to mention but know who you are, so thank you for your constant encouragement and support.

Charles Brandon was a fascinating man. He has become deeply entrenched in my own life and I have enjoyed every moment researching and exploring his life.

Sarah Bryson

October 2015

List of Illustrations

Introduction

Charles Brandon was an enigmatic, charismatic man, rising from a mere boyhood friend of a future king to flirting with a European duchess, marrying the Dowager Queen of France, being created a Duke of Suffolk, and not to mention becoming the leading magnate in Lincolnshire by the end of his life. How did this man, whose father died at the Battle of Bosworth, rise to such heights and manage to stay both loyal and close friends with the ever-changing, sometimes tyrannical King Henry VIII? It has been suggested that Brandon's achievements at court were wholly due to his father, Sir William Brandon. While his father's death defending the first Tudor king certainly set Brandon upon the track to success, I would argue that it was the future duke's own talents, skills, wit and abilities that kept him in favour throughout his life.

It has also been claimed that the only way Charles Brandon was able to stay in favour at court was by letting King Henry VIII win at jousting. It is true that Brandon was one of the best, if not the best jousters during the reign of Henry VIII. He was tall, well-built and powerful, and had all the abilities to joust with great talent and skill. He was able to beat his opponents and yet, interestingly, he always seemed to lose to the king. Because of this it has been asserted that jousting was the only thing that Brandon was good at and, thus, he used this talent to keep within his king's good books.

Charles Brandon was clearly a clever man. He did all the leg-work when it came to jousting. He beat everyone and then let the king beat him, essentially making the king the best jouster in the land without the king having to do any heavy work. But the question remains, was this Brandon's only skill, or was there more to this man than just being a brilliant jouster?

Through carefully studying Brandon's life, his decisions and actions when it came to war, to expanding his estates, to marriage and, of course, his reactions towards his king, it has become clear that it was far more than just his jousting talents that kept him as one of the leading courtiers during Henry VIII's reign.

Clearly, Brandon knew how to play his cards well. He became close friends with Henry VIII, sharing many interests with the king, including hunting, hawking and the courtly fashion of wooing lavish and beautiful ladies. Charles was an incredibly smart man. He knew what to say to please the king, when he had to comply with his king's wishes, and when he could push the boundaries. Brandon knew Henry VIII, he knew not just the king but the man underneath, and it was this knowledge, this skill that kept him in favour.

I argue that it was not simply his skill in jousting that kept Charles Brandon in favour and helped him avoid the great trials and tribulations at court, but his ability to read the temperamental king, his skill in responding appropriately and, most of all, always being loyal and faithful in an ever-changing court until his death.

It is no secret that Charles Brandon always seemed to walk a fine line. Born into relative obscurity in 1484, not even his exact birth date was recorded.

Brandon would often overstep what was considered acceptable for the age. He married a woman almost twice his age only to take her money and have the marriage annulled before returning to his first wife, with whom he had two daughters. He flirted with a European duchess to the astonishment of all those around, except King Henry VIII, who tried to convince the duchess to marry Brandon. He then went on to marry Henry VIII's younger sister Mary without the king's permission – an act considered treason at the time.

He spoke out against the king's marriage to his second wife Anne Boleyn. Not only did he survive, but he went on to have a successful court and military career and died one of the king's most beloved and dearest friends. Why? Because of the great and lasting friendship that he had formed with the king when they were younger and because of Brandon's ability to read the king, to inflate his ego and to know what to say and when to say it. No matter his personal thoughts and beliefs, Brandon was always loyal to the king and Henry VIII came to rely heavily upon this loyalty.

Much has been written about Charles Brandon over the centuries yet so little has been compiled into one singular book about his life. We learn about Charles Brandon, Duke of Suffolk, through biographies about his third wife, Mary Tudor, Dowager Queen of France, younger sister of Henry VIII, or his fourth wife Katherine Willoughby, Duchess of Suffolk. We also gain information about the duke from reading through biographies and sources related to the king himself. Charles was often at Henry VIII's side, participating in tournaments with him, sharing intimate conversations, hunting, hawking, attending council meetings, travelling overseas or leading the king's wars in France. From these sources we see glimpses of Charles participating in courtly life as well as the more intimate moments where he relaxes his more public persona and allows the real man to shine through.

It is my aim in this book to give new life to Charles Brandon, Duke of Suffolk, to detail the man's life, to pull back the layers and explore just who he was. Through reading personal letters that he wrote and letters that were written about him, I hope to share Brandon as a man with thoughts, feelings, desires and fears, as well as a courtier who had to present a certain image to those around him. I also aim to set Charles Brandon within the greater England and Europe in which he lived, so that the reader can gain a more rounded understanding of what life was really like during the fifteenth and sixteenth centuries.

Charles Brandon was a man born into relative obscurity yet died most beloved and best friend to one of England's most famous Kings. This is his story, this is his life.

The Beginning (1484 – 1485)

Charles Brandon's early years are shrouded in mystery, uncertainty and confusion. What is known is that he was born in 1484.[1] The exact date and location, as with many children born during the Tudor period, has not been recorded. However, what is certain is that Brandon was born during a turbulent time in English history. To fully understand the England that Brandon was born into we must first explore the years before his birth.

The Wars of the Roses still continued, upheaval resonating throughout England. The great factions of York and Lancaster battled for the throne, each side believing it was their God-given right to claim the English throne. The Lancastrian side was headed by King Henry VI, his wife Queen Margaret of Anjou, and his son Prince Edward. The king was suffering from some form of mental illness that made him completely incapable of ruling for long periods of time, requiring his wife and other members of the council to step in and govern while he was incapable.[2] The York side was headed by Richard of York, 3rd Duke of York, and his son Edward. Richard was the great grandson of King Edward III and governed England as lord protector while King Henry VI was unwell. However, the duke and the queen fell out with one another and the duke sought to take the throne for himself and his heirs due to his royal ancestry.[3]

The two factions battled fiercely with many losses. However, with Henry VI's death on 22/23 May 1471,[4] the Lancastrian hopes were crushed. Edward IV claimed the throne and became king bringing some stability once more to England. That was until Edward's early death on 3 October 1483.[5] Edward's successors were his two young sons, Edward and Richard. Understanding the turmoil that a young boy might have in his early reign, Edward left his own younger brother, Richard, Duke of Gloucester, as protector to guide his nephew, the future Edward V. To keep the future king and his brother safe after the death of their father, Richard took the boys to the Tower of London. Then, just before Edward's coronation, Richard had the boys declared illegitimate. He claimed that his brother was pre-contracted to marry Lady Eleanor Butler and thus the children Edward IV had with Elizabeth Woodville were illegitimate.[6] As his brother's only legitimate heir, Richard claimed the throne for himself and on 26 June 1483 was crowned king.[7] Both Edward and Richard, the young Princes in the Tower, were never seen nor heard from again.

Now there was a new Yorkist king upon the throne, but there was another man who felt he had a stronger claim. Henry Tudor, born on 28 January 1457, was the son of Edmund Tudor, 1st Earl of Richmond, and his wife Lady Margaret Beaufort. Edmund Tudor was captured in one of the battles of the Wars of the Roses and died of the plague on 3 November 1456, just two months before his son's birth.[8] Edmund was the oldest son of Owen Tudor, whose wife was the Dowager Queen Catherine of Valois. Catherine's first marriage was to the great English King Henry V, and her son, Henry VI, was the half-brother of Edmund Tudor.[9] As one of the last male heirs in the Lancastrian line, Henry Tudor and his mother both strongly believed that Henry had a claim to the English throne.

Henry, along with his uncle, Jasper, 1st Duke of Pembroke, escaped to Brittany in 1471 when Edward IV ascended the throne.[10] It was here that Henry and his uncle would spend the next fourteen years, slowly building up support, mostly gained from Duke Francis II of Brittany, until 1485, when they returned to England to lay claim to the throne. It was during these years in exile that Henry Tudor met William Brandon, father of Charles Brandon.[11]

There appear to be very few facts related to Charles Brandon's family. His grandfather was Sir William Brandon of Wangford and Southwark (born approximately 1425, died 1491).[12] William Brandon rose from relative security under the service of John de Mowbray, Duke of Norfolk. Before the duke died in 1476, he granted Sir William a seat in the local parliament and also marriage to Elizabeth Wingfield (died 28 April 1497).[13] William had a long list of accomplishments including becoming Marshal of the King's Bench, Burgess (MP) for Shoreham, knight for the Shire of Suffolk, and Collector of Customs at Kings Lynn and Great Yarmouth, Norfolk. William Brandon was also present at the Battle of Tewkesbury, one of the most decisive battles in English history where Prince Edward, Henry VI's son, was killed and the Lancastrian forces, of which William was a part, were decisively defeated. Despite their loss, William Brandon was knighted for his efforts. William must have been able to come to terms with the Lancastrian loss as he was present at the coronation of Richard III, brother of Yorkist King Edward IV.[14]

Sir William and Elizabeth Wingfield had three sons, Robert Brandon, William, and the youngest Thomas. It has also been proposed that the couple had several daughters, two of those being Anne and Elizabeth, although there is contradictory evidence to support this claim. William Brandon the Younger was born around 1456, making him about twenty-eight years of age when his son Charles was born. [15]

There appears to be some scandal surrounding the younger William Brandon. In 1478 Sir John Paston wrote that:

> Yonge William Brandon is in warde and arestyd ffor thatt he scholde have by fforce ravysshyd and swyvyd an olde jentylwoman, and yitt was nott therwith easysd, butt swyvyd hyr oldest dowtr, and than wolde have swyvyd the other sustr bothe; wherfforr men sey ffowle off hym, and that he wolde ete the henne and alle hyr chekynnys; and som seye that the Kynge entendyth to sitte upon hym, and men seye he is lyke to be hangyd, ffor he hathe weddyd a wedowe.[16]

John Paston's letter suggests that some time during or before 1478, William Brandon forced himself upon an older woman and made an attempt to have some sort of relationship with the woman's daughters. In addition to this great offence, the letter claims that the king, Edward IV, was not pleased by this news and that the punishment for such horrible crimes was to be hanged. It is interesting to note that there does not seem to be any record of William Brandon serving time in prison or being punished accordingly. It could be that it was mere gossip or hearsay, or that those who alleged the crimes did not have enough power behind them to see Brandon fully punished. Whatever the case, Brandon was not punished and he returned to King Edward IV's good graces.

William had strong Lancastrian ties and supported Henry VI during the Wars of the Roses. However, when Henry VI was defeated and eventually murdered, and Edward IV came to the throne, the Brandons changed sides. They pledged their support to the new Yorkist King Edward IV. Upon his death, though, his brother

Richard III came to the throne and the Brandon's loyalty quickly began to fade. William Brandon and his brother Thomas soon became dissatisfied with the new king, and the shock deposition of the future Edward V, and decided to joined the Duke of Buckingham's rebellion in 1483. The rebellion was led by Henry Stafford, 2nd Duke of Buckingham, and aimed to have Richard III removed from the throne and replaced by his nephew Edward, oldest son of Edward IV. However, rumours abound that Edward was dead and the plan was changed to replace Richard III with Henry Tudor. It was at this time that Henry made his first attempt to lay claim to the throne. He sailed with a small army from Brittany, but due to poor weather, Henry and his men had to return. Without Henry Tudor's men, Buckingham's own army floundered and a bounty was put upon his head. He was eventually captured, convicted of treason and beheaded in Salisbury on 2 November 1483.[17]

Despite supporting the Duke of Buckingham and his failed rebellion, both William and Thomas Brandon managed to remain in England. But by 1484, both became dissatisfied with Richard III once more and left the country. The brothers headed to Brittany to join Henry Tudor and support his claim to the throne. In the spring of 1484, King Richard III issued a general pardon to several men who had rebelled against him, one of those being William Brandon.[18] It is unclear if this pardon was issued before or after William Brandon left to join forces with Henry Tudor. If it was before, William may have not trusted the king's words after the failed rebellion and the execution of the Duke of Buckingham. If the pardon had been issued after William had left for Europe, it may be that he had no knowledge of the pardon or if he had then he might have felt it simply too late as he had already cast his lot with Henry Tudor. Whatever the reason for not accepting this pardon, it was believed at this time that William's wife Elizabeth was pregnant with their son Charles.

Elizabeth Bruyn of South Ockendon was the daughter and co-heiress of Sir Henry Bruyn. Elizabeth was first married to Thomas Tyrell Esquire, who had died in 1473. Sir Bruyn died in 1466 leaving Elizabeth a portion of her father's wealth. Elizabeth and William Brandon married between 1473 and 1476.[19] Elizabeth survived the death of her husband in 1485 and lived on until March 1493/4, dying when her son Charles was approximately nine or ten years of age. After William Brandon's death, Elizabeth went on to marry William Mallory Esquire.[20]

It is unclear exactly how many children William Brandon and Elizabeth Bruyn actually had. There have been suggestions that Charles Brandon was their only child, while other sources state they had four children,[21] and others state three.[22] It does seem most likely that William and Elizabeth had at least three children, a first born son named William after his father, a daughter named Anne and, of course, Charles, the youngest. The exact birth-dates of William and Anne remain unknown, although it can be strongly assumed that William was the oldest, then Anne and lastly Charles.[23] It is also difficult to detail the lives of both William and Anne. It does appear that Anne married Sir John Shilston and, after his death, Sir Gawain Carew.[24] However, the date of Anne's death or if she had any children remain unknown. William's life is also difficult to track and it is unknown if he married or fathered any children. He appeared to have died in the late 1490s[25] when Charles was a young teenager. Where William and Anne were when their parents fled to Brittany is unknown. It is possible that they travelled across the Channel with their parents or they may have stayed with relatives or trusted friends in England.

To William and Elizabeth Brandon, Henry Tudor must have signified hope and a future. The Wars of the Roses had brought a great deal of upheaval to England and now, leaving the country, they placed all their hope in Henry Tudor and his campaign. Laying claim to the English throne was one thing, but obtaining it was another. Throughout 1483/84, Henry and his ever-growing group of supporters relied heavily upon Duke Francis of Brittany for support and received payments from the duke to help pay for their day-to-day upkeep. In September 1484, Henry Tudor threw himself upon the mercy of King Charles VIII of France and begged him for support for his campaign. The king agreed and helped Henry and his supporters purchase resources and mercenaries.[26]

Henry Tudor and his group of exiles, including William and Elizabeth Brandon, were first in Vannes[27] in Brittany and then at the French Court, and therefore it is uncertain when or where Charles Brandon was born. There are no reports on how far along with child Elizabeth was when they left England and headed to Brittany. Nor are there any reports from where exactly William, his brother

Thomas and Elizabeth departed from England. One possibility was from Dover to Calais and then they travelled overland to Brittany. Another is they left England from a more westerly point such as Southampton. Wherever they departed and wherever they arrived in Europe, they had to travel across the Channel, and this must have been quite an ordeal for Elizabeth, no matter how far along she was in her pregnancy.

Despite not knowing where Charles Brandon was born we are able to make a few assumptions about what his birth would have been like. Giving birth in the middle ages was dangerous for women, and childbirth did not discriminate. Young, old, poor or rich women could die not only in childbirth but also due to complications afterwards. There was no way of monitoring the baby's heart-rate or of taking blood pressures, and thus women replied heavily on other experienced women to support and help them. Childbirth was predominantly women's business and physicians and doctors only attended under extreme circumstances. If a woman had the funds or contacts she would have sought advice and support from a midwife, a woman who had a great deal of experience and knowledge in delivering babies.[28]

Women of noble birth or of higher classes would close themselves off from the world for a period before they gave birth, commonly known as lying-in. The mother's rooms would be closed off and tapestries would be hung over the windows to block out as much light as possible. Only a single window would be left open to allow fresh air into the room. The room would be hung with calming tapestries and images so as not to upset the mother, which could in turn harm the unborn child. Religious crosses and other related items would have been kept within the room to provide spiritual support. Other women, especially those of the common and lower classes, would have worked right up until they went into labour if this was possible.[29] Whether Elizabeth Bruyn had the opportunity to retreat from the male dominated world before the birth of her son, we do not know. Hopefully she would have had the support of a midwife or other women about her to help ease her pain and guide her through the difficult time. What we can know is that she would have relied heavily upon her Catholic faith.

England during the fifteenth century was a strongly devoted Catholic nation, paying tribute to the pope in Rome. Religion and faith were closely entwined with birth, life and death. With the

Figure 1. The Battle of Bosworth
Cassell's Illustrated History of England, 1865

strong possibility that a mother in labour could die, women often turned to their religious beliefs to help support them throughout childbirth.[30] Elizabeth would have done the same, possibly holding a small cross or reciting prayers as she went into labour and delivered her son.

Wherever he was born, Charles Brandon would have been baptised shortly afterwards. It was vitally important that a young child was baptised, as an unbaptised soul could not go to heaven. This ritual of baptism was conducted by priests who were male and thus not allowed into the birthing chamber. Due to this, the church gave permission for a midwife to christen a baby only under extreme circumstances (if the baby was about to die).[31]

William Brandon must have been overjoyed at the birth of his son Charles. Why the boy was given such a name remains unclear. Perhaps he was named after a family friend, or perhaps, as is often tradition, he was named after a king. It could be possible that Charles was named after King Charles VIII of France, who was supporting and financing Henry Tudor's claim to the English throne.

Despite William and Elizabeth's happiness at the birth of their son, joy would soon turn to heartbreak as within a year of his birth, Charles's father would be dead.

William Brandon died at the Battle of Bosworth, a battle that has gone down in record as one of the most pivotal battles in English history. The aftermath changed the course of England and saw a new monarch and dynasty come to the throne.

The first day of August 1485 was to be the day that Henry Tudor would finally leave France after fourteen years of exile in Brittany and France, aiming to lay claim to the English throne.[32] He set sail from Harfleur, France accompanied by approximately 2000 soldiers.[33] This would be Henry's greatest push to date and by his side would be William Brandon.

Landing on 7 August at Mill Bay, 6 miles west of Milford Haven, located along the Pembrokeshire coastline, it is said that when he reached the coast Henry knelt down and kissed the sand reciting *Psalm 43*, "Judge me, O Lord and favour my cause." He then made the sign of the cross.[34] At Mill Bay, Henry was met by his half uncle, David Owen, illegitimate son of Owen Tudor, Henry's grandfather. Gathering his men, Henry headed off across land to lay claim to the English throne.[35]

Their first stop was the village of Dale, of which its castle surrendered easily. Henry and his men camped here and the future king made sure to remind them not to get up to any trouble.[36] The troops moved on through Haverfordwest and Cardigan, then northward to Llwyndafydd.[37] After this they claimed the garrison at Aberystwyth Castle, and then turned to march inland. On 13 August they reached Machynlleth, and the next day they made a 30-mile trek across rough terrain to Dolarddun.[38] Following this the growing army headed to Mynydd Digoll (Long Mountain), where Henry met with Rhys ap Thomas, an important man who carried a great deal of sway with the Welsh people. Rhys pledged his loyalty to Henry and brought approximately 2,000 troops to Henry's cause.[39]

With his growing number of troops, Henry headed to Shrewsbury. However, the portcullises were closed and Henry and his men were not given permission to pass. The next day Henry sent a messenger to negotiate with those in charge, and after a mysterious message from an outside source was sent to the head bailiff. Henry and his men were allowed to pass through and a number of men from the town joined Henry's forces.[40]

From Shrewsbury, Henry travelled through Shropshire and Staffordshire. It was in Staffordshire that Sir Gilbert Talbot and a troop of about 500 men joined Henry.[41] The men marched to Stafford, where Henry would meet Sir William Stanley, younger brother of Henry's stepfather. Throughout this time the Stanleys had been sitting on the fence, not making their allegiances clear to either Henry or King Richard III. Although it is interesting to note that Thomas Stanley, Henry's stepfather, had been following Henry and his men under the pretence of keeping an eye on them for the king.[42] In addition to this, it became known that it was William Stanley who sent a message to the Mayor of Shrewsbury to convince him to open the gates to Henry and his men. Had the Stanley brothers' allegiance already been decided?

From Stafford, Henry and his men marched through Lichfield arriving at Tamworth on 20 August. The next day his men marched over the River Anker to Atherstone, where Henry is reported to have had a secret meeting with his stepfather. It was at this meeting that Thomas Stanley allegedly pledged his formal support for his stepson.

However, the next day, on 22 August, Henry Tudor sent a message to his stepfather asking him to send his men to join Henry's troops.

To this, Stanley replied that he needed to prepare his men and for now it would appear he was keeping his distance.[43] Also on this day, Henry chose to knight several men who had shown great loyalty to him throughout his time in exile. These men included Sir Richard Guildford, Sir John Hastoy, Sir John Risley, Sir John Trenzy, Sir William Tyler, Sir Thomas Milborn and now Sir William Brandon.[44] It must have been a great honour for William Brandon to be knighted. He may have felt that his loyalty to Henry was being rewarded and if Henry were to win against Richard III that his own prospects would continue to rise. Little did William Brandon know that he only had one more day to live.

There is great debate as to exactly where the Battle of Bosworth took place. There is also a great deal of debate as to how the battle played out and where Henry Tudor and Richard III's armies were placed and deployed.[45] It is estimated that Henry had an army of approximately 5,000 – 8,000 soldiers to King Richard III's 12,000 – 20,000 men. Thomas and William Stanley had a combined force of approximately 6,000 men, yet neither brother had made a definitive move as to which side of the battle they would join.[46] Richard III held the higher ground upon Ambion Hill, while Henry and his men were on the lower ground next to marshes.

Henry Tudor, lacking experience in military action, appointed the Earl of Oxford to command his troops and lead the vanguard. Behind the vanguard was Henry, flanked by Gilbert Talbot, Sir John Savage and the rest of his men.[47] Close to Henry was Sir William Brandon. Brandon had been chosen to be Henry's standard-bearer, a great honour for a man who continued to display his loyalty. It is unclear as to exactly why he was chosen. Perhaps it was due to Brandon's unfaltering loyalty to the man he hoped would become king, or perhaps, as one historian suggests, it was because of Brandon's physical toughness.[48] We have no description of what he looked like, although his son Charles grew up to be tall, handsome, well-built and extremely suited to physical pastimes such as hunting and jousting. This may be an indication that William Brandon too was physically fit and able to fight in battle, protecting his king while bearing Henry's standard high.

A standard bearer is "one who bears a standard or banner"[49]. It was Brandon's duty to carry the flag that represented Henry and his troops. The standard that Henry chose was white and green, representing the Tudor colours. Upon this was the red cross of St George, patron saint of England and soldiers, and the red dragon of Wales. Henry Tudor had strong ties with Wales through his grandfather Owen Tudor as well as his uncle Jasper Tudor. This identification with Wales and its people helped Henry to recruit many Welsh men and soldiers along his campaign towards London.

On King Richard's side he ordered the Duke of Norfolk and Sir Robert Brackenbury to lead his vanguard. The rear-guard was commanded by Richard III and comprised his personal bodyguard and other soldiers. Behind him was the Earl of Northumberland and his men.[50]

When the battle cry was called, arrows fired and Oxford's men clashed with the Duke of Norfolk's. The two were old foes. Both sides paused, perhaps to regain their breath and positions. Oxford formed his men into a wedge and charged forward.[51] At this second charge, Henry's French troops joined the attack on Norfolk's men. Soon Norfolk's men were in trouble and many were killed, including the duke himself. Others fled while some defected to Henry Tudor's side.[52]

Northumberland and his men did not move into the fight and it is believed that the earl decided to leave the battle without employing any of his men into the fray. Amongst the chaos, some of his loyal supporters begged Richard III to flee, but the king would be no coward. Oxford's men had pushed forward leaving a gap. Richard III saw an opportunity to get to the man who caused such a great threat to his throne, and he and his men charged forward aiming to strike Henry down.[53]

Reports say that Henry Tudor was surrounded by a group of his most trusted knights, one being Sir William Brandon, who proudly held Henry's standard. Richard III charged at the standard bearer with his lance, the lance pierced through Brandon and broke in half.[54] History records that William Brandon "hevyd on high" Henry Tudor's standard, "and vamisyd it, tyll with deathe's dent he was stryken downe".[55] William Brandon drew his last breath fighting for Henry Tudor to become king. Little would he know the great legacy that his death left for his one-year-old son Charles.

Richard III and his men continued forward, the battle was fierce and heated and Henry, with little support, must have feared for his life. However, it was at this moment that the Stanley brothers, who had been watching the battle, decided to act. William Stanley and his men charged down in support of Henry Tudor.[56] It was at some point during this battle that Richard III was killed. Despite history recording him as a hunchback and a coward, Richard III fought bravely until his final breath.[57]

After the battle and Henry was declared victorious, he ordered that the dead and wounded be tended to. He declared that every man should be given a decent burial and many of those who died were buried at the nearby church of St James, Dadlington.[58] Although it is unknown exactly where William Brandon was buried, it was reported that he was the only one of nobility on Henry Tudor's side who died that day.[59]

After fourteen years in exile, having marched halfway across Wales and England in just two weeks and vastly outnumbered, Henry Tudor and his men went against insurmountable odds and won. Within just two short hours the man who had tenuous ties to the throne had defeated a king and claimed the crown for himself. However, for Elizabeth Bruyn and her son Charles, things were not quite so victorious and happy. Elizabeth had lost her husband and Charles had lost his father. Suddenly life was thrown into uncertainty. But from these humble and uncertain beginnings, Charles Brandon would go on to forge a life of great responsibility and power.

The Early Years (1485 – 1509)

It was not until the reign of Henry VIII that Charles Brandon's actions and whereabouts started to be recorded in detail, therefore it is difficult to piece together the first few decades of his life.

It is assumed that after the death of his father, and Henry Tudor came to the throne, that Elizabeth Bruyn returned to England with her infant son. When this was remains unknown. It has been suggested that when she did return, Charles went to live with his grandfather, Sir William Brandon of Wangford and Southwark, or even his uncle, Thomas Brandon, who had fled England along with his brother.[1] It was most likely either with his grandfather or uncle that the young Brandon learnt the skills necessary to become a man. He would have had a tutor or joined other boys of a similar age to be educated. We know that Brandon was able to read and write, as he wrote many letters throughout his life. However, his handwriting was of very poor quality. It was messy and, as was usual for the time, the man spelt phonetically.[2] It has been suggested that Brandon had a strong Suffolk accent as many of his letters were spelt to reflect this dialect.

With the introduction of the printing press into England, access to books and pamphlets was becoming easier. Such works as *Le Morte d'Arthur* by Sir Thomas Malory emphasised chivalric adventures, personal combat and heroic wars, while upholding the knightly value of honour.[3] These tales were translated into everyday life in the form of jousting and other events, at which Brandon grew to be extremely skilled. Brandon became the perfect, heroic knight – tall, broad-shouldered, strong, skilled at jousting and hand-to-hand combat. It was these qualities that drew the future Henry VIII to him[4] and it is possible that, as a boy, Brandon read stories of chivalry and valour as part of his education.

As well as some formal education during the early years of his life, Brandon would have been taught all the important aspects of the Catholic faith. He would have been taught about participating in mass and also the Eucharist and transubstantiation, where the bread and wine of communion would have been turned into the flesh and blood of Christ. He would have learnt about confession and the need to admit sins to a priest and repent for wrongs. He would have been taught about the idea of needing to do good deeds for others and the concept of taking pilgrimages in order to pray to God.[5] Brandon would have believed that the pope was the head of the Catholic church and that his position was appointed by God.

Brandon would have also learnt a range of skills and pastimes that were common to young men at the time, including how to ride a horse, how to play tennis, how to joust, hunt and hawk, and possibly how to wrestle.[6] Archery was also an important part of a young man's education and it is likely that Brandon would have been efficient in using a bow. As an adult, Brandon proved to be a very physical and active young man, and he appeared to enjoy sports and outdoor pastimes, activities that were also favoured by Henry VIII.[7]

Brandon's grandfather died in 1491, and his lands and inheritance went to his oldest son and heir, Robert Brandon.[8] If Charles Brandon was not already living with his uncle, Thomas Brandon, it is proposed that around this time he moved from his grandfather's home to go live with him.[9] Thomas had already proved his support for the new Tudor king when he had been in exile in Europe with his brother William. During this time, Thomas helped to conduct a raid that would see more men join Henry's forces. The story is that the Earl of Oxford, loyal supporter of the Lancastrian cause, had previously been imprisoned in the garrison in Hammes. On 28 October 1484, the earl escaped and met with Henry Tudor, joining his growing forces. The decision was made for Oxford, Thomas Brandon and others to return to the garrison to free fellow supporters. While Oxford and his men attacked the garrison from outside, Thomas Brandon and thirty-strong men entered and, after some harsh fighting, a truce was called. This allowed the Earl of Oxford and Thomas Brandon to take seventy loyal men from the garrison to join Henry Tudor.[10] Interestingly, shortly after this time Richard III issued a general pardon for Thomas Brandon and the other thirty-seven men involved in the storming of the garrison at Hammes.[11] This may have been another attempt to win back supporters. Once again it is unclear if Thomas Brandon knew of this pardon and, if he did, it would be highly doubtful that he would have accepted, as by this time he had firmly thrown in his lot with Henry Tudor.

There are no records of Thomas Brandon travelling across Wales and England with Henry and his men in August 1485, or of him participating in the Battle of Bosworth. It may be that he did take an active part in the battle, or perhaps he stayed behind in France with his brother's wife to protect her and his nephew.

However, Thomas Brandon was beginning to build an illustrious career for himself, and taking young Charles under his wing served the boy well. In September 1486, Thomas became an esquire of the body for Henry VII, a position that required him to be close to the king's person, and in the spring of 1487 he was commanding a naval force. Six years later he was serving in the French campaign and was knighted after the Battle of Blackheath in 1497.[12] Thomas Brandon was an active member of court and even sat on the king's council on several occasions, as well as acting as a diplomat for the king. He was involved with Henry VII's horses and hawks, and from around 1499 was appointed master of the horse, having complete control over the care and maintenance of the king's horses, a position that, once more, brought him into close proximity to the king. Thomas Brandon must have been extremely good at his duties as he was reappointed master of the horse by Henry VIII after the death of his father.[13]

In addition to all of this, Thomas Brandon participated in the baptism and knighting of Prince Arthur, Henry VII's first son and heir with his wife and queen, Elizabeth of York. He was also present at the knighting of young Prince Henry, the future Henry VIII. Thomas regularly participated in court jousts. This knowledge and the fact that Charles Brandon too was well-suited to jousting suggests that the Brandon men were well-built and extremely fit and strong. It is most likely from Thomas that Charles Brandon first learnt his skills at jousting. As well as this, in 1501 Thomas took part in the magnificent wedding of Prince Arthur to Katherine of Aragon. It is reported that at the wedding Thomas wore a gold chain worth around £1,400.[14] (Approximately £680,540.00 in today's currency.)[15] Although one cannot help but think that after the wedding Thomas would have had to have given the gold chain back to the king.

Thomas Brandon was honoured with leading a party of courtiers who were sent to meet Philip the Handsome when a storm wrecked his ship on the coast of England. Thomas was also marshal of the King's Bench prison in Southwark, and it is thought that he lived in Southwark in a manor rented from the Bishop of Winchester. To add to this impressive list, Thomas Brandon was elected into the Order of the Garter in April 1507.[16]

Thomas married twice, both women wealthy widows in their own right. Through these marriages and his services to the king, Thomas Brandon came into a considerable amount of wealth as well as ownership of a great many estates.[17] It can be suggested that Charles Brandon used his uncle's model of marriage throughout his own life to increase his own revenue and to bring more wealth and land to his name.

Even after the death of Henry VII in 1509, Thomas Brandon's career continued to flourish under the new king, Henry VIII. As previously stated, he retained his title of master of the horse and on 2 June 1509, was created warden and chief justice of the royal forests south of the Trent. On 24 June 1509, Thomas Brandon had the great honour of participating in Henry VIII's coronation procession.[18] According to Edward Hall, Brandon was:

> [...] clothed in tissue, Broudered with Roses of fine Gold, and traverse his body, a greate Bauderike of Gold, greate and massy, his Horse trapped in Golde, leadyng by a rayne of Silke, the kynges spare Horse trapped barde wise, with harneis Broudered with Bullion Golde, curiously wroughte by Gold Smithes.[19]

With such an active and illustrious court career it is no wonder that Charles Brandon followed in his uncle's footsteps and climbed the ladder of the royal court to become one of the highest ranking men in England by the end of his life. It was during this time that the young man started to make his first appearances at court. In 1501 in the wedding celebrations of Prince Arthur and his marriage to Katherine of Aragon, Charles Brandon was first recorded as participating in the celebratory jousts. He also had the honour of waiting upon the prince the morning after his wedding.[20] In 1503, Brandon was recorded as waiting upon Henry VII at his table and around 1507, when Brandon was around twenty-three years of age he was appointed as an esquire of the

Figure 2. Engraving of Henry VIII from
Cassell's Illustrated History of England, Volume II (1865)

body, just as his uncle had been.[21] More importantly, around the years 1505/06, Brandon was part of the king's spears, a group of men who were active in participating in jousts and courtly displays.[22]

It would seem that Charles followed closely in his uncle's footsteps as, towards the end of Henry VII's, reign he became master of the horse for Henry Bourchier, Earl of Essex, who was one of the most prominent nobles at Henry VII's court.[23]

Surprisingly, Charles did not hold a post in either Prince Arthur's household or that of the king. Yet this did not stop him forming a close bond with the future Henry VIII. Despite being almost ten years older than Henry, Brandon would become one of his bosom buddies.[24] With the death of Arthur in 1502, Henry was moved within close proximity to the king and kept under a close watch as he was now the sole heir to the throne of England.[25] Without having a great deal of freedom,[26] it is quite possible that Henry lived vicariously through Charles Brandon. He was able to watch Charles joust and participate at the lists while he himself was forbidden to participate due to possible injury. He was also able to gossip about romantic interests and women with Brandon because Brandon was quite a ladies' man at court.[27]

Brandon first attracted the attention of Anne Browne, daughter of Sir Anthony Browne, around 1505/06 when Charles was around twenty-one years of age. He confessed to Walter Devereux that "he was in love and resorted muche to the company of Anne Browne".[28] Brandon proposed marriage to Anne and the couple slept together, conceiving a daughter who would be named Anne after her mother. However, Brandon saw better prospects for himself with Anne's aunt, and he broke off the betrothal and made a proposal to Margaret Neville, Dame Mortimer, an older widow of some wealth. On 7 February 1507, Brandon had licence of Margaret's lands and began to sell them off in quick succession, profiting over £1,000. (Around £483,770.00.)[29] But with the land sold and a wealthy profit made, Brandon was looking to annul his marriage to Margaret on the grounds of consanguinity, due to his previously relationship with her niece and also being related to the grandmother of Margaret's first husband.[30] Unfortunately, Margaret would continue to play a role in Brandon's life for many more years to come as she bitterly fought the annulment of her marriage. Finally, on 20 August 1529, the pope had to step in and he granted Brandon an annulment. This, in turn, saw the legitimisation of the children he had with Anne Browne and also those he had with his third wife, Mary Tudor.[31]

In 1508, Brandon returned to Anne Browne and the couple married in secret at Stepney Church. They later repeated the marriage ceremony publicly at St Michael, Cornhill. In 1510, Anne gave birth to the couple's second daughter, Mary. Sadly, Anne died shortly afterwards, in approximately 1510, and Brandon was left a widower at the age of twenty-seven with two young daughters.[32]

There is some debate as to whether Brandon fathered several illegitimate children during his early years. It has been suggested that he fathered Charles, later Sir Charles Brandon of Sigston, Mary, who married Robert Ball of Scottow, and lastly Frances, who married William Sandon and, after his death, Andrew Bilsby.[33] There seems to be no information regarding who this Mary Ball or Frances Sandon/ Bilsby were and even the names of their husbands are difficult to track down.

There is mention of a Sir Charles Brandon in the *History of Parliament Trust*. These records state that Sir Charles Brandon was the illegitimate son of Charles Brandon, Duke of Suffolk, born by 1521. This would put the boy's conception around the time that Brandon was married to Mary Tudor, Dowager Queen of France and sister to King Henry VIII. Unfortunately, it makes no reference to who his mother was. There is absolutely no information regarding Sir Charles's younger years, although the records state that he served with his father protecting the northern borders between January 1543 and February 1544. From his birth-date this would suggest that Sir Charles was in his twenties when he served with his father protecting the northern borders. The records suggest that Sir Charles married an Elizabeth Strangways, although who exactly this woman is remains unknown. Sir Charles was made steward and constable of Sheriff Hutton in January 1544 and fought in Boulogne where he was knighted, presumably by his father on 30 September. He died on 12 August 1551, sadly only a month after the death of his two younger half-brothers.[34] If indeed Sir Charles Brandon was the illegitimate son of Charles Brandon, it remains unknown if he had any relationship with his siblings while growing up or how much contact he had with his father in his early years.

It is not impossible that Brandon had illegitimate children. After all by 1514 he was a duke and one of the most powerful men in

England. He was known to have been very handsome, athletic and certainly had a way with women. Unfortunately, there is very little information regarding Brandon's two daughters and thus it must be taken with some scepticism if they were actually the illegitimate daughters of Brandon. Sir Charles, however, does appear to have been his illegitimate child but it is interesting to note that Brandon makes no reference whatsoever to this illegitimate son in his will. This is surprising as surely Brandon would have wished to have provided in some small way for a son, even if he was illegitimate.

Life at Court and a War with France (1509 – 1513)

The next four years would see a dramatic rise in Brandon's prospects and position at court. He would rise to become one of King Henry VIII's most trusted and beloved friends and confidantes. His position at court would also be elevated and by the end of 1513, Brandon was on the very cusp of becoming one of the highest ranking men in England.

On 21 April 1509, at Richmond Palace, King Henry VII died.[1] His death was kept secret for several days as preparations were made to usher Henry Tudor to the throne. Naturally, Henry was informed of his father's death and he played along with the charade that his father was still alive until it was proclaimed that the old king had passed to be succeeded by his only living son.[2] At the funeral, Brandon was appointed one of ninety-three esquires of the body, alongside such men as Thomas Knyvett and William Parr.[3]

While there was a great deal of vying for position and power at this time, it seemed as though Brandon passed effortlessly from the service of the old king to his friend and new king. In fact, it would seem as though with the coronation of King Henry VIII Brandon's prospects had only one way to go, and that was up.

Henry Tudor took Katherine of Aragon, his late brother's widow, to be his wife on 11 June 1509 in a small ceremony in the Queen's Closet at Greenwich. Unlike his brother's lavish wedding ceremony at St Paul's this was a low-key affair with only a few attending.[4] There is some debate as to why Henry took Katherine to be his wife when, as a man approaching eighteen years of age and a new king, he could have any foreign princess he desired. He stated that he chose Katherine to fulfil his father's dying wish, although it could quite simply be that Katherine was young, cultured, intelligent and extremely beautiful, that Henry had simply fallen for her, and she was, after all, readily available.

While the couple's wedding was a quiet affair, their coronation on 24 June was a magnificent event that heralded in not only a new king and queen, but also the dawning of a new age. By the end of his reign, Henry VII had become known as a miser. With the knowledge of his end ever in mind, he was desperate to ensure the safe passage of kingship to his son. He did not want a repeat of the Wars of the Roses or any challenge to his son's reign. With the coming of a young, extremely handsome, almost eighteen-year-old who greatly resembled his late grandfather King Edward IV, the people of England held great hope for a new beginning, the ushering in of a new era of hope and prosperity.[5]

Brandon was selected to be one of the six challengers in the grand tournaments that were held to celebrate the king and queen's coronation. For a man of just twenty-three/four, and who was only an esquire of the body and a member of the king's spears, this was a huge honour and only the beginning of things to come. In addition, Brandon was also given the position of chamberlain of the principality of North Wales in November 1509.[6]

The early years of Henry VIII's reign were filled with entertainment and celebration. The king was young, athletic and found it difficult to keep still. He held little interest in politics and council meetings and thus left the running of his kingdom to his trusted advisers and privy council members. Through his love of sport and entertainment, the king built up a close group of friends around him who all shared similar interests and skills. These men included Edward Howard, Nicholas Carew, Francis Bryan, William Compton, Thomas Knyvett, Henry Guildford and, of course, Charles Brandon. They formed the inner core of the king's great household and soon became the staff of his privy chamber. These men spent a great deal of time with the king, sharing in his love of sports, entertainment, gambling and other pastimes. Many of them, especially Brandon, were extremely talented within the tiltyard and shared a great skill and passion for jousting. It was these men who held the king's ear. In fact, many of them would spend almost every waking moment with him and together they would create an Arthurian ethos in which the young king thrived.[7] Henry VIII lavished his close friends with gifts including patronage and rich, expensive clothing.[8]

After Henry VIII ascended the throne, Brandon remained an esquire of the body to the new king.[9] This meant that Brandon was responsible for such activities as dressing the king each morning and tending to his personal needs. It is easy to imagine both Brandon and Henry VIII spending their days hunting, playing card games, gambling, playing tennis, taking part in archery, practising in the tiltyard, observing beautiful women at court or getting up to general antics that young men like to do. Both Henry VIII and Brandon had a natural talent for all things athletic, and it is easy to see how, through these endless days of activity and close proximity, Brandon formed a close bond with the king that would go on to span his entire life. [10]

Despite these days of entertainment, laughter and joy, the new king and queen did face a tragic loss in January 1510 when Katherine gave birth to a stillborn daughter, and the death of Henry's first-born was a great loss for the king.[11] However, he believed that he and Katherine were still young and that they had plenty of time to produce sons.

Only a few weeks later, on 27 January 1510, Sir Thomas Brandon passed away at Blackfriars. He was buried two days later.[12] At Sir Thomas's funeral, his oldest brother Robert was chief mourner, followed by Anthony and Humphrey Wingfield, and John Brews.[13] Brandon is not recorded at being at his uncle's funeral, but it is not unrealistic to think that he was there considering how close they were. As Sir Thomas had no male heirs of his own, a great sum of his fortune was left to his nephew. Sir Thomas's will consisted of land, plate and coin totalling almost £1,000 (approximately £483,770.00),[14] although not all of that went to Brandon. Sir Thomas left a sum of money to Lady Jane Guildford whose servants had cared for Sir Thomas in his final illness.[15] Even a large portion of the £1,000 left would be a considerable sum for Brandon, who was starting to make a name for himself at court.

Upon his uncle's death, Brandon also succeeded him as marshal of the King's Bench and, in November 1511, he also became marshal of the king's household. These positions gave him control over the prisons in Southwark and helped to make Brandon an influential figure in the borough. It should also be noted that after his uncle's death, Brandon continued to live in the manor that Sir Thomas rented from the Bishop of Winchester.[16] It can be assumed that Brandon either bought the residence at this time or continued to rent it.

On 1 January 1511, the great joy that Henry had been waiting for finally arrived. At approximately 1:30am, Katherine of Aragon delivered a son, who was quickly named Henry after his father. After eighteen months on the throne, Henry VIII finally had a son and heir. Four days later the little boy was baptised at the Chapel of the Observant Friars at Richmond.[17]

To celebrate the young prince's birth, an extravagant tournament was held at Westminster in which Brandon had the great honour of participating. The tournament consisted of a magnificent pageant, jousting, and was followed by a huge feast. At the joust the king appeared at one end of the field from his great pavilion of cloth of gold, his horse also draped in cloth of gold. At the other end of the field, for the defenders, appeared Brandon riding his horse. He was wearing a long robe of russet satin and appeared to be in the form of a recluse or a religious person. His horse was also draped in the same colour cloth.[18] He entered the arena without pomp or minstrels playing and rode to where the queen was sitting. Brandon pleaded with the queen for permission to be allowed to joust in her honour, and if she did not give licence he would depart without further noise. Naturally, the queen gave him permission to joust and when she did this Brandon threw off his robe to reveal that he was wearing a rich suit of armour. The sight must have been one to behold and Brandon rode to the opposite end of the tiltyard to the king, where he was met by several servants wearing russet satin.[19]

After this came Henry Guildford, wearing cloth of gold and silver completely surrounded by what appeared to be a small castle. The castle was beautifully decorated with mystic rhymes, which were said to evoke blessings upon the young king and queen. Following him came the rest of the men who would joust for the queen, wearing cloth of silver and, once permission was granted for them to participate, they made their way to where Brandon was waiting. Following from this came the Marquis of Dorset and Sir Thomas Boleyn (father of the famous Anne Boleyn), who were dressed in black velvet as though they were pilgrims from St James's shrine. They carried staves and a number of men also wearing black followed behind them. After this came the Duke of Buckingham and his horse, dressed in cloth of silver. The procession was finished with several lords apparelled in ornate armour.[20]

The joust was a spectacular event with many courses run and multiple lances broken. The queen and her ladies cheered and waved their honours while the crowds watched on with great excitement. Naturally, the king won first prize[21] and, while it is not recorded just how Brandon got on, it can be assumed as a skilled jouster that he did well, although he was smart enough to never beat the king.

Tragically, Henry and Katherine's son died just fifty-two days after his birth, at Richmond Palace of unknown reasons.[22] Despite the great loss, the king was once more hopeful that the queen would give him a son and heir.

After having the great honour and privilege of jousting for the queen, Brandon's accolades continued to grow. In January 1511, Brandon was named a Justice of the Peace for Surrey,[23] and in April 1512, he was granted for life the office of Ranger of the New Forest and, in May, he was made keeper of Wanstead in Essex.[24] Then, on 6 October, he was created master of the horse, the same title once held by his uncle. This granted him £60 13s (£29,340.65)[25] from the chamber and an additional £40 (£19,350.80)[26] from the exchequer.[27] The role gave him responsibility for the king's horses, including the horses used for hunting and jousting.[28] Naturally, as an accomplished rider, Brandon would have taken easily to this role and, in addition, it gave him more time with the king. It is possible to imagine Brandon assisting the king, choosing which horse he would take out to hunt, and then joining in the hunt. Such closeness gave Brandon even more opportunity to speak personally with the king. Perhaps they spoke of the lovely women at court, both men young and dashing in their looks and seeing themselves holding all the chivalry of King Arthur. It is also possible that they spoke about the upcoming war against France.

Tensions were starting to mount in Europe. Towards the end of 1508, Pope Julius II created the League of Cambrai, which was joined by most European nations (not including England). The league set itself to oust Venice from mainland territories that it had acquired over many years. Pope Julius II vowed to reduce Venice to nothing more than a fishing village for daring to encroach upon papal territory, not to mention its desire to have spiritual independence from the Holy See. France played a major role in this war stripping

Venice of most of its territory. However, once the French sacked Venice, the armies did not leave. In addition to this, King Louis XII of France also summoned an ecumenical council, which was designed to examine not only the reform of the church but also of Pope Julius II, who the French King thought to be corrupt and self-indulgent. Pope Julius II was livid and seeing his very position challenged, he sought to make a new alliance to drive the French back and out of the Holy lands. As a true Christian, Henry VIII joined the Holy League towards the end of 1511.[29]

King Henry saw the great advantage of participating in the Holy League against France. The pope had promised him the French crown once King Louis XII was defeated. This, of course, would have appealed to Henry and would have harked back to the great military triumphs achieved by Henry V. The pope also promised to bestow upon Henry the title of "the most Christian king", which had recently been stripped from Louis XII.[30]

Soon preparations for war were being made and, once again, while the royal coffers funded a great deal of the war, many high lords and nobles throughout England had to raise and arm their own men. Much of the planning was left to Thomas Wolsey, a man who would soon become a cardinal and right hand man to the king. An English/ Spanish invasion was planned, which would take place at Guyenne, in south-west France. King Ferdinand, Katherine of Aragon's father, Henry VIII's father-in-law, would supply Henry with additional cavalry, cannons and wagons with the aim of conquering Aquitaine, which had once belonged to the English.[31]

Part of the campaign was to be naval and Charles Brandon and Henry Guildford were given the joint captaincy of the *Sovereign*, one of the king's largest ships. Edward Howard, brother of Thomas Howard, was made admiral of the fleet. His duty was to ensure that the Channel was kept clear of French warships. Howard set his fleet on seek-and-destroy missions designed to find French ships and eliminate them. In August he located several enemy ships at the port of Brest. The English and French ships engaged one another and, as was the style of the time, the ships were designed not to shoot cannons at one another but to lock together so that the sailors could board the enemy's ship. The French ship, the *Marie la Cordeliere*, and the English ship, the *Regent*, became locked in battle and, somehow, the *Cordeliere's* gunpowder store was ignited. With such a huge explosion both ships began to burn profusely and the men aboard, including Henry VIII's companion Thomas Knyvett, either burned or drowned. [32]

Two months previously, in June, Thomas Grey, Marquis of Dorset, and 12,000 men[33] landed in San Sebastian near Biarritz.[34] Without any support from Edward Howard and his fleet, Dorset and his men were trapped at St Jean de Luz. King Ferdinand reneged on his promise to send the supplies and equipment he had previously promised. He also began to try and persuade Dorset to take his army to the Pyrenees rather than continue with his instructions from the English king, which were to march north and invade Bayonne. Instead of marching forward, Dorset remained and soon his troops became ill with dysentery. Around 1,800 men died and some even mutinied. Dorset too fell ill and he and his men returned home, although once back in England, Dorset made multiple excuses not to meet with his irate king. Henry VIII did not wish to offend Ferdinand and publicly accepted the king's explanation of English incompetence for the failure of the attack. Although privately no real punishments were handed out to his men[35] as it was most probable that Henry realised it was due to Ferdinand's lack of holding up his side of the agreement that the campaign failed.

In early 1513, Brandon had the honour of being selected to lead an army that was to land at Brittany. However, the expedition was soon called off. In the autumn of that year, Henry VIII decided to invade France personally with an army of 30,000 men,[36] of which Brandon raised 1,831 men, mostly from his offices in Wales. Brandon was also appointed as high marshal and lieutenant of the army, in which he was responsible for discipline, including dispensing the death penalty, selecting camp sites, and creating knights. This was an extraordinary position for Brandon as, at the time, he was a mere knight, yet he had power over the Duke of Buckingham, earls and more experienced knights and men.[37] He also had the honour of leading the vanguard of the king's ward, which consisted of around 3,000 men. The English army took the city of Therouanne in Artois without a great deal of difficulty and went on to besiege Tournai. Brandon led the assault upon one of the city gates of Tournai, and this led to the people of the city surrendering to Henry VIII on 24 September 1513. When Henry VIII was handed the keys to Tournai, he handed them to Brandon, who led his men in to occupy the city. This in itself was an extraordinary honour for a man who was only knighted on 30 March 1513. In addition, Brandon was rewarded the castle of Mortain by the king.[38]

After this there were several weeks of celebration in which Brandon was to cause one of the greatest scandals of the time. Henry VIII and his men met with Margaret of Austria, Duchess of Savoy, and daughter of Maximilian I, Holy Roman Emperor. Twice widowed and vowing to never remarry, Margaret was the governor of the Habsburg Netherlands and an extremely well-educated and influential woman.[39] During these lavish celebrations it was reported that King Henry suggested a marriage between his best friend Brandon and Margaret of Austria. The duchess, unwilling to marry again, deflected any suggestion of marriage saying it would deeply offend her father.[40] Whether there was any real prospect of marriage remains unclear but it seems as though Brandon was willing to push the boundaries.

Margaret of Austria stated that:

> One night at Tournay, being at the banquet, after the banquet he [Brandon] put himself upon his knees before me, and in speaking and him playing, he drew from my finger the ring, and put it upon his, and since shewed it me; and I took to laugh, and to him said that he was a thief, and that I thought not that the King had with him led thieves out of his country. This word laron he could not understand; wherefore I was constrained to ask how one said in Flemish laron. And afterwards I said to him in Flemish dieffe, and I prayed him many times to give it me again, for that it was too much known. But he understood me not well, and kept it unto the next day that I spake to the King, him requiring to make him to give it me, because it was too much known—I promising him one of my bracelets the which I wore, the which I gave him. And then he gave me the said ring.[41]

Surely Brandon must have known he was stepping outside his boundaries and pushing the limits of courtly love. It was not uncommon for a lady to give a man a gift to show her favour, but Margaret was a duchess and an extremely influential and important woman and Brandon was a mere knight. Yet Brandon continued to push his luck and another time at Lille, Brandon once more got down on his knees before the duchess and took another ring from her finger.[42] Margaret spoke with Henry VIII and begged for the ring back, saying it was not for the love of the ring but for the fact that Brandon had stepped out of line and pushed far above his status. It would seem that Henry was willing to play along with his friend's game and, instead of getting Brandon to return the ring, he gave Margaret another more beautiful ring set with diamonds and rubies.[43]

The whole incident caused quite a scandal and there was some outrage from Maximilian I, Margaret's father, at the idea that Brandon would marry his daughter.[44] Outwardly, Henry VIII denied any inclination to see Brandon married to Margaret of Austria. In March 1514, Henry VIII wrote to Maximilian I stating:

> Is much displeased to hear that there is a common report
> that the Archduchess of Austria is to be married to the Duke
> of Suffolk; will make enquiry if it originated in England, that
> the authors may be punished.[45]

It is interesting to note that despite this whole scandal Brandon did not receive any punishment, nor does there seem to be any punishment handed out to anyone in regards to spreading the rumours about a supposed marriage between Brandon and Margaret.[46] Perhaps the whole incident was put down to an over-dramatic game of courtly love, or maybe Henry VIII realised he had let his friend push a little too far and wished for the whole incident to be forgotten.

On a less scandalous note, on 23 April 1513, Brandon was elected as a Knight of the Garter.[47] The Order of the Garter is the oldest and highest British order of chivalry, founded in 1348 by King Edward III,[48] and consisting of the king (or queen), their spouse, the Prince of Wales and twenty-four knights. Other members of the order are known as royal knights companions and extra or stranger knights. While the Order of the Garter is a small group, a new member can be chosen if a vacancy becomes available. A new member of the order is chosen personally by the ruling sovereign, at the time Henry VIII, and has to be someone who has served the sovereign faithfully.[49] Brandon had already shown throughout his service not only to Henry VIII but to his late father that he was a loyal and dedicated servant. As a member of the Order of the Garter, Brandon was required to display his banner of arms, helmet, crest and sword as well as a stall plate within the stalls of St George's Chapel.[50] Upon Brandon's death his banner of arms, helmet, crest and sword were removed, leaving only the stall plate.[51]

Also in 1513, Brandon was contracted to marry Elizabeth Grey, Viscountess Lisle. Elizabeth Grey was the daughter of John Grey, 2nd Baron Lisle.[52] When her stepfather, Sir Thomas Knyvett, died on the *Regent* in August 1512, she became the ward of Brandon.[53] Brandon organised with the king to purchase Elizabeth's wardship for the sum of £1,400[54] (a staggering £677,278),[55] which he could take seven years to pay off. While this was a huge sum to lay out Brandon would receive around £800 (£387,016.00)[56] a year from Elizabeth's lands and Brandon would hold Elizabeth's wardship until she came of age, which was at least six years, and thus Brandon would more than make his money back.[57] At twenty-eight years of age, Brandon was a widower and a young, attractive man, who was a close favourite of King Henry VIII. Brandon, ever seeking to further his prospects proposed marriage to the eight-year-old Elizabeth when she came of age. On 15 May, Brandon was created Viscount Lisle and received a number of grants to signify his new position.[58] He would also have access to the coin and lands that his intended, Elizabeth, inherited. The marriage between Brandon and Elizabeth never came to pass because less than two years later Brandon would once more create an ever bigger scandal by marrying Henry VIII's younger sister.

By the end of 1513, it was clear to anyone at court that Brandon was the king's favourite. Even Margaret of Austria noted "the great love and trust that the king bare and had" towards Brandon.[59] If the past four years had seen the dramatic rise of Brandon through the ranks at court then 1514 would see him reach the pinnacle of his career and become one of the most powerful and respected men in all of England.

The Duke and the French Queen
(1514 – 1515)

On Candlemas Day, 2 February 1514, Charles Brandon, Viscount Lisle, was formally invested as the Duke of Suffolk. The ceremony took place at Lambeth and was conducted by the king. In addition, Thomas Howard, Earl of Surrey, was created 2nd Duke of Norfolk. His son, also Thomas, was created Earl of Surrey, and Charles Somerset was created Earl of Worcester.[1]

This was a huge advancement for Brandon and a signal of his rise and great favour with the king. At the time that Brandon was created Duke of Suffolk there were only two other dukes in the realm, the newly created Duke of Norfolk and the Duke of Buckingham. Thomas Howard, Duke of Norfolk, came from noble family. His father, John Howard, 1st Duke of Norfolk, was head of Richard III's vanguard at the Battle of Bosworth[2] when he was slain by an arrow through the brain.[3] Thomas Howard also fought at the Battle of Bosworth but was injured and captured by Henry VII.[4] Over time, Howard proved his loyalty to the new Tudor monarch and was restored to his title of Earl of Surrey.[5]

There seems to have been little love between the newly created Duke of Norfolk and Brandon. Brandon was from mediocre stock while Norfolk from a prestigious and well-known family. In addition to this, Brandon had been elected as leader of the king's vanguard in the war against France the previous year and had been made high marshal of the whole army, a huge responsibility for a mere knight and master of the horse.[6] The Duke of Norfolk may also have been resentful and jealous of Brandon's friendship and position with the king knowing that Brandon not only had regular access to the king but also had his ear. While the pair would be forced to form a somewhat amicable working relationship, the next decade would show that there was clearly underlying resentment and tension.

Along with the dukes of Suffolk and Norfolk, the only other duke in the kingdom was Edward Stafford, Duke of Buckingham. Buckingham was a descendant of Thomas Woodstock, youngest son of Edward III. In addition to this, his mother was Katherine Woodville, sister of the late Queen Elizabeth Woodville. At the time Buckingham was also the richest peer in England with an annual income of around £6,000 per year (£2,902,620.00)[7] as well as being high steward of England and a privy councillor.[8]

Unlike the dukes of Norfolk and Buckingham, Brandon did not come from royal blood nor did he come from a noble family. Instead, Brandon's rise was due to his friendship with Henry VIII and his proven skills in military service.[9] Being created Duke of Suffolk was a huge step upwards in social standing as Brandon was now one of the most powerful men in England.

In January, Brandon was granted custody of the lands and marriage of Roger, son and heir of Sir Robert Corbett. This allowed Brandon to control all the lands and property of Roger until the boy came of age, which totalled around £150[10] (£72,565.50).[11] Then in February, the king granted Brandon the manor, castle and park of Donnington, Berkshire, and an annuity of £40[12] (£19,350.80 today).[13] Although this did not bring Brandon a great deal of money, it added to his land base. Also on 28 February, Henry VIII wrote to the great wardrobe from Lambeth requesting a saddle and harness for the Duke of Suffolk.[14] This may have been a present for the newly created duke.

While being elevated from a viscount to a duke in 1514 may have seemed like a huge affair, in 1515 Brandon would cause the greatest scandal of his career, causing such a stir throughout Christendom that it made his flirtation with Margaret of Savoy look like a mere blip in social standing.

In 1500, King Henry VII and Philip I of Castile negotiated a treaty of friendship, which was signed in early June. Part of this treaty was that Henry VII's youngest daughter Mary would be pledged to marry Philip's son Charles. Mary was just five years old at the time and Charles just four months – age clearly had no factor in international negotiations.[15] However, the treaty would not last long. Events throughout Europe would see constant changes in alliances and soon Philip I was seeking a French bride for his son Charles, namely King

Louis XII of France's daughter Claude. Yet this was not to be, as Louis XII withdrew from the treaty with Philip I and married his daughter Claude to Francis of Angoulême.[16] Once more Philip I was on the lookout for a beautiful and influential bride for his son, and it seemed that fate would intervene.

On 16 January 1506, Philip and his wife Juana were sailing for Spain when a fierce storm blew them off-course and they had to take refuge in England. Never one to overlook an opportunity, Henry VII jumped on his royal guests and welcomed them warmly. Philip and Juana were presented with almost three months of entertainment and lavish celebrations. While this was happening, Henry VII and Philip I negotiated a new treaty of friendship and once more discussion of a marriage between Mary and Charles was presented.[17] Finally, on 21 December 1507, Maximilian (Holy Roman Emperor), Prince Charles of Spain and Henry VII of England signed an agreement of marriage between Charles and Mary.[18]

At just eleven years of age, Mary was betrothed. What Brandon thought about this future marriage is unknown. At twenty-three years of age it is doubtful that Brandon had any romantic feelings towards the young princess. After all, he was caught up with his own marital problems at the time, although it is possible that Brandon would have been aware of the beautiful Mary and that she too was aware of the up-and-coming friend of her brother. Brandon had participated in the celebratory jousts for the wedding of Arthur Tudor and Katherine of Aragon and would have participated in other sporting events at court. The chances that Brandon and Mary had seen and knew of each other would have been quite high, although it is doubtful that Brandon would have had cause to speak with or spend time with a princess.

On 17 December 1508, Mary, now thirteen, was married by proxy to Prince Charles. Standing in for the young prince was the Sieur de Berghes. Both Mary and Berghes exchanged vows and then Berghes placed a ring upon the middle finger of Mary's left hand. According to the law, both Mary and Charles were married, but the fact that Charles was under-age and the wedding never legally consummated brought the whole affair into question. At the time, after the proxy wedding, there was a huge banquet and three days of celebrations and jousting,[19] in which, no doubt as one of the king's spears, Brandon would have participated.

However, the marriage was not to be. After Henry VII's death on 21 April 1509, Henry VIII came to the throne[20] and had different plans for his sister and European alliances. During 1515, the Holy League against France was created and England ended up going to war with France.[21] King Ferdinand, as we have heard, did not hold up his side of the agreement and Henry VIII felt betrayed and let down. In addition to this, Ferdinand signed a one-year truce with the French king.[22] At the same time, Pope Julius II died and when Pope Leo X succeeded he showed no wish to continue the Holy League's feud with France.[23] Also, Thomas Wolsey, Henry VIII's right-hand man, was vying for England to create peace throughout Europe.

Henry VIII was growing angry at the emperor for the delay in the marriage between his sister and Prince Charles. Soon Henry VIII was looking for an alliance elsewhere, and Mary would play a vital role in this. Henry VIII turned his attention away from a treaty between England and the Empire and sought one with France. King Louis XII of France was also eager for an alliance with England, as there was conflict between France and the Empire. Part of this alliance was to be a marriage between Henry's sister Mary and the fifty-two-year-old King Louis XII.[24]

On 30 July 1514, Mary Tudor formally renounced her marriage with Prince Charles of Spain:

> In the royal manor of Wanstead, and in the presence of Thomas duke of Norfolk, Charles duke of Suffolk, Thomas bp. of Lincoln postulate of York, Richard bp. of Winchester, Thomas bp. of Durham, Charles earl of Worcester, and Sir Ralph Vernay, the Princess Mary solemnly renounced her compact of marriage with Charles prince of Spain.[25]

Then only two weeks later, on 13 August, Mary was married via proxy to King Louis XII. The Duke of Longueville, who had been captured in the 1513 campaign of France, acted as proxy for the French king: [26]

> Duke of Longueville, taking with his right the right hand
> of the Princess Mary, read the French King's words of espousal
> (recited) in French. Then the Princess, taking the right hand
> of the Duke of Longueville, read her part of the contract
> (recited) in the same tongue. Then the Duke of Longueville
> signed the schedule and delivered it for signature to the
> Princess Mary, who signed Marye; after which the Duke
> delivered the Princess a gold ring, which the Princess placed
> on the fourth finger of her right hand.[27]

Brandon was present at both Mary's renouncing of her marriage
to Prince Charles of Spain and to her proxy marriage to the French
king. By now Mary was eighteen years of age and reported to be one
of the most beautiful princesses in all of Christendom.[28] It would be
ridiculous to think that Brandon did not see Mary's beauty and one
cannot help but wonder if, at this time, his interest turned towards
the young queen-to-be.

Things moved swiftly for Mary after her proxy wedding. No
expense was spared for the new French queen's wardrobe, and it
is reported that Henry VIII spent around £43,000 (an almost
unthinkable £20,802,110.00)[29] on clothing, mostly in the French
fashion for Mary and her servants. In addition to this, liveries for her
servants and other trappings were made.[30] On 2 October, Mary left
Dover for France. Henry VIII walked his sister down to the waterside
and it was here that allegedly Mary made her brother promise that if
she should outlive King Louis XII, then she would be able to choose
her second husband for herself. At this time Mary would most likely
have been aware that the often ill and ageing Louis may not have long
to live.[31] It is interesting to note that Mary made her brother agree to
this arrangement.

The journey from Dover to Boulogne was rough and many of
Mary's ships were scattered. The poor queen had to be carried to shore
in the pouring rain.[32] On 5 October, Mary and her entourage reached
Montreuil, where she spent several days resting. Then on the 7th,
Mary set out for Abbeville, where she would meet her new husband.
Along the way Mary was greeted with pageants and celebrations.
Many dignitaries from the towns welcomed the new queen with
much flattery and gifts.[33]

Mary was not supposed to meet her husband until she officially
arrived at Abbeville, but it seemed the French king was eager to see
his new bride. Pretending to be out hawking, the king bumped into

Mary and her entourage. Upon the sudden meeting, Mary acted the part and initially pretended to be surprised before greeting her new husband warmly. The ageing king, naturally, was smitten with his beautiful young bride.[34]

Later that day Mary formally entered Abbeville, and on 9 October 1514, she was married to Louis XII at nine o'clock in the morning in the great hall of the Hotel de la Gruthose. Mary wore a French gown made of gold brocade and trimmed with ermine. She was covered in beautiful jewels and was given away by the Duke of Norfolk and the Marquis of Dorset. Louis XII wore gold and ermine to match his bride. After the wedding, the pair were separated and dined in their own apartments before they came together once more in a lavish ball. At eight o'clock, the newly married couple were escorted to their bed for the official bedding ceremony.[35]

The morning after the wedding, King Louis XII dismissed most of the English women in the queen's household. Naturally Mary was quite distressed about this and sought advice from Thomas Wolsey. When Brandon heard the news, he laid the blame squarely on Norfolk. He believed that Norfolk went along with the French king, as most of the women in service of Mary were servants of Wolsey and Brandon, and thus dismissing them would mean they could not feed information to either man close to Henry VIII. Brandon went on to state that if Henry VIII found out how unhappy his sister was, Norfolk would not hesitate to lay the blame on Brandon and/or Wolsey.[36] It is interesting to note that at this early stage of his career, Brandon and Wolsey had a close working relationship and the tension between Brandon and Norfolk, which would continue throughout their lives, was already manifesting.

Brandon was not present during Mary's journey to France or for her wedding to the French king. Henry VIII chose to keep his friend behind. It may have been that Henry was aware of Mary's affections for Brandon and did not wish to cause any discomfort having the man his sister desired at her wedding. Ultimately, Henry had another mission for the duke. Brandon's mission was twofold. First he was to help organise the jousts that were to celebrate the coronation of Mary and Louis XII and also represent the English, but more importantly he was to begin negotiations for Henry and Louis XII to meet in the spring to hopefully arrange a mutual attack against Ferdinand of Aragon.[37]

Brandon was sent to France in mid-October and he first met with the French king at Beauvais on 25 or 26 October. Unfortunately, the king was ill and had to meet Brandon while he was lying down in bed. Mary was also present, sitting beside her new husband.[38] It must have been quite a sight for Brandon to see the beautiful young Mary now married to an old king battling with gout.

Brandon continued negotiations with the French king over the next few weeks. Initially, Louis XII pretended to be interested in a joint attack against Ferdinand but he was really only interested in recovering Milan for France. Louis XII welcomed England's support in this campaign, but at first seemed vague in setting an actual date for a meeting with Henry.[39] Despite Brandon's lack of diplomatic experience, and having to organise the jousting events in his spare time, he did manage to get the French king to agree to a meeting with Henry VIII as well as to start to discuss some possible strategies for a joint attack.[40] Louis was impressed with Brandon's efforts[41] and stated that "no prince christened hath such a servant for peace and war".[42]

On 25 October, Brandon wrote to Henry VIII to inform him of the discussions he'd had with the French king and of the upcoming jousting tournaments, of which Brandon was partly responsible for organising. In an addition to the end of the letter he writes:

> I bysche yovr grace to [tell my]sstres Blount and mysstres Carru [the] next tyme yt I wreth un to them [or se]nd them tokones thay schall odar [wre]th to me or send me tokones agayen.[43]

It is interesting to note that Brandon makes reference to Mistress Blount, *aka* Elizabeth "Bessie" Blount, and to Mistress Carew, *aka* Elizabeth Carew, wife of Nicholas Carew. Both women were part of Queen Katherine's court at the time and both were said to be extremely beautiful and close friends.[44] There has been some suggestion that this letter meant that Brandon was in a sexual relationship with Bessie Blount and/or Elizabeth Carew, but this may not be the case. It was not unusual as part of the game of courtly love for a man to send tokens, poems or letters to young, beautiful women and to receive them in return. As part of the game, it was not expected that there would be a full, physical relationship between the pair and it was often played as a means for expressing love and desire in court aimed at emulating the Arthurian legends of old. It is known that Henry VIII lavished expensive gifts upon both Elizabeth Carew and Bessie Blount and that he began a sexual relationship with Bessie Blount some time after 1514. Yet to suggest that Brandon had a full affair with either woman simply cannot be assured with any certainty. It also seems highly doubtful that Brandon would sleep with the wife of Nicholas Carew, one of his close friends and a member of the king's inner circle.[45]

On 5 November 1514, Mary was crowned Queen of France by the Bishop of Bayeux at the Abbey Church of Saint-Denis.[46] The whole court attended, including Brandon and those of his entourage. Afterwards another great feast was held for the new queen. Shortly after this, on 9 November, Brandon received a French pension of 1,000 crowns.[47]

The official celebratory tournaments began on Monday 13 November.[48] Naturally, as England's representative and having helped to organise the jousts Brandon took part:

> My Lord of Suffolk and he ran three days, and lost nothing. One Frenchman was slain at the tilt, and divers horses. On Saturday the 18th, the tournay and course in the field began as roughly as ever I saw; for there was divers times both horse and man overthrown, horses slain, and one Frenchman hurt that he is not like to live. My Lord of Suffolk and I ran but the first day thereat, but put our ayds thereto, because there was no noblemen to be put unto us, but poor men of arms and Scots, many of them were hurt on both sides, but no great hurt, and of our Englishmen none overthrown nor greatly hurt but a little of their hands. The Dolphyn himself was a little hurt on his hand. On Tuesday, the 21st, the fighting on foot began, to the which they brought an Almayn that never came into the field before, and put him to my Lord of Suffolk to have put us to shame if they could, but advantage they gat none of us, but rather the contrary. I forbear to write more of our chances, because I am party therein. I ende[d] without any manner hurt; my Lord of Suffolk is a little hurt in his hand.[49]

Records show that Brandon performed excellently at the jousts and at the hand-to-hand combat. He was reported at the time to be the best jouster in all of Europe, after Henry VIII of course.[50] In fact, he did so well that there seemed few Frenchmen who could compare to his skills at the tilt. On the first day, Brandon ran fifteen courses, thirteen of them as the challenger. On the second day, Brandon unhorsed his opponent three successive times.[51] To try and outshine Brandon, the French brought in an enormous German of great strength and skill, but Brandon was not to be beaten. After unhorsing his German opponent, Brandon struck him with the butt-end of his spear causing the German to stagger. But the fighting continued. After lifting their visors to draw breath, Brandon and the German continued to fight with blunt-edged swords. Despite such a fierce opponent, Brandon was able to out-skill the German and beat him about the head until blood came out of his nose.[52] He seems to have shone at the events, coming out with only a sore hand.[53] Mary would have been present at these tournaments, able to watch Brandon joust and fight.

Brandon's response was modest. He wrote a short note to Henry VIII:

> My lord at the Writing of this lettre the Justes were doon and blissed be god alle our englissh men sped well as I am sure ye shall here by other.[54]

Instead of trying to build himself up in the king's eyes, Brandon kept his success a low-key affair, instead choosing to praise the victories of the English in general. Despite such a modest reaction, Brandon's achievements helped secure him support amongst many of the French noblemen and also helped to secure trust with King Louis, so much so that now Louis XII was more than willing to negotiate with Henry VIII through Brandon.[55]

After the celebrations Brandon was recalled home where he was greeted warmly by Henry VIII and Thomas Wolsey,[56] who in 1515 would be created a cardinal by Pope Leo X. The next time Brandon returned to France would be to return the newly widowed Mary back to England.

On 1 January 1515, less than three months after his marriage, King Louis XII died.[57] He had been sick for several weeks and his death was no surprise, although it was reported that when Mary was told she fainted. Mary was sent to the Hôtel de Cluny where she wore white, the French colour of mourning.[58] She was to stay in seclusion for forty days so that it could be worked out if she were pregnant or not. If she was pregnant and gave birth to a son, he would be the next King of France. However, no one really believed this and Francis, husband of Louis XII's daughter Claude, was quickly accepted as the next king.[59]

On the same day that the French king died, Brandon participated in a masque in the queen's chambers. Eight dancers were involved, four men and four women. The men were Nicholas Carew, Lord Fellinger, Henry VIII and Charles Brandon. The four women were Elizabeth Carew, Bessie Blount, Lady Guildford and Lady Fellinger. They were dressed in cloth of silver and blue velvet with the letters H and K embroidered on them. The king was partnered with Bessie Blount and it is possible that Brandon was partnered with Elizabeth Carew.[60]

Once news of the French king's death reached England, Brandon was sent to France to return the Dowager Queen and, hopefully, to retrieve as much of Mary's coin, plate and jewels as possible.[61] It is reported that before Brandon left, Henry VIII made him swear not to act foolishly and marry the young Mary until after the pair had returned to England.[62] It could have been that Henry VIII did intend to fulfil the promise he made to his sister and, knowing of her affection for Brandon, would allow her to marry him, but not until they returned home. It could also be that Henry VIII agreed to the marriage face to face, but that when Mary returned home he would not allow Brandon to marry his sister and would seek a far more diplomatic marriage for her elsewhere.

It is interesting to note that just before Brandon arrived in Paris to meet Mary, two friars met with the Dowager Queen to turn her mind against Brandon. They informed Mary that the English council would never let her marry Brandon and, worse, that Brandon and Thomas Wolsey performed witchcraft to turn Henry VIII's mind towards their will. They even went so far as to suggest that Brandon's witchcraft caused a disease in William Compton's leg, Henry VIII's groom of the stool. Later, when he heard this news, Brandon immediately informed Wolsey. He proposed that someone must have been coaching the friars and suggested that this person was the Duke of Norfolk, Brandon's rival. Once again this was a case of Norfolk and Brandon's clear dislike for one another. While publicly for the sake of the king they appeared to get along, clearly there was a constant simmering rivalry between the two.[63] However, it is poignant that if it was Norfolk who sent the friars, the Duke of Norfolk must have been aware of some feelings from Brandon towards Mary, or vice versa.

Brandon finally arrived in Paris on 31 January 1515. Brandon met with Mary the same day and reported that Mary was eager to return home so that she may see her brother.[64] Brandon was to face two major difficulties in the negotiations to see Mary returned to England. The first was regarding her jewellery. If the late king had given any to her as queen, it was to stay in France as the jewels belonged to the future queen. But if they were given to Mary as personal gifts, then she would be entitled to take them home with her to England.[65] The second difficulty was that the new King Francis I was reluctant to let Mary leave.

Mary was only eighteen years old, young, beautiful and available to marry again. While still in France, she was left vulnerable as Francis I could use her as a bargaining tool. He could have her married to another French nobleman to continue the alliance with England, or even have her married to another member of nobility from another country to form an alliance. There was also speculation that Francis I was worried that if Mary returned to England, Henry VIII would once more seek a treaty with the Holy Roman Empire and betroth Mary to Prince Charles, with whom she had previously been betrothed. There was also the fact that if Mary remained in France, Francis could keep her jewels and other travelling expenses.[66] It was rumoured that Francis even had an interest in marrying the beautiful young Mary,[67] but that seems unlikely has he would have had to divorce his current wife, the late king's daughter, to do so.

With such uncertainty, stress and fear surrounding her, Mary Tudor decided to take matters into her own hands. The young Dowager Queen proposed marriage to Brandon and the duke accepted.[68] Whether this was a spontaneous decision or thought about for several days remains unknown. However, matters were finally decided and Mary and Brandon married in secret, without Henry VIII's permission. Although the exact date of their wedding remains unknown it has been suggested that the couple married sometime between 15 and 20 February, before approximately ten witnesses.[69] The newlyweds then consummated their marriage to make it legally binding.

Despite having just committed high treason, Brandon would not shy away from what he had done and accepted full responsibility for his actions. He wrote to Henry VIII stating that when he met with Mary he found that her mind was made up and that she did not want anyone else but him.[70] Francis I fully supported this marriage, as it allowed Mary to return home without any fear or concern that she would be used in negotiations against him.

On 5 March 1515, about a month after he had secretly married Mary, Brandon wrote to Thomas Wolsey:

> Begs Wolsey to help him now as he has done always. When he came to Paris he heard many things which put him and the Queen in great fear. And the Queen would never let me [be] in rest till I had granted her to be married; and so, to be plain with you, I have married her. Fears lest the King should know it and be displeased with him; had rather be dead than that he should be miscontent. Entreats Wolsey not to let him be undone, which he fears he shall be without his help.[71]

Wolsey passed on the letter to Henry VIII and the king was greatly displeased. Not simply because Brandon had committed treason by marrying his sister, but also because he had broken his promise. A man's word was of great importance.[72] Wolsey wrote back to Brandon:

> The King would not believe it, but took the same grievously and displeasantly, not merely for Suffolk's presumption, but for breaking his promise made to the King at Eltham in Wolsey's presence, and would not believe he would have broken his promise had he been torn with wild horses.[73]

Knowing that he had got himself into a most grievous situation, Brandon threw himself at Wolsey's mercy, seeking any advice that the man could give. Mary too wrote to her brother, seeking to remind him that she had agreed to marry the sickly and ageing Louis XII and that he had promised her that for her second marriage she could take a man of her choosing. She also sought her brother's forgiveness and promised to give him the plate, coin and jewels of her dowry:

> Begs he will remember that she had consented to his request, and for the peace of Christendom, to marry Lewis of France, "though he was very aged and sickly," on condition that if she survived him she should marry whom she liked. Since her husband was dead, remembering the great virtue in my Lord of Suffolk, "to whom I have always been of good mind, as ye well know," she has determined to marry him without any request or labor on his part. She is now so bound

to him that for no earthly cause can she change. Begs his good will. Trusted him as one who had always honorably regarded his word. Has come out of France and is at Calais, where she will wait till she hear from him. Binds herself to give up to him her "dote," all such plate of gold and jewels as she had with Lewis, and to give such securities for repayment of her dower as he shall think fit. [74]

Then, in an attempt to win Henry VIII over, Mary had the magnificent Mirror of Naples, a huge pearl, smuggled out of France as a gift for her brother.[75] Mary's letters to her brother are interesting as, while she seeks his forgiveness, she also reminds him repeatedly of his promise to allow her to marry a man of her choosing. Mary's letters indicate that the young woman was headstrong and clearly felt that her brother had at least in some way already given permission for this marriage. Again, when the evidence is examined, Henry VIII must have been aware, at least at some level, that Brandon held a strong interest in Mary and that she too reciprocated these feelings. However, at this point it suited the king to deny this knowledge as he wished to benefit as much as possible from Brandon's treason.

Next Brandon decided to write directly to the king, throwing himself at the king's mercy and begging his forgiveness:

Begs the King's forgiveness for his offence in this marriage and intreats "for the passion of God" that it may not turn his heart against him: "but punish me rather with prison or otherwise as may be your pleasure. Sir, rather than you should have me in mistrust in your [he]art that I should not be true to you as thys may by accusseun, [str]yke of me hed and lyet me not lyef. Alas! Sir, my Lord of York hath written to me two letters that [it] should be thought that the French King would make ... es hand with your grace, and that a would occupy me as [a]n instrument thereunto. Alas! Sir, that ever it should be thought or said that I should be so; for, Sir, your grace not offended, I will make good against all the world [t] o die for it that ever I thought any such thing or did thing, saving the love and [ma]rrag of the Queen, that should be to your displeasure, [I p]ray God let me die as shameful a death as ever did man." But for this he might have said there was never man that had so loving and kind a master as himself, or master that had so true a servant as the King had in him.[76]

On 22 April, Brandon, upon learning what was happening back in England, once more threw himself at the king's mercy. This time he wrote to Henry:

> All the Council, except my Lord of York [Thomas Wolsey], are determined to have Suffolk put to death or imprisoned. This is hard; for none of them ever were in trouble but he was glad to help them to the best of his power, and now in this little trouble they are ready to destroy him. "But God forgive them, whatsoever comes of me, for I am determined; for your grace is he that is my sovereign lord and master and he that has brought me up of nought, and I am your subject and servant and he that has offended your grace in breaking my promise that I made your grace touching the Queen your sister." Will undergo what punishment Henry pleases. Knows the King is of such nature that it will not lie in their powers to destroy him through malice.[77]

Brandon's letter is emotional and dramatic. He throws himself at Henry's mercy, acknowledging that he was and is nothing without all that Henry had done for him. He also recognises that he has committed a great sin by breaking his promise to Henry not to marry Mary. In breaking his promise Brandon had betrayed the code of honour for a man, one of the most important beliefs for Henry VIII. Most important of all, Brandon places Henry VIII, his king and master, above all others. By marrying the sister of a great king, Brandon put himself into a very precarious position, not just because he had committed treason but because such actions could be perceived as trying to set himself up as the next king. At this time Henry VIII had no living male heir and if Brandon could produce a son with Mary, then their child would be next in line for the throne. Brandon was in a dangerous position but by professing his loyalty to Henry he placed himself in a position of weakness and showed that he had no intention of ever betraying Henry or the trust the king held in him. Henry VIII has always been and would always be his king and master.

It is interesting to note that Brandon writes that he is willing to take any punishment given to him by Henry but also realises that Henry won't punish him because of the evil words and malice of others. Why the other members of the council sought to have Brandon imprisoned or put to death remains unknown. Throughout his time at court the only person that Brandon seemed to feud with was the

Duke of Norfolk, who he competed with for position, and who in addition opposed the French alliance that Brandon and Wolsey fully supported.[78] Perhaps Norfolk whispered to the other members of the council and sought to turn them against Brandon, or maybe they were simply astounded that Brandon would be so presumptuous as to rise from so little to marry the king's sister.

Whatever the reason behind the English council's lack of support for Brandon, he and Mary were married in a more public wedding in France on 31 March.[79] The couple landed in Dover on 2 May. They were met by Henry VIII and a great retinue at nearby Birling House. The king warmly welcomed the couple and accepted his younger sister's explanation that it was she who was responsible for the marriage and not Brandon.[80]

In return for the king's blessing, Brandon and Mary were ordered to not only return Mary's full dowry, as well as all her plate and jewels, but to also pay £24,000 (£11,610,480.00)[81] in yearly instalments of £1,000 (£483,770.00)[82]. Brandon was also required to give up the wardship of Lady Lisle, with whom he had previously been contracted to marry.[83] While this was a staggering sum that would have certainly seen Brandon close to poverty, records show that by 1521, six years after their marriage, the couple had only repaid £1,324[84] (£640,511.48)[85]. Clearly the king was more interested in making a show rather than actually enforcing the regular repayments.

Having gained the king's blessing, Brandon and Mary were formally married at Greenwich on 13 May in front of Henry VIII and Queen Katherine of Aragon.[86] Yet despite being the Duke of Suffolk and now married to the Dowager Queen of France and the king's sister, Brandon's financial base was fragile. Compared to the dukes of Buckingham and Norfolk, he had little land of which he could draw revenue from. Without Mary's plate, jewels or coin, which she had signed over to her brother, Brandon's new wife was relatively poor and relied heavily upon her own pension from France as the Dowager Queen.

Brandon in turn drew upon his Welsh holdings as well as the £40 a year (£19,350.80)[87] he was granted in his creation as Duke of Suffolk in addition to his small pension from France to support himself and his household.[88] Yet this was not enough and Brandon also had to beg Wolsey to ask the king for a loan of £12,000[89] (£5,805,240.00).[90]

Brandon had to draw upon the de la Pole estates in Suffolk that had been given to him by the king in February 1515. Richard de la Pole had been a constant thorn in Henry VIII's side as he had a distant claim to the English throne. He had fled to Europe and was at times used by the French as a possible means to take over England.[91] The king may have granted Brandon some of the de la Pole estates as a means to squash any further thoughts of uprising in the area and to ensure a man he trusted oversaw the happenings in Suffolk.

In 1524, Brandon's uncle, Sir Robert, died, leaving Brandon the manor of Henham, which the duke incorporated into his East Anglia estates.[92] Brandon continued to purchase estates and manors within this area in an attempt to become one of the largest magnates in East Anglia, although he never quite managed to secure the entire de la Pole estates. His chancellor Oliver Pole and his general attorney Humphrey Wingfield spent £100 (£48,377.00)[93] on four manors in an attempt to secure Brandon's power base in Suffolk.[94] As well as his personal status, the people of the area greatly loved Mary and welcomed her warmly wherever she went. In addition to this, in December the Bishop of Ely made Brandon steward of the estates of the diocese, which only added to Brandon's position.[95] It is interesting to note that over the next few years Brandon's reputation throughout East Anglia clearly advanced. In the Norwich episcopal registers in 1517, Brandon was simply referred to as "the Duke of Suffolk". However, by 1524 he was "the most powerful man, Charles Duke of Suffolk, great marshal of England", and in September of the same year he was "the noble and most powerful prince, Charles Duke of Suffolk and Great Marshal of England".[96]

As well as lavishing such titles upon Brandon, the people of East Anglia recognised the importance and influence the duke held and were now calling upon him to present their requests and causes to Wolsey or the king. An example of this is when there was a grain shortage in January 1528 and the people begged Brandon for support. He wrote to Wolsey:

> The inhabitants of the Suffolk coast, who are destitute of grain fit for man's use, have asked him to request Wolsey for a licence for them to carry white and red herrings and sprats to Flanders, to barter for corn.[97]

The outcome of such a crisis remains unknown but it is significant to note that, in desperation and hunger, the people of the Suffolk coast pleaded with Brandon for support knowing that he would be able to take their cause to Wolsey and hopefully obtain them the help they required.

Brandon was aware that his position was heavily reliant upon his favour and position with the king. After their wedding, both Brandon and Mary took some time away from court, but both knew how important it was to return to court and also to the king's side, and thus by the end of the year they had resumed normal life at court. [98]

If the Duke of Norfolk, Brandon's rival for the king's attention, thought he could use Brandon's dramatic marriage to Mary Tudor to discredit Brandon and see him removed from court, he was sorely mistaken. By the end of 1515, Brandon had weathered the storm of his betrayal and come out of it strong, if not stronger than before. He was now not only the Duke of Suffolk but also the king's greatest friend and brother-in-law, a highly influential position.

The King's Man (1516 – 1532)

The following sixteen years would see Brandon involved with a war against France, the birth of four of his children, the appearance of a new queen and a constant struggle with income. Yet underlying it all would be his ever-present loyalty to Henry VIII and an ever-increasing rise in his status and position at court.

Despite thinking that Mary might have been pregnant in early 1515, she did not in fact give birth to her first child until 1516. On 11 March 1516, between ten and eleven o'clock at night, Mary gave birth to a healthy boy at Bath Place, London, a house belonging to Cardinal Wolsey.[1] There is some question as to why Mary gave birth at Bath Place rather than her home of Suffolk Place. It may be that her labour came upon her unexpectedly and she did not have enough time to go into her lying-in. Or it may simply be that due to the duke's relationship with Wolsey and all the cardinal had done for them in seeing their favour restored to the king that Bath Place was offered to Mary for the birth of her first child. Either way, Brandon now had a son and heir.

The baby boy was christened Henry after the king. The christening ceremony took place at Suffolk Place and was conducted with great splendour and ceremony. The hall was lavishly decorated with wall-hangings of red and white Tudor roses, torches were lit and the christening font was warmed for the special occasion. The christening was performed by John Fisher, Bishop of Rochester, and he was assisted by Thomas Ruthall, Bishop of Durham. The king attended the ceremony as did Cardinal Thomas Wolsey, the Duke of Norfolk and other important members of the court. The king and Cardinal Wolsey stood as godfathers while Catherine, Dowager Countess of Devon, a daughter of the late King Edward IV, stood as godmother.[2]

After the ceremony, Lady Anne Grey carried little Henry to his nursery and Sir Humphrey Banaster, Mary's vice chamberlain, carried his train. After this, spices and wine were served by the Duke of Norfolk and presents were given in celebration. The king gave the child a salt cellar and a cup of solid gold and the queen gave two silver gilt pots. As was usual, Mary was not in attendance as she had not yet been churched. The whole event was full of pomp, ritual and lavish celebration, which signified the importance of the birth of the king's nephew as well as Brandon's favour with the king.[3]

With his chequered marital career, Brandon worked hard to ensure the legitimacy of his children and his marriage to Mary Tudor. He appealed to Pope Clement VII to issue a bull stating the legitimacy of his marriage and in turn his children. Yet it was not until 20 August 1529 that a bull was finally granted, legitimising Brandon and Mary's marriage. The bull stated:

> That Suffolk in the days of Henry VII. had married Margaret Mortymer alias Brandon, of London diocese, on the strength of a dispensation which was not valid, and with her had cohabited although he had previously contracted marriage with Ann Browne, and was related to the said Margaret in the second and third degrees of affinity. Besides, the said Anne and Margaret were related in the second and third degrees of consanguinity, and Suffolk's grandmother was the sister of the father of a former husband of Margaret's (ac etiam ex eo avia tua et genitor olim conjugis dictae Margaretae frater et soror fuerant). For these causes, feeling that he could not continue to cohabit with Margaret Mortymer without sin, he caused his marriage with her to be declared null by the official of the archdeacon of London, to whom the cognisance of such causes of old belongs. After this sentence Suffolk married the said Anne, and had some daughters by her, and after her death he married Mary queen dowager of France. The bull ratifies this sentence, and supplies all defects both of law and fact, and visits with ecclesiastical censure all who call it in question.[4]

On 19 and 20 May 1516, another spectacular jousting event was organised. Henry VIII, Brandon, Sir George Carew and Henry Bourchier, Earl of Essex were to be on one team; Sir William Kingston, Sir Giles Capell, John Sedley and Edmund Howard on the other.[5] On the first day both Brandon and Henry scored well, the king scoring slightly better. On the second Brandon continued to gain high scores and he ended the day with the highest total.

However, the king had not done as well and his opponents were not on par with his skills.[6] Frustrated, the king vowed "never to joust again except it be with as good a man as himself".[7] It is important to note that when Brandon returned to court and jousting, he returned as the king's opponent rather than on the same team.

After this Brandon was away from court until February 1517. With tensions between Charles V the Holy Roman Emperor and Francis I of France, Wolsey thought it best to keep Brandon, clearly pro-French, away from court. Brandon was always aware that his favour and position was heavily reliant upon the king's favour, and in turn was concerned about what those around the king were saying about him. He was probably most worried that the Duke of Norfolk had free access to the king and could be whispering any lies about Brandon. Brandon wrote to Wolsey on 14 July 1516 stating that: "Though he is far off by the King's commandment, his heart is always with him."[8]

Brandon need not have worried as, during Henry VIII's summer progress that year, he stopped to visit the Brandons at Donnington, which brought the duke great comfort.[9] In addition to this, the king bestowed upon Brandon the wardships of Sir Thomas Knyvett's two sons. (Knyvett died on board the ship *Regent* in 1512.)[10] It is also possible that the king or Thomas Wolsey decided to keep Brandon from court to ease his financial burdens, as it would have cost the duke far less to keep his own household than maintain his household as well as that of his household at court.

After Brandon's return to court in February 1517, he resumed his normal position with the king and attended council meetings (although sporadically) and participated in regular jousting events, although now as the king's leading opponent rather than his teammate.[11] Meanwhile, Mary was pregnant again. In July she had set out on a pilgrimage to Walsingham, most likely to pray for the safe delivery of her child, when her labour came upon her quite suddenly. She was forced to stop and stay with the Bishop of Ely, at Hatfield, and on 16 July, between two and three o'clock in the morning, she gave birth to a healthy baby girl. The child was named Frances, as she was born on St Francis's Day, yet her name also allowed Mary and Brandon to pay tribute to King Francis I, who had supported them in their marriage several years earlier.[12]

Due to the suddenness of the labour and birth, Frances's christening was a low-key event compared to her brother's and was held in the local parish church. Frances's godmothers were Queen Katherine and Princess Mary, although since both could not attend Lady Boleyn was sent to stand in for the queen and Lady Elizabeth Grey stood in for the princess. Frances's godfather was the Abbot of St Albans.[13]

Oddly, there are very few details about the birth of Brandon's next child, a daughter named Eleanor, who quite possibly may have been named to honour Emperor Charles V's favourite sister, Eleanor of Austria. Eleanor was born some time between 1518 and 1521, although there are no records surrounding the circumstances of her birth, location or her christening. It can be assumed that she was christened, as all babies were at the time, and that godparents were appointed.[14]

From 1519, Henry VIII started to "grow up". He was moving away from the fun-loving sportsman who filled his time with entertainment and left the running of the kingdom to his advisers, specifically Thomas Wolsey. Now the king was starting to show more of an interest in politics and how he and England were viewed by the rest of Europe. Henry VIII was competing on a political stage against the likes of Francis I of France and Charles V, who had recently been created the Holy Roman Emperor. Both men were younger than Henry and had achieved great military successes across their respective countries. In the first ten years of Henry's reign the king had neither the military glory nor the male heir he so desperately desired.[15]

In addition to this the king's coffers, which had been overflowing when he came to the throne, were starting to run low and the common people did not want to be taxed so the king could go to war. Instead of seeking military glory, Thomas Wolsey persuaded his king to seek peace across Europe.[16]

Throughout the previous year, hostilities between France and Spain had been bubbling and both King Francis I and Emperor Charles V were seeking the support, or at least the neutrality, of Henry VIII and England.[17] In 1518, the Treaty of London was signed between the major European nations including France, England, Spain, the Holy Roman Empire, the Papacy, Burgundy and the Netherlands. The treaty stated that none of the signatories should attack one another and if they should, the others would come to the aid of any who were under attack. [18]

To solidify the Treaty of London, a magnificent (and costly) event was organised between King Henry VIII of England and King Francis I of France. The event was arranged for 7 to 24 June 1520. The meeting was held on land between the English stronghold of Guînes and the French town of Ardres, and became known as the Field of Cloth of Gold.[19]

While the purpose of the meeting was to solidify the Treaty of London and strengthen relations between the two countries, it ended up as a means for each king to try and impress the other (and at times to attempt to out-do each other). Henry VIII spared no expense and sought not only to impress but to wow the French.[20]

In the months leading up to the meeting, Henry VIII ordered many lavish furnishings to be gathered, lavish clothing to be made, events to be organised and a magnificent pavilion to be created that the king would occupy over the course of the meeting. The royal coffers paid for many of these expenses but many of the noble men and women who attended had to pay their own expenses. This included their clothing, which was designed to impress, and those who participated in jousting had to pay for their own weapons and armour. Some nobles mortgaged their estates, sold manors and property and even organised loans in order to have the funds to attend the magnificent Field of Cloth of Gold. Approximately 5,000 men and women accompanied the king across the English Channel as well as around 3,000 horses.[21]

Of course, as Duke of Suffolk and one of the leading men of court, Brandon was not only required to go to the meeting but it was expected of him. In addition to this since his wife was the Dowager Queen of France – even though she had been queen for only a period of a few months – Mary was invited to attend the meeting between her brother and stepson-in-law Francis I.

On 16 March 1520, Brandon replied to a letter written by Wolsey where the king's man asked how many horses and people Mary would be taking with her to France. Brandon rests the details with Wolsey and replies for Wolsey:

> to take the peyne to ordre the same as ye shall think shall
> stonde moost with the kinges pleasur and her honor.[22]

Unfortunately, the list containing the details of who attended Mary no longer survives but it is known that Brandon took with him five chaplains, ten gentlemen, fifty-five servants and thirty horses. All of these would have been paid out of Brandon's own pocket, and the sheer expense of transporting, feeding and clothing these men appropriately would have been extremely high. It is also known that Brandon brought along his own armour for jousting as, throughout the celebrations, Brandon participated in multiple jousts.[23]

On Thursday 7 May, Henry VIII and Francis first met. In a small valley between the English-held Guînes and the French Ardres, the two kings rode towards each other. Both men were clearly set on impressing one another. Henry VIII wrote cloth of silver with rich jewels and white plumes, while Francis I wrote cloth of gold frieze, rich jewels and a bonnet with white plumes. When both kings approached each other they removed their bonnets and embraced before dismounting their horses and embracing once more. They then went to an English pavilion to talk.[24]

Over the course of the next seventeen days, various events and entertainments were held in an attempt to display the skill and splendour of each country. These events included jousting, archery, wrestling, singing, exotic and magnificent feats, and the exchanging of lavish and extravagant gifts.[25] Brandon participated in multiple jousting events where he represented his king and the English. On Thursday 14 June, Brandon ran a staggering twenty-four courses and, in the process, broke eighteen staves and scored three hits. This was a remarkable result and records state that Brandon did marvellously well and was deserving of the prizes he received.[26]

Another notable event was a wrestling match between Henry VIII and Francis I. Unfortunately, Francis I tripped Henry and the English king lost. It was reported that the two kings nearly came to blows over this wrestling match, but others were able to calm the kings down. Perhaps Brandon was one of those men who had to intervene and help calm his king!

One of the most magnificent displays at the Field of Cloth of Gold was the splendid pavilion built to house Henry VIII.[27] The pavilion consisted of a series of wood and canvas tents that could be separated by hangings of rich cloth to create separate rooms, including chapels and private apartments. The pavilion is shown to be made out of red cloth with a fringe of gold, decorated with Tudor roses and fleur-de-lis. Along the eaves was a frieze beating the royal mottoes *Dieu et mon droit* and *semper vavat in eterno*. On top of the pavilion poles were the models of the king's beasts (lions, greyhounds, dragons and antelope).[28] It has been proposed that around 6,000 workers were employed to build the king's and the other English quarters.[29] Brandon had the great honour of staying with his wife Mary in one wing of this great pavilion.[30]

On 24 June, the grand meeting came to an end and both kings departed. However, before Henry VIII returned home to England he went to Gravelines to meet with Charles V to discuss a possible alliance. At the end of May, only a few days before the Field of Cloth of Gold, Charles V travelled to England and met with King Henry VIII and his aunt, Katherine of Aragon. Henry V and Charles rode to Canterbury, where they feasted and most likely discussed a possible treaty with the Holy Roman Empire.[31] At Gravelines, Brandon was appointed to tend to the king with several other members of nobility.[32] More discussions were held but a treaty of friendship was not finally agreed until 25 August 1522.[33]

The Treaty of London declared that none of those who signed the treaty should attack another and if they should, the others would come to the aid of any that were under attack. In the spring of 1521, France attacked Navarre and an attack was made against Imperial Luxembourg in the name of France.[34] While both attacks were unsuccessful France had broken the Treaty of London and Henry VIII was forced to make a decision: would he support France or the Holy Roman Empire?

While such events were unfolding across Europe and England, tragedy was to hit the Brandons. During 1522, their first born son Henry died.[35] There are no details surrounding the boy's death or the reasons why. At just five or six years of age the little boy could have died from a number of illnesses or accidents. One can only imagine how devastated Brandon must have been over the loss of his son and heir. However, Mary was pregnant for a fourth time, and during 1522 she gave birth to another son. He was also named Henry, once more after the king, although no further information about his birth, location or christening survives.[36] One can imagine that, just as the first Henry, the newborn was christened with some pomp and that once more the king stood as godfather. At least Brandon once more had a son and heir who he hoped would carry on his title and bloodline.

As well as having three children with his third wife, Brandon also had to think of the other two daughters born to his first wife, Anne Browne. By now, Anne was sixteen and Mary was twelve. Brandon's attention turned to finding suitable husbands for his daughters, and by March 1525, Anne married Edward Grey, Lord Powis.[37] Brandon purchased Grey's wardship in 1517 for the sum of £1,000[38] (£379,580.00).[39] Previously, Anne had been at the court of Margaret of Austria, of whom Brandon was very familiar, to further her education. However, at the insistence of Mary Tudor, Anne was recalled to England.[40]

Mary, Brandon's other daughter with his first wife, was married to Thomas Stanley, Lord Monteagle, in 1527 or early 1528. As with Edward Grey, Brandon purchased Thomas Stanley's wardship, but for what amount remains unknown. Stanley was to be appointed as a Knight of the Bath during the coronation of Henry VIII's second wife Anne Boleyn. Ironically, he also took part in Anne Boleyn's trial in May 1536, which found her guilty of treason. Mary was to give her husband six children: three sons – William, Francis and Charles – and three daughters – Elizabeth, Anne and Margaret. Mary would also go on to serve as a lady-in-waiting to Henry VIII's third wife Jane Seymour.[41] During her marriage there was some allegation from Grey regarding Mary's misbehaviour, although exactly what that was and if there was any truth in the rumour remains unknown.[42]

Unfortunately, Brandon was to have difficulties with his son-in-law throughout his life. Thomas Stanley was to prove unreliable with his money and, in 1533, Brandon was forced to intervene in Stanley's financial business and had to pay the sum of £1,452 (£467,689.20)[43] to pay off his debts, of which over half were owed to Brandon himself. However, only fifteen days later Monteagle asked to borrow another £300 (£96,630.00)[44] from Brandon. Clearly, Monteagle could not cope and thus Brandon took charge of Stanley's finances. He declared that Monteagle's debts were to be paid in regular instalments and that Brandon would oversee his son-in-law's expenditures.[45] In addition to this Stanley had to promise to "honestly handle and entreat the said lady Mary as a noble man ought to his wife".[46] This promise may also suggest that Stanley was not treating his wife accordingly and that his financial messes were affecting Mary.

However, Brandon was not completely strict with his son-in-law and, on 27 September 1534, he granted Stanley and his daughter Mary the lavish and costly gifts of:

> An egg of diamonds, with 90 great pearls at 20s., and 14 diamonds at 40s., 118l.; a "lasce" of 23 rubies at 20s., and 11 score 7 pearls at 10s. the score, 28l. 13s. 6d.; a pattlett with 17 diamonds, two rubies at 20s., 216 pearls at 5s. the score, 22l. 5s. 4d. A pattlett of 19 score pearls at 5s. the score, and other jewels, of which one chain is in the hands of the countess of Worcester, amounting in all to 523l. 19s. 9d. 25.[47]

For his son, however, Brandon sought a greater marriage. Little Henry, after all, was in the line of succession and, as such, Brandon needed to find a future wife befitting such a position. In March 1528, Brandon bought the wardship of Katherine Willoughby, daughter and heiress of the late Lord Willoughby de Eresby, who had died in October 1526, from the king for a staggering £2,266 13s 4d[48] (£860,381.33).[49]

By 1522, Henry VIII and Queen Katherine had only one living child, a daughter named Mary born in 1516. The queen had lost five children, three sons who were either stillborn or died shortly after birth and two daughters who had both been stillborn. While the king was still somewhat hopeful of the birth of a son and heir, he did have an illegitimate son.[50]

In 1512, when Henry VIII was approximately twenty-one, a beautiful young woman came to court. Her name was Elizabeth "Bessie" Blount and at that time she had no idea the future that lay ahead of her. Bessie is first linked to Henry VIII during the Twelfth Night celebrations in 1514, when the king chose Bessie to be his dancing partner.[51] At this time Bessie was thirteen and the king around twenty-three. While it may seem like an extreme age difference, it was not uncommon at the English court for a man to partake in courtly love with a younger woman. After all, Brandon had married Dame Mortimer who was considerably older than himself. This was the same Bessie Blount that Brandon had made mention of in a letter he had written to the king in 1514.

On 15 June 1519, Bessie Blount, Henry VIII's mistress, gave birth to a healthy baby boy who was named Henry Fitzroy, after his father the king. The name Fitzroy is a Norman-French surname meaning "son of the king", and it was common for illegitimate children of the king to receive this name. Henry VIII publicly acknowledged the boy as his own and his godfather was Cardinal Thomas Wolsey.[52]

On 18 June 1525, at Bridewell Palace, Fitzroy was created Earl of Nottingham as well as given the double dukedom of Richmond and Somerset. During the creation the young boy came out and knelt before the king. Once he was created Duke of Richmond and Somerset, Fitzroy took his place on the dais beside his father. On the same day, Henry Brandon, Brandon's son, now only two or three years old, was created Earl of Lincoln.[53] The title was prestigious for the young boy, who was not even old enough to read or write, yet it may have been granted to him as the earldom was closely associated with the de la Poles. By granting the title to Brandon's son, the king may have been further distancing not only the title but the people of East Anglia from the rebellious de la Pole family.

With the elevation of Brandon to Duke of Suffolk in 1514, and then his son's title of Earl of Lincoln in 1525, there was some hushed talk that if anything should happen to the king and he died without a legitimate male heir that Brandon would seek to put his own son upon the throne, as he was the nephew of the king and born in wedlock. In addition to this, it was suggested that Brandon would rule through his son until the boy came of age. There were no truths to these rumours and they were quickly squashed. Brandon was proving himself a loyal friend and courtier to Henry VIII and, after all, the king had no intention of dying without a male heir.

Four years previously Edward Stafford, Duke of Buckingham, had been executed. He was accused of wishing the king's death and seeing himself on the throne. With royal blood running through his veins and an arrogant attitude, Buckingham had been a regular member at court but often made those around him feel uncomfortable.[54] When he applied for a licence to raise 400 armed men, Henry VIII was immediately suspicious and Buckingham was quickly arrested. At his trial at Westminster, Brandon stood as one of the judges where Buckingham was found guilty and sentenced to death.[55] On 17 May, the Duke of Buckingham was executed on Tower Hill.[56] With Buckingham dead and Henry Fitzroy only six years old in 1525, it was now only the Duke of Norfolk and Brandon who were, in effect, England's leading peers.

On 25 August 1522, the secret Treaty of Bruges was signed between Charles V and Thomas Wolsey on behalf of Henry VIII, declaring that Henry would support Charles V in the war against France. Then in May 1523, England officially declared war on France.[57] This may have been a difficult situation for Brandon, as his wife had been the Queen of France and was receiving a pension of £4,000 (£1,518,320.00)[58] a year now that she was Dowager Queen.[59] Brandon himself was receiving a pension from Francis I,[60] and both Brandon and Mary owed a great deal to the French king for supporting their marriage. Yet Brandon was ever the opportunist and when Charles V visited England, he had the great honour of hosting Henry VIII and the emperor at Suffolk Place, where the men dined and hunted. When war with France was declared and his French pension stopped, Brandon was luckily able to secure an imperial pension.[61]

At the end of August, Brandon was appointed lieutenant-general[62] and was sent to Calais at the head of an army of 10,000 men.[63] He was to be paid 100s a day while footmen received 6d a day and on horseback 8d a day.[64] Brandon reached Calais on 24 August, but there were difficulties with supplies and there was plague in the area that infected some of the men in Brandon's army.[65] The campaign finally started on 1 October.[66] Brandon's initial aim was to head to Boulogne. However, on 26 September, Henry VIII, with support from Thomas Wolsey, decided to order Brandon to march straight for Paris.[67] The aim was for a triple attack upon the capital. The Duke of Bourbon, who was rebelling against the French king, would attack from the south, Charles V and his army would attack from the east, and Brandon and his men from the north. After receiving Burgundian reinforcements, Brandon's army went on to destroy the river crossings at Ancre and Bray on 18 and 20 October. Then, on 28 October, Brandon's army captured Montdidier.[68] Along the way other towns also surrendered and, despite marching such a huge number of men and even larger numbers of supplies, soon Brandon was within 80km of the city of Paris.[69] Unfortunately, events did not pan out as they were planned.

It seems that Charles V was more interested in securing his Pyrenean frontier and focused much of his time and supplies on the war in Northern Italy. In addition to this, once Charles V captured Fuenterrabia, he stopped his army. The Duke of Bourbon's revolt fell apart and the aid that Margaret of Savoy, with whom Brandon was familiar in 1513, had previously offered, did not appear.[70] Suddenly Brandon was left at the head of 10,000 men with no reinforcements or extra supplies.

By November, winter was upon the English army. There was heavy rain followed by an intense frost. Many man died from the cold or the plague, and Brandon had the choice of digging in for the winter just outside of Paris, or returning to Calais – naturally he chose the latter. By mid-December Brandon and his men were back in Calais waiting to sail to England, and Brandon returned to England in the New Year. Sadly, of the 10,000 men who had left for the campaign in August, less than half returned.[71]

Henry VIII openly blamed the Duke of Bourbon for the failure of the attack and no blame was laid upon Brandon. In fact, despite the setback and failed attempt to take Paris, Brandon had proved himself as a keen military expert. He had deferred to his war council at times but had also made crucial decisions regarding the invasion that had proved valuable. His military efforts both in 1513 and 1523 were showing the king that Brandon was an effective, skilled and trustworthy military commander. [72]

Another military expedition was tentatively made in April 1524, and once more Brandon was named military commander. He was enthusiastic for another campaign against France and sent his man, Sir Richard Jerningham, to the Low Countries to start organising the necessities. However, the final go-ahead was never granted and the whole idea came to nothing.[73]

War with France was once again proposed in early 1525. In February of that year, French troops had suffered a devastating loss against the imperial troops of Charles V outside of Pavia. To make matters worse for the French, their king, Francis, had been captured in the battle and was now a prisoner of Charles V.[74] When the messenger brought the news of Francis I's capture to Henry VIII, the king is reported to have likened him to the Archangel Gabriel such was his happiness and excitement at hearing the news. Henry VIII, ever the opportunist, saw another chance at military glory and quickly proposed war against France. The English king believed that the idea to go to war had been blessed by God and, unlike two years previously, he had visions of reclaiming the French throne for England.[75]

However much the king desired to go to war, his coffers were greatly reduced due to the war England had undertaken against France only two years previously.[76] Naturally money, and a lot of it, was needed to fund a war and it was needed quickly. Thomas Wolsey quickly proposed an "amicable grant", hoping to gain an estimated £800,000 (around £303,664,000.00)[77] for the proposed war.[78] However, this amicable grant was not passed through Parliament. Rather, it was proposed as a means for people to give monetary gifts to fund the king's war. [79] Of course, people did not have a say if they wished to donate to the king's war fund. The grant was proposed as a nice way of demanding coin, hence the title.

Clergy were ordered to pay a third of their income if it was more than £10 (£3,795.80)[80] a year or a quarter if it was less.[81] Laity (essentially everyone else not in the service of the church) were required to pay 3s 4d in the pound if they earned over £50 (£18,979.00)[82] a year, those earning between £20 and £50 a year (£7,591.60 – £18,979.00)[83] were required to pay 2s 8d per dollar, and those earning less than £20 (£7,591.60) a year had to pay 1s per dollar.[84] Naturally, the everyday person was not impressed. These so called offers to the king were nothing of the sort. Instead, they were demands upon people who more often than not struggled to make ends meet. In addition to this, in 1522 – 1523 a huge loan of £250,000 (£94,895,000.00)[85] had been forced upon the people and as of yet had not been paid back.[86]

Discontent quickly spread through the country. People claimed they could not afford to pay the tax and that it was unconstitutional as it had not been approved by Parliament, while the clergy protested as they had not agreed to such a tax in convocation.[87] Soon there were widespread rumblings in Essex, Kent, Norfolk, Warwickshire and Huntingdonshire.[88] However, the greatest protests were in Lavenham, where around 4,000 people gathered to protest against the grant.[89] The king quickly sent Brandon and the Duke of Norfolk to try and deal with the protesters but the rebels greatly outnumbered their own army. While Brandon waited for the Duke of Norfolk and his men to arrive, he began to burn bridges in an attempt to stop the rebels. He also informed Wolsey that his troops would defend him against all perils but he doubted they would fight against their own countrymen.[90] Luckily for Brandon and his army, the rebels did not turn up and several leaders of the so-called rebellion returned with Brandon and the Duke of Norfolk to London. They were quickly put in Fleet Prison. [91]

Henry VIII, ever conscious of the opinion of his people quickly turned face. Organising a council meeting the king stated "that his mynd was neuer, to aske any thyng of his commons, whiche might sounde to his dishonor, or to the breche of his lawes".[92] Whether in an act of clemency or the realisation that it was not possible to gather such funds from the people, and with the threat of rebellion on their hands, the amicable grant was quickly dropped. The king claimed he knew nothing about the grant[93] and that he had not authorised it. A general pardon was granted for the rebels and those held in Fleet Prison were released. In the end Wolsey took the blame for the whole affair and the idea of going to war with France was dropped.[94]

It is interesting to note that Brandon and the Duke of Norfolk wrote to the king informing him that the common people blamed Wolsey for the heavy taxation.[95] Leading a small group of men against 4,000 rebels and hearing that they laid the blame fully with Thomas Wolsey may have been one of the first indicators for Brandon that Wolsey was not popular or liked by the common people. It may have been at this time that Brandon started to sense that things were changing at court and that people were slowly turning against the Cardinal.

Over the next several years Brandon would have to play a difficult balancing role keeping himself amicable with both France and Spain, despite the on-and-off-again threats of war, in an attempt to continue to receive the pensions he was receiving from both countries. This was a difficult balancing act yet one Brandon appeared to maintain.

In addition to an unwanted tax and the threat of rebellion, in 1524 Henry was involved in a life-threatening jousting accident, one caused by Brandon himself. Brandon and Henry VIII were undoubtedly the two best jousters in all of England. Their skills and abilities were well-known, both men shared a mutual love for the sport and had been jousting together and against one another for years. On 10 March, Brandon was set to joust against the king. With one man at each end of the tilt the signal was given to start and both men surged their horses forward. Brandon was wearing a helmet that gave him very little vision and, alarmingly, the king had forgotten to lower his headpiece. People cried for Brandon to "hold" but with limited vision and unable to hear he surged forward and struck the inside of the king's helmet, sending splinters exploding over the king's face.

In his *Chronicle*, Hall recounts the incident in more detail:

The 10th day of March, the king having a new harness [armour] made of his own design and fashion, such as no armourer before that time had seen, thought to test the same at the tilt and appointed a joust to serve this purpose.

On foot were appointed the Lord Marquis of Dorset and the Earl of Surrey; the King came to one end of the tilt and the Duke of Suffolk to the other. Then a gentleman said to the Duke, "Sir, the King is come to the tilt's end." "I see him not," said the Duke, "on my faith, for my headpiece takes from me my sight." With these words, God knoweth by what chance, the King had his spear delivered to him by the Lord Marquis, the visor of his headpiece being up and not down nor fastened, so that his face was clean naked. Then the gentleman said to the Duke, "Sir, the King cometh".

Then the Duke set forward and charged his spear, and the King likewise inadvisedly set off towards the Duke. The people, perceiving the King's face bare, cried "Hold! Hold!", but the Duke neither saw nor heard, and whether the King remembered that his visor was up or not few could tell. Alas, what sorrow was it to the people when they saw the splinters of the Duke's spear strike on the King's headpiece. For most certainly, the Duke struck the King on the brow, right under the defence of the headpiece, on the very skull cap or basinet piece where unto the barbette is hinged for power and defence, to which skull cap or basinet no armourer takes heed of, for it is evermore covered with the visor, barbet and volant piece, and so that piece is so defended that it forceth of no charge. But when the spear landed on that place, it was great jeopardy of death, in so much that the face was bare, for the Duke's spear broke all to splinters and pushed the King's visor or barbet so far back by the counter blow that all the King's headpiece was full of splinters. The armourers for this matter were much blamed and so was the Lord Marquis for delivering the spear when his face was open, but the King said that no-one was to blame but himself, for he intended to have saved himself and his sight.

The Duke immediately disarmed himself and came to the King, showing him the closeness of his sight, and swore that he would never run against the King again. But if the King had been even a little hurt, the King's servants would have put the Duke in jeopardy. Then the King called his armourers and put all his pieces together and then took a spear and ran six courses very well, by which all men might perceive that he had no hurt, which was a great joy and comfort to all his subjects there present.[96]

Naturally Brandon was alarmed. After all, his actions might have killed the king. Luckily, Henry was not badly hurt and laid no blame upon Brandon, and their friendship remained intact. Brandon swore that he would never joust against the king again, but this did not last and in December of the same year the pair challenged each other to another joust, coming out disguised in silver beards. After this Brandon only occasionally participated in jousting events, only when the king chose to, and Henry VIII seemed to only take part on occasions he deemed to be important.[97]

Brandon did continue to take part in courtly events and in November 1527 was recorded as dancing with the king. In addition to this he had the honour of being allowed to have three ostrich feathers in his cap when all others were only allowed two. Clearly, Brandon was still high in the king's favour.[98] It is interesting to note that in 1527 Brandon was approximately forty-three years old, certainly a good age for a man of the Tudor period who had access to an extremely rich diet of meats and few vegetables, and yet he appeared to be in robust health. He participated in sporting events as well as dancing, and was still strong and vigorous.

As well as war against France and jousting accidents during the early 1520s there were people who were starting to challenge the Catholic faith. Their thoughts and opinions started to send waves throughout Europe and England, which would have dramatic effects upon England and the lives of its people, including Brandon.

The subject of Charles Brandon's religion is a difficult one to tackle without having a greater understanding of what was happening in England and Europe during his life, especially in the late 1510s and 1520s. Brandon was born into a Catholic England. King Henry VII was a devout Catholic and England had been a Catholic nation for hundreds of years. During the formative years of his life, Brandon would have been taught all the important aspects of the Catholic faith and also that the pope was the head of the Catholic church, that his position was appointed by God, and his word was law.

In 1517, though, things began to change. Martin Luther, a professor of theology at Wittenberg University in Germany, posted his *Ninety Five Theses*[99] to the church door. In his theses Luther attacked the Catholic concept of salvation through good deeds and argued that the way to salvation was through Christ by faith and repentance. He argued that true repentance was the way a person lived his or her life and not simply through confession. He also attacked he sale of indulgences and emphasised that the pope had limited powers upon earth. These ideas were drastically different to what the Catholic church taught and caused a great deal of upheaval, not just in England but throughout Europe.[100]

Henry VIII was outraged by such ideas and in 1521 wrote (with the help of leading theologians and churchmen) his *Assertio Septem Sacramentorum* (Defence of the Seven Sacraments), which he sent to the pope and which earned him the title *Defensor Fidei* (Defender of the Faith).[101] However, over the next decade Henry's religious views and opinions would begin to change.

By 1526, Katherine of Aragon had failed to give Henry VIII a living male heir. In 1516, she had given birth to a healthy baby girl, but she had a string of miscarriages and stillbirths behind her and at forty-one was well past her child-bearing years.[102] With the birth of his illegitimate son in 1519, Henry had shown that he was capable of fathering a living son and in his mind the problem lay with his wife and not himself.

In addition to this, Henry's attention had turned to another. His eye fell to Anne Boleyn, an intriguing woman who had received an excellent education at the French court and, while not classically beautiful, had dark and intriguing eyes that could captivate a man. As Henry fell further in love with Anne Boleyn, his mind turned to separating from Katherine of Aragon. He wanted to marry Anne and have male heirs with her. In order to do this, Henry would need an annulment of his marriage, which could be granted by Pope Clement VII. But this was not as simple as he hoped.

The tale of Henry VIII's "Great Matter" and his desire to seek an annulment of his first marriage in order to marry Anne Boleyn has been told many times over in countless books. The purpose of this book is not to retell that story but to provide the few glimpses of Brandon's role within such a complicated and detailed part of English history.

Pope Clement VII was reluctant to grant Henry VIII his heart's desire. On 1 June 1527, the city of Rome had been ransacked by the Imperial army, led by Katherine of Aragon's nephew Charles V, and Pope Clement had been captured.[103] The pope was in no position to see his captor's aunt removed from her position as queen. However, continual pressure from Thomas Wolsey and the pope's final release saw him agreeing to send a papal legate to England to decide upon the king's matter. Cardinal Lorenzo Campeggio was chosen for this task but he was under instructions to stall the hearing for as long as possible.[104] Campeggio was an old man riddled with gout and, frustratingly for Henry VIII and Thomas Wolsey, his journey to England was slow and painful.[105] The cardinal finally arrived in London on 7 October, where he lodged overnight at Brandon's home, most likely at Southwark, before being taken to Bath House the next evening.[106] The hearing for Henry VIII's great matter officially started on 31 May 1529.[107]

However, the trial, which both Henry VIII and Anne Boleyn hoped would secure the annulment of Henry's marriage, did not go as planned. Cardinal Campeggio and Cardinal Thomas Wolsey were to lead the trial and, despite Wolsey's strong desire to serve his king, things were not to go the cardinal's way. After almost two months of to-ing and fro-ing, Henry VIII's hopes relied heavily upon his right-hand man, on 23 July 1529, Cardinal Campeggio announced that he could not give a final judgement until he had discussed the matter further with Pope Clement VII. He then adjourned the court indefinitely.[108]

Needless to say, Henry VIII was furious. All his hopes of having a quick annulment of his marriage to Katherine of Aragon so that he could marry Anne Boleyn and produce a legitimate heir had just been dashed. Brandon, it would seem, was equally furious at the results. He had attended the trial that day, sitting with the king in a gallery above the door. After the king had stormed out in anger Brandon rose and shouted from the gallery: "By the mass it was never merry in England whilst we had cardinals amongst us!" to which Cardinal Thomas Wolsey replied "If I, a simple cardinal, had not been, you should have had at this present time no head upon your shoulders wherein you should have a tongue to make any such report in despite of us".[109]

Wolsey's retort was sharp and, more-so, to the point. After all, it was Thomas Wolsey who had interceded with Henry when Brandon had committed treason and married the king's sister without permission. Brandon did not reply to Wolsey's remark and quickly hurried out in search of his king. This was not the first time that any animosity or anger between Brandon and Wolsey had arisen. On 4 February of the same year, Don Íñigo López de Mendoza, the Spanish ambassador, had written to his king to state that he believed Anne Boleyn thought Thomas Wolsey was trying to hinder the trial rather than aid it. He also noted that he believed Brandon had joined with the Boleyns and the Duke of Norfolk to bring about the fall of Wolsey.[110]

Mendoza wrote:

> This suspicion [of the lady] has been the cause of her forming an alliance with her father [Viscount Rochford], and with the two Dukes of Norfolk and Suffolk, to try and see whether they can conjointly ruin (desbaratar) the Cardinal. Hitherto they seem to have made no impression on the King, save that the Cardinal is no longer received at Court as graciously as before, and that now and then King Henry has uttered certain angry words respecting him.[111]

Clearly Brandon was smart enough to see which way the wind was blowing. Henry VIII was desperate for an annulment of his marriage and he had put all his hopes and faith in Thomas Wolsey. Wolsey was not able to get the job done and Brandon, although having supported him, did not wish to be brought down with the cardinal. It was perhaps not so much that Brandon was against Wolsey directly, but that he was wise enough to side with his king when he saw that Wolsey's writing was on the wall.

Meanwhile, in May 1529, rumours started to spread of a possible peace treaty between Francis I and Charles V, which was to be held at Cambrai. Desperate to see England represented, the king sent Brandon and Sir William Fitzwilliam across the Channel. After a short briefing the pair left on 17 May with the offer to provide Francis I English troops and money to go to war against Charles V.[112]

Upon arriving in France, Brandon and Fitzwilliam were entertained lavishly in an attempt to stop both men from attending the peace talks.[113] Brandon alone was sent with another, far more secret mission. He was to seek out Francis I's thoughts regarding Wolsey and to see if Francis thought that the cardinal was obstructing Henry's divorce. Francis's reply is interesting and he seems to walk a fine line as Brandon writes in a letter to his king:

> Campeggio, who told Francis he was going to England and afterwards to Spain by commission of the Pope. On which Francis asked him how he could go into Spain, and yet do what the king of England wished for the divorce; and he replied that he did not think that the divorce would take effect, but should be dissembled well enough. Thinking that the King was deceived, he told the bishop of Bath what the Cardinal had said, desiring him to advertise you of it. I then proceeded to inquire of him, promising that what he said should never be revealed, What say you of the cardinal of England in this matter? and he replied, When he was with me, as far as I could perceive, he desired that the divorce might take place, for he loved not the Queen; but I advise my good brother not to put too much trust in any man, whereby he may be deceived, and the best remedy is to look to his own matters himself;—saying further that the cardinal of England had great intelligence with the Pope and with Campeggio, and, as they are not inclined to the divorce, it is the more needful for the King to have regard to his own affairs.[114]

In the end both Brandon and Fitzwilliam were recalled from France as no matter their presence a peace treaty between Francis I and Charles V was inevitable.[115] However, Brandon was able to obtain Francis I's thoughts on Wolsey and the divorce for his king.

In the end Henry VIII would have the annulment of his marriage, but Thomas Wolsey would not live to see it. On 9 October 1529, Wolsey was officially charged with praemunire, which is asserting the power of papal jurisdiction over the supremacy of the English monarch, in this case Henry VIII. The cardinal was also stripped of his role as lord chancellor.[116] He was sent to Esher, Surrey, but was officially arrested in early November 1530 and died on 29 November on his way to London for his trial.[117]

There are no records of Brandon's thoughts regarding the arrest and subsequent death of Wolsey. Brandon owed a great deal to the cardinal in 1515 when he had desperately sought his help and support after his treasonous marriage to Mary. Brandon begged the cardinal for support and had openly stated that he felt Wolsey was the only one who could help him, yet fourteen years later Brandon had turned against his supporter. Although this might seem quite disloyal, Brandon was no fool. He knew that if he tossed his lot in with Wolsey, he could be brought down along with him, especially since his own rival the Duke of Norfolk was against Wolsey. Brandon was smart enough to know that his position at court relied heavily upon the king's good graces, and if the king was against Wolsey then so too was Brandon. In the end, Brandon would receive his share of spoils from Wolsey's fall. He was granted Wolsey's prize mules as well as the manor of Sayes Court in Deptford. He also took in the clerk of Wolsey's kitchen.[118] Brandon was appointed as president of the king's council, a role that suited him well as he was one of the king's closest friends. However, Brandon's attendance was sporadic and a Venetian ambassador reported in 1531 that Brandon:

> Has the second seat in his Majesty's Privy Council, which he rarely enters, save for the discussion of matters of a certain importance, passing his time more pleasantly in other amusements.[119]

Ultimately Henry VIII would have his own way. Henry VIII turned from the pope to his own parliament and from October 1529 to April 1536 "The Reformation Parliament" sat. The parliament was created on the idea that there was only one supreme head in England, the king, and that all matters of church and state needed to be referred to the monarch and not the pope. It enforced the idea that no foreign power (e.g. the pope) could dictate law in England and that any laws enforced by the monarch were binding.[120]

The king went on to accuse the clergy of supporting Thomas Wolsey and, in return, the clergy offered the king a bribe of £100,000 (£32,210,000.00)[121] to drop any charges against them. Then on 7 February 1531, Henry VIII demanded that he be known as the supreme head of the English church. Naturally the clergy were against such an idea, but the king was insistent. After some argument the clergy granted the title with one slight alteration. Convocation granted Henry VIII the title of singular protector, supreme lord, and even, so far as the law of Christ allows, supreme head of the English church and clergy.[122] By the end of 1532, Parliament was the only legal legislative body in England. Henry VIII could now have his annulment.

Over the next decade what is known as the "Reformation" would sweep across England changing the face of religion within the country forever. Henry VIII was orthodox in his beliefs and his faith would remain devout throughout his life. However, he became more interested in the running and organisation of the church. He, along with his new right-hand man, Thomas Cromwell, would also oversee the dissolution of the monasteries. Religious houses that were hundreds of years old would ultimately have to surrender to the king. They were closed, pulled down and their wealth absorbed by the king's coffers. Henry VIII then sold much of the land belonging to the former monasteries to his courtiers. Brandon would be one of those who benefited from the dissolution of the monasteries. He purchased Vaudey Abbey and its land and used the demolished abbey to extend his castle in Lincolnshire.

It is difficult to assess Brandon's personal religious beliefs during this time of upheaval in England. On 28 October 1537, Sir Richard Bulkeley wrote to Thomas Cromwell stating:

> My cousin Doctor Arthur Bulkeley, of the number of the Arches, has been chaplain to the duke of Suffolk this seven years. He now desires "to appertain to your Lordship, to do you service at his Grace's request." And as Mr. Bedell who was of your spiritual council is now dead, he would be the rather glad to do you service because of his former acquaintance with your goodness. I pray that at my request he may be the more acceptable.[123]

From this letter we can assume that Arthur Bulkeley was chaplain to Brandon from around 1530. It is unclear when he left Brandon's services but Bulkeley was appointed as Bishop of Bangor in 1541 and was consecrated 19 February 1542. He died the following year on 14 March.[124] In addition to having Bulkeley as his personal chaplain, Brandon's chapel was also graced with statues of saints and he hired Nicholas Cutler to be the master of six choir boys.[125] Brandon was known to patronise former monks.[126] Towards the end of his life John Parkhurst, a reformer, was also briefly chaplain to Brandon and his fourth wife Katherine Willoughby.[127]

Katherine was known to have strong reformist beliefs and would become close friends with Queen Catherine Parr, Henry VIII's sixth and final wife, who also shared similar religious beliefs. Parkhurst too was known to have reformist friends such as Miles Coverdale.[128] What did this mean for Brandon and his personal religious beliefs? It seems that the duke had both reformist and conservative people within his service. It may be that, at heart, Brandon was conservative in his personal religious views. However openly, as he had done throughout most of his life, he followed the religious will and desires of his king.

Despite siding with the Duke of Norfolk and the Boleyns against Thomas Wolsey, Brandon was opposed to the king marrying Anne Boleyn. Mary, Brandon's wife, had been close friends with Katherine of Aragon and when the king openly separated from her in 1531, Mary, it seemed, also removed herself from appearing at court.[129]

Eustace Chapuys, ambassador to Charles V wrote to his master that Anne "had been accused by the Duke of Suffolk of undue familiarity with a gentleman who on a former occasion had been banished on suspicion".[130]

This gentleman was Sir Thomas Wyatt, poet, courtier and long-time friend of the Boleyn family and from his poetry it is quite probable that he had a crush on Anne. However, there is no evidence to suggest that Anne returned these feelings. While there turned out to be no truth in the rumour, Henry was furious at his best friend and banished him from court for a time. In response to this accusation, Anne Boleyn made one of her own declaring that Brandon was sleeping with his daughter Frances.[131] Yet this did not teach Brandon a lesson and, later in the year, he spoke with the treasurer of the king's household, Fitzwilliam, in the hopes to work with him to persuade the king against marrying Anne Boleyn.[132]

Then in 1532, Mary spoke publicly about her opposition to the marriage and where her loyalties lay, speaking about Anne Boleyn in unfavourable terms. This resulted in a quarrel between some of the Duke of Norfolk's men (the duke being Anne Boleyn's uncle) and Brandon's men. On 23 April, Carlo Capello reported:

> At the moment of his arrival at the Court, one of the chief gentlemen in the service of said Duke of Norfolk, with 20 followers, assaulted and killed in the sanctuary of Westminster Sir (D'no) William Peninthum (sic) chief gentleman and kinsman of the Duke of Suffolk. In consequence of this, the whole Court was in an uproar, and had the Duke of Suffolk been there, it is supposed that a serious affray would have taken place. On hearing of what had happened, he (Suffolk) was on his way to remove the

assailants by force from the sanctuary, when the King sent the
Treasurer [Thomas Cromwell] to him, and made him return,
and has adjusted the affair; and this turmoil displeased him.
It is said to have been caused by a private quarrel, but I am
assured it was owing to opprobrious language uttered against
Madam Anne by his Majesty's sister, the Duchess of Suffolk,
Queen Dowager of France.[133]

The murderers were pardoned and in 1533 the Duke of Norfolk
demanded that Brandon relinquish the office of earl marshal to
Norfolk, which Brandon had held since the death of Norfolk's
father in 1524. The king complied with this request and in turn
granted Brandon the warden and chief justice of the royal forests
south of Trent:[134]

> The King hears that [Suffolk] is content to surrender his
> patent of Earl Marshal, and has accordingly granted it to the
> duke of Norfolk, whose ancestors long held it, in place of
> which he shall have the justiceship of the Forests on this side
> of the Trent for life. The King is pleased with him for so kindly
> parting with the office, and that he has more zeal to nourish
> kindness and love between Norfolk and himself than to that
> or any other office. Advises him to come to Court, as Norfolk
> is shortly going "towards his great journey in ambassade".[135]

After this, Brandon and his wife removed themselves from court
and it took the influence of Thomas Cromwell and even a visit from
the king to smooth things over.[136] Brandon must have learnt a lesson
as, when he returned to court, he made sure to keep his thoughts
and opinions to himself rather than risk losing the king's favour
once more.

During this time Brandon appears to have been everywhere at
court and yet not directly involved with anything. He was petitioned
by various people for help but he did not seem to play any direct
role with the happenings of court throughout the early 1530s. He
continued to entertain the king and take part in various forms of
entertainment and pastimes. But when the king required any real
business to be done, he turned to Thomas Cromwell.[137]

It could be that Brandon was uncomfortable with the missions
Henry VIII sent him on in relationship to the annulment of his
marriage to Katherine of Aragon. Brandon clearly had a poor
relationship with Anne Boleyn and the Duke of Norfolk. With his

wife adamantly opposed to her brother's marriage, Brandon may have thought it prudent to appear at court to keep his presence known and friendship with the king while at the same time distancing himself from the political events unfolding around him.

Between 1515 and 1519 Brandon's income was around £3,000 (£1,138,740.00)[138] a year, yet upon his marriage to Mary Tudor he lost the title of Viscount Lisle and the wardship of Elizabeth Grey, and thus all the lands that went along with that. This reduced his income to around £1,500 (£569,370.00)[139] a year. Still, holding various offices would have brought in income from other areas but this is hard to calculate and would not have amounted to any more than £1,500 (£569,370.00)[140] a year. He would have also received payments for his French pension, although the exact sum that this would have been cannot be calculated accurately. In addition to this, Brandon would have received his wife's dowager payments from France, which amounted to £4,000 (£1,518,320.00)[141] a year. Therefore, Brandon's financial income would have been around £7,000 (£2,657,060.00)[142] a year if all payments were received.[143] However, things were not quite as simple as they appeared.

The war with France in the 1520s greatly affected both Mary and Brandon's pensions from France. The payments had come intermittently throughout this period, and Brandon was constantly chasing his and his wife's income. Brandon wrote that his wife's payments "restith much of her honour and profit, and mine also".[144] Clearly Brandon was heavily reliant upon Mary's dowager payments for his financial dealings. Without regular payments, Brandon was forced to borrow £12,000 (£4,554,960.00)[145] from the crown in 1515/1516 and an additional £3,000 (£1,138,740.00)[146] from the revenues in North Wales, which he had access to due to his offices in Wales.[147] However, in 1525 Brandon lost his position as Chief Justice of North Wales under a new scheme by Thomas Wolsey where the council in the marshes was incorporated into the council of Princess Mary. Brandon's position was granted to his deputy. Brandon was compensated with the castle at Ewelme, although it was not so much the loss of income but the loss of military status that affected the duke. No longer could he be the one to call upon the people in the north to march to war.[148] Brandon and Mary also had to make payments of £1,000 (£379,580.00)[149] a year to Henry VIII for their marriage, although these payments do not appear to have been regularly enforced. [150]

In all, Brandon was living beyond his means. His wife was the Dowager Queen of France and had a reputation to live up to. She required clothing and servants suitable for her position and all of this cost money. In 1524, Brandon had fifty-one servants who earned 26s 8d each. His physician, Master Leonard, was the highest paid member of Brandon's household earning £20 (£7,591.60)[151] a year.[152] Mary had more than double this number of servants. While this is not a staggering number of servants, it did put pressure on the Brandons to see everyone clothed, fed and paid accordingly, and he was spending around £1000 (£379,580.00)[153] a year just on his own servants. Mary paid her servants from her own pension from France.[154]

Brandon also had a reputation to live up to. He was a duke and close friends with the king and, thus, always had to dress and look the part. Cloth suitable for a duke was expensive and Brandon sought to build and extend his lands and powerbase. In the late 1510s, Brandon rebuilt his late Uncle Thomas's house in Southwark and turned it into a large brick palace, which was decorated with terracotta. In 1527, he decided to build a similar palace in East Anglia, which would become his main country residence. It was to be called Westhorpe Hall and was a moated brick courthouse of considerable size that had terracotta plaques and battlements. It also had beautifully decorated chimneys, a chapel with cloisters that contained a magnificent stained glass window[155], oak-panelled rooms, and even a statue of Hercules. The surrounding parks were well-stocked with deer for hunting, and the gardens were designed in the French fashion. Brandon stated that the building costs for Westhorpe Hall were £12,000 (£3,865,200.000)[156], much of which much would have come from Mary's French pension, which was now being received once again.[157]

Tragically, Westhorpe Hall was demolished in the 1760s. Thomas Martin, a historian at Thetford noted that he:

> Went to see the dismal ruins of Westhorpe Hall, formerly the seat of Charles Brandon, Duke of Suffolk. The workmen are now pulling it down as fast as may be, in a very careless and injudicious manner. The coping bricks, battlements and many other ornamental pieces, are made of earth, and burnt hard, as fresh as when first built. They might, with care, have been taken down whole, but all the fine chimneys, and ornaments were pulled down with ropes, and crushed to

pieces in a most shameful manner. There was a monstrous figure of Hercules sitting cross legged with his club, and a lion beside him, but all shattered in pieces. The painted glass is likely to share the same fate. The timber is fresh and sound, and the building, which was very lofty, stood as when it was first built. It is a pity that care is not taken to preserve some few of our ancient fabrics. To demolish every piece of old architecture is quite barbaric.[158]

To end 1532, on 24 October, King Francis I of France elected Brandon and the Duke of Norfolk as Knights of the Order of St Michel.[159] The Order of St Michel was the French equivalent of the English Order of the Garter, which Brandon had been elected to in April 1513.[160]

For fourteen years Brandon had continued to remain close with the king. While not hugely influential in politics, he was extremely smart at playing the game, which meant that ultimately he knew his king. He had weathered the great religious upheaval in England, seen the birth of four of his children and the tragic death of his first-born son. He had survived political changes at court, led a war against France and battled constant financial difficulties. By the end of 1532, Brandon's position was secure, yet the following few years would test his beliefs and see great personal loss.

The Tempestuous Years
(1533 – 1535)

The years 1533 to 1535 were difficult for Charles Brandon, with the duke facing many emotional ups and downs. In two short years, Brandon was forced to take actions against his conscience, lost a great deal of cash and property as well as, tragically, both his wife and his son.

On 25 January 1533, just before dawn, Henry VIII married his second wife Anne Boleyn at Whitehall Palace.[1] Unfortunately, records do not state exactly who was in attendance. If Brandon attended the wedding, he would have been sworn to absolute secrecy as, at the time, many still considered that Henry was still legally married to Katherine of Aragon.

After the marriage, it was left to the Dukes of Norfolk and Suffolk to carry the news to Katherine of Aragon. They met the queen on 9 April 1533 at her residence at Ampthill and informed her that she was no longer Queen of England, and from that day forward she had to style herself as the Dowager Princess of Wales. Katherine took the news with grace but refused to use the new title or to believe that Henry's marriage to Anne was valid.[2] Again on 3 July, Katherine was given the papers stating that her marriage to Henry VIII had been annulled and that the king was lawfully married to Anne Boleyn. As the king could not have two wives, it was essential that Katherine now style herself Princess Dowager.[3] This time Katherine was outraged and declared that she did not recognise any judgement made except that of the pope.[4]

In December, Brandon was once more sent to try and convince Katherine that she was no longer to style herself Queen of England and, in addition, she must be moved from her present lodgings to Somersham. It is reported that Brandon wished some mischief would happen to him so he did not have to go.[5] Clearly the duke was not looking forward to the task ahead, already seeing first-hand the outrage that Katherine of Aragon had expressed at being informed she was no longer queen. When Brandon advised Katherine of her upcoming move, Katherine stated that she would rather be hewn into pieces than be called Dowager Princess, she absolutely refused to go to Somersham, and she slammed the door in Brandon's face. The duke was left standing outside, imploring Katherine to see reason and to accept her new position. Brandon went on to question Katherine's servants, who also refused to refer to her as Dowager Princess and insisted that Katherine was queen. Five days passed, in which time Brandon's men removed the furniture and hangings from the house and dismissed most of Katherine's servants. During this time he continued to try and persuade Katherine to leave, but she insisted that the only way she would go was if he broke down the door, an action Brandon would not undertake for fear of ramifications.[6] Brandon was at a complete loss and wrote to Henry explaining the situation, even going so far as to say that he thought the only way they could transport Katherine was if they bound her with ropes. He requested the king's guidance as to what he should do.[7] Brandon had to wait until 31 December, when he received instructions from the king that he should leave Katherine where she was and return to court. [8]

The whole situation was uneasy and uncomfortable for Brandon, and while he thought Katherine was being stubborn, he was also aware of her failing health and the ever-decreasing living conditions she was forced to endure. He was not unsympathetic to her cause and he conveyed to the king the poor health that Katherine was suffering when he returned to court.[9] This information had no effect on the king, and Brandon was left once more in the difficult situation of harassing the former queen while secretly being sympathetic to her cause. Katherine continued to style herself as queen until her death almost three years later.

While these events were unfolding, Brandon and his wife Mary also managed to find time to organise the wedding of their oldest daughter Frances. Brandon and Mary Tudor's children were highly prized within the marriage market. Previously a marriage between the Duke of Norfolk's son Henry Howard, Earl of Surrey, and Frances Brandon had been proposed, but Norfolk turned down the idea due to Frances's small dowry. This was another sign that while Brandon was the Duke of Suffolk and a leading man at court his financial status was still quite precarious. However, another marriage prospect soon arrived. In October 1530, Thomas Grey, Marquis of Dorset, died leaving his son Henry Grey as heir. Brandon sought the approval of the dowager marchioness and then bought the wardship of Henry Grey for 4,000 marks. Henry and Frances were married in May at Suffolk Place in a spectacular wedding attended by the king. It was Mary Tudor's last public appearance.[10]

On Saturday 12 April 1533, Anne Boleyn was finally presented at court as queen. She attended mass dressed in robes of state and wearing beautiful jewels.[11] Following this, on 28 May, Archbishop Cranmer declared that Henry VIII's marriage to Katherine of Aragon was invalid and his marriage to Anne was lawful.[12] Now there would be no doubt as to who was the lawful Queen of England, at least in Henry and Anne's minds.

Anne Boleyn's magnificent coronation was set for Sunday 1 June. Wearing a gown of crimson velvet edged in ermine, and a purple velvet mantle with her hair loose and hanging down to her waist, Anne Boleyn made the journey barefoot from Westminster Hall to Westminster Abbey under a canopy of cloth of gold. Brandon's duty was to walk before the queen carrying her royal crown and then during the coronation he stood close to the queen holding a white staff of office.[13] Afterwards, a great banquet was held at Westminster Hall, where Brandon acted as lord high steward and constable. It was his responsibility to organise all the details of the coronation, including Anne's procession through London the previous day. Wearing a doublet covered in pearls and riding a charger covered in crimson velvet Brandon rode through the banquet, consisting of 800 people and approximately thirty-two dishes.[14] Whatever Brandon's thoughts on the marriage, where he did his duties to the fullest, and Anne Boleyn's procession through London, her coronation and her lavish banquet afterwards were of great opulence, and no expense was spared.

To secure Anne Boleyn's place as queen and to see the heir of her body as the next King of England, Henry VIII had his parliament pass the Act of Succession on 23 March 1534. The Act stated that any heirs born to Anne Boleyn would become first in line to the throne and that Mary Tudor, Henry VIII's daughter with Katherine of Aragon, was declared illegitimate and no longer able to inherit the throne. The Act also stated that, if anyone was asked, they were required to swear an oath recognising the Act as well as affirming that Henry VIII was now the supreme head of the Church of England (so far as the law allows). Anyone disagreeing with the Act and refusing to take the oath were charged with treason.[15] Charles Brandon, along with other important and high-ranking members of parliament and the church, signed the oath on 30 March 1534.[16] No matter what Brandon's thoughts were regarding the marriage, his signature was now attached to the oath stating that he not only believed in the marriage but would also uphold it as well as the king's right to be the supreme head of the English church. Once more Brandon was showing his loyalty first and foremost to his king.

Despite the great triumph and majesty of Anne Boleyn's coronation, it could not be missed that Mary Tudor was not present. Some have suggested that Mary's absence at Anne's coronation was a firm statement against the new queen. It was common knowledge that Mary openly opposed her brother's desire to seek an annulment from his marriage to Katherine of Aragon. Initially, Brandon had spoken similar words, but quickly learnt to keep his thoughts to himself and toe the political line at court.

However, it was most likely that Mary was not in a fit enough state to attend the magnificent event. The dowager queen had been ill for some time and in May 1533, Brandon returned to Westhorpe to visit his wife. Tragically it would be the last time he would ever see her alive. Brandon was soon recalled to London to continue the organisation of Anne's coronation and it was likely that he was there when Mary died between seven and eight o'clock in the morning on 25 June 1533.[17]

The cause of Mary's death is unknown. One suggestion is that she may have suffered from angina. Mary had been ill for some time and several years earlier had complained of a constant pain in her side. Another suggestion is grief over her brother's dismissal of Katherine of Aragon and his marriage to Anne Boleyn.[18] However, it would seem that, despite the current events of the time, Mary still loved her brother as she wrote him a letter in June shortly before her death stating she:

Figure 3. The grave of Mary Tudor
Photo Copyright © Natalie Grueninger 2015

Has been very sick "and ele ates" (ill at ease). Has been fain to send for Master Peter the physician, but is rather worse than better. Trusts shortly to come to London with her husband. Is sure, if she tarries here, that she will never "asperre the sekenys." Will be glad to see the King, as she has been a great while out of his sight, and hopes not to be so long again.[19]

Whether it was the pain in her side, angina or some other cause, Mary's death would shake Brandon's world.

As Dowager Queen of France and Duchess of Suffolk, Mary Tudor's funeral was a lavish affair. Her body was embalmed and for three weeks the coffin, draped in deep blue or black velvet, lay in state at Westhorpe, candles burning day and night. On 10 July, Henry VIII ordered a requiem mass to be held for his sister at Westminster Abbey. A delegation was sent from France and joined the English delegation for the funeral on 20 July 1533. Mary was interred at Bury St Edmunds and her chief mourner was her daughter Frances, who was accompanied by her husband, and her brother Henry, Earl of Lincoln. Also attending the funeral was Mary's youngest daughter Eleanor and her ward Katherine Willoughby.[20]

For the journey from Westhorpe to the abbey church at Bury St Edmunds, Mary's coffin was placed upon a hearse draped in black velvet embroidered with Mary's arms and her motto "the will of God is sufficient for me".[21] The coffin was covered in a pall of black cloth of gold, atop this was an effigy of Mary wearing robes of state, a crown and a golden sceptre, which signified Mary's status as Dowager Queen of France. The hearse was drawn by six horses wearing black cloth and the coffin was covered by a canopy carried by four of Brandon's knights. Surrounding the coffin, standard-bearers carried the arms of the Brandon and Tudor families.[22]

At the head of the procession walked 100 torch-bearers, comprising members of the local community who were paid and dressed in black for the funeral. Next came members of the clergy, who carried the cross. After them came the household staff followed by the six horses pulling the hearse. Behind the hearse followed the knights and other noble men in attendance, followed by 100 of the duke's yeomen. Lastly came Mary's daughter Frances, the chief mourner, and the other ladies. Along the way the funeral procession was joined by other members of the local parishes.

Figure 4. The Duchess of Suffolk, Katherine Willoughby
by Francesco Bartolozzi, 1884

At two o'clock in the afternoon, Mary's coffin was received at Bury St Edmunds by the abbot and the monks. The coffin was placed before the high altar and surrounded by the mourners in order of precedence and a mass was said. Afterwards, a supper was held for the noble members of Mary's funeral entourage.[23]

Overnight eight women, twelve men, thirty yeomen and some of the clergy were appointed to watch over Mary's body. The next day a requiem mass was sung and Mary's daughters, her two step-daughters, her ward Katherine Willoughby and Katherine's mother brought forward palls of cloth of gold to the altar. The funeral address was conducted by William Rugg, the officers of Mary's household broke their white staffs, and finally Mary was interred. Mary's body lay at peace at Bury St Edmunds until 1784. Her remains were disturbed when her altar monument was removed because it obstructed the approach to the rails of the communion table. Her resting place is now marked by a slab on the floor.[24]

Mary was greatly loved by the people of Suffolk and after her funeral alms of meat, drink and coin were given to the poor.[25] As was custom neither Mary's brother Henry VIII nor her husband attended the funeral. However, since Mary had been a dowager queen of France and a princess of England, a funeral at court was required. Therefore, on 10 and 11 July, another funeral was held at Westminster with all official duties being performed, except there was no body. It is believed that Brandon attended this funeral for his wife.[26] We do not have any record of his feelings towards the death of his wife of eighteen years. He had risked all, even facing treason charges and the possibility of death by marrying a member of the royal family without the king's permission. Surely he must have felt something towards his wife, be it love or a close companionship.

With the death of Mary Tudor, Charles Brandon was left in quite a financial situation. The king did step in and cancelled £1,000 (£322,100.00)[27] of Brandon's debt, as well as providing him with the fruits of the vacant see of Ely for the year 1533/34, which amounted to around £2,000[28] (£644,200.00)[29]. But Brandon was still strapped for cash and the duke needed to look elsewhere for financial assistance. Fortunately he did not need to look far.

Brandon's eyes turned to Katherine Willoughby. Born on 22 March 1519, Katherine was the daughter of William, 11th Baron Willoughby, and his wife Maria De Salinas, one of Katherine of Aragon's ladies who had come from Spain with her in 1501 when she came to England to marry the late Prince Arthur. When Katherine was just seven years of age, her father died and, with no male son surviving, Katherine became his heir.[30] In March 1528, Brandon bought the wardship of Katherine from the king with the intention of marrying Katherine to his son Henry.[31] Katherine had then come to live with the Brandons to be raised.

To be sent to live with a prominent member of court or someone of importance and to become their ward was quite common during the Tudor age. For example, Anne Boleyn gained a position within the Duchess of Austria's court to learn the skills required to be an intelligent and dutiful woman.[32] Brandon himself had sent his oldest daughter Anne to serve Margaret of Savoy for a period of time before she was recalled in 1515.[33] To be taken in as a ward was also helpful to the family, as they no longer had to provide food and clothing for the child, and also were not required to pay for the child's education. Another example of this is when Mary Boleyn's husband, William Carey, died in 1528. She was left in quite a precarious position and with little money and two children to raise, her son, Henry, became a ward of his aunt, Anne Boleyn. It would have been Anne's responsibility to see the boy clothed and educated, and this helped to relieve the financial burden for Mary Boleyn. [34]

By being sent to live with the Brandons, Katherine would have had the opportunity to learn many skills, including what it was like to be the lady of the house and how to run a household. Katherine did not have to wait long to learn these valuable lessons as only a mere three months after the death of his third wife, Brandon married Katherine on 7 September 1533.[35]

There has been some debate over Brandon's actions in such a rushed marriage. Brandon needed cash, though, and quickly, and could not afford to wait until his son came of age to marry Katherine. With his son's marriage, Brandon would not have acquired the properties and financial benefits that were left to Katherine from her father. Instead these would have gone to his son and Brandon was ever the opportunist and in desperate need for money.[36]

At the time of the marriage Brandon was forty-nine and Katherine was fourteen. Looking back with a modern perspective, Brandon was old enough to be Katherine's father. But for the age it was not uncommon for an older man to marry a much younger woman.

However, it is said that there were still some mutterings surrounding Brandon's actions, and people were well-aware of the real reasons Brandon married Katherine.[37]

Katherine had been raised to seek out a good and prosperous marriage, and by marrying a duke she would become a duchess and, in turn, become one of the most prominent women in England. Despite the vast age difference, there seems to have been a close relationship of some sorts as Katherine would go on to give Brandon two sons in a short period of time.

As well as the couple's marriage on 7 September, another event, far more important, was taking place on the same day. In the queen's apartments at Greenwich, Anne Boleyn gave birth to a baby girl at approximately three o'clock in the afternoon.[38] While the birth of a daughter was not what Henry and Anne had desperately longed for, the fact that the little girl was born healthy and that Anne recovered quickly gave hope that soon they would soon have a son.

The baby was named Elizabeth and on 10 September, she was christened at the Chapel of the Observant Friars. Neither Henry nor Anne attended the christening. It was not traditional for the father to attend the christening and Anne had not yet been churched. Brandon, however, attended the christening and had the great honour of escorting the baby girl, along with the Duke of Norfolk. The christening was conducted by Archbishop Thomas Cranmer, and Elizabeth's godparents were the archbishop, the Dowager Duchess of Norfolk, the Dowager Marchioness of Dorset and the Marquis of Exeter.[39]

Brandon's financial troubles were not so easily swept away by gaining his new wife's inheritance. In fact, the duke would have to battle for two more years before finally he was able to settle the majority of his debts. Katherine's uncle, Sir Christopher Willoughby, challenged his niece's inheritance and claimed that before Katherine's birth his brother had stated he was to inherit some of his properties upon his death. Brandon and Katherine's mother, the Dowager Lady Willoughby, joined forces to contest this and after interference by the king, Brandon was able to retain much of the inheritance.[40] Yet Katherine's lands only brought in approximately £900 a year[41] (£289,890.00),[42] and even with this win, Brandon's financial woes were not over as, at the time, he was not entitled to the full amount. Katherine's mother still had control of much of her lands and income and it was not until a formal grant after her death in July 1540 that Brandon was able to obtain the full £900 and incorporate it into his own finances.[43]

On 19 July 1535, the late Mary Tudor's debts were cancelled,[44] but Brandon still had to pay a staggering sum of £6,700 (£2,158,070.00)[45]. In an attempt to pay off this debt, Brandon handed over a great deal of plate and jewel amounting to £4,360 (£1,404,356.00)[46] as well as exchanging some of his lands and property with the king. Brandon lost his Oxfordshire and Berkshire manors as well as his house at Westhorpe. In return, Brandon gained land in Lincolnshire, which was worth a mere £175 (£56,367.50)[47] a year, a manor in Essex, a house in London, and £3,183 (£1,025,244.30)[48] in cash and the final cancellation of his debts.[49]

Brandon also wrote to Nicholas de St Martin in an attempt to obtain his French pension, which at the time of his wife's death was four months overdue:

> I have written to Sir John Wallop to speak to the Great Master that I may have the arrears due to me at May last; trusting that the French king and his council will not stop my dues, if the King forbear his. If Sir John Wallop cannot obtain this from the Grand Master he is to speak with the King, and advertise you of the result. The king (of England) intends to send one of his Council shortly to Francis. When he arrives in Paris, you are to declare to him the effect of my business, and be ordered accordingly, as I wish to have all my causes determined. At the coming of the King's ambassador send me word, that I may give you directions.[50]

Unfortunately it seems that the duke's efforts came to naught. Despite having revenue of around £2,500 – £3,000 (£805,250.00 – £966,300.00)[51] a year, Brandon still owed money to the crown.[52] He also continued to live beyond his means as he was required to keep up appearances as one of the highest ranking peers of the land and it would seem that the duke's financial issues would be constant throughout his life.

Tragically, Brandon's son Henry, Earl of Lincoln, died on the morning of 1 March 1534,[53] just six months after his father's marriage to Katherine Willoughby and at the age of just eleven. Rumour was that Henry died of a broken heart after having his wife stolen from him, but there seems to be little truth in this. Young Henry may have been sick for a period of time leading up to his death. Whatever the cause of the young earl's death, Brandon was left with four daughters but no male heir to succeed him. Anne Boleyn is reported to have said that "My Lord Brandon kills one son to beget another".[54] If there is any truth in this report, then clearly Anne still held a great deal of resentment towards the duke for trying to break up her engagement to the king. Brandon's thoughts on Anne Boleyn's comments are not recorded.

Just over a year later, in September 1535, Brandon wrote to Cromwell advising him of the birth of his first child with Katherine, a son. He also asked if Cromwell could be one of the godfathers:

> It has pleased God to send me a son. I beg you will ask the King to be so good to me as "to make a Corssten solle," and that you also will be one of the godfathers.[55]

Katherine had given birth on 18 September 1535.[56] We do not know what sort of labour Katherine had or how long it lasted, but she was able to deliver a second son a short period later, so it is presumed that she recovered well after the delivery of her first child.

A short time later the little boy, named Henry after the king, was christened. Henry VIII stood as one of the godfathers[57], a great honour for Brandon, and even gave the midwife and nurse £4 (£1,288.40)[58] for their efforts.[59]

Brandon and Cromwell appeared to have held a good working relationship and, thus, it was natural that he should seek the king's right-hand man to be godfather to his son. Brandon often wrote to Cromwell seeking support for his servants,[60] and the pair also hunted together in August 1535, when Brandon gifted Cromwell a stag.[61] However, it does not appear that the pair had as close a relationship as Brandon had once held with Cardinal Thomas Wolsey.

After three years of ups and downs, Charles Brandon was once more a married man with a new-born son and heir. Things were finally settling down for the duke and, perhaps, he even hoped for some peace. If this was the case he was to be mistaken as 1536 and 1537 would be two of the most turbulent years of Henry VIII's life, and by his close relationship with the king and his status as one of the highest peers in the kingdom, Brandon would be drawn into these events with powerful force.

Rebellion (1536 – 1537)

In 1536 England was to face the death of two queens, the marriage of a third and a major rebellion that would shock the country to its very core. It was during these years that Henry VIII would turn to his most trusted friend and appoint Charles Brandon as the man to protect England from rebellion.

On 7 January, Katherine of Aragon died.[1] Katherine's death had a huge impact on both Henry VIII and Anne Boleyn as they now considered themselves to be free of the woman who had loomed in the shadows of their marriage. Although Henry and the English law considered the king's first marriage to be annulled, the Catholic church in Rome and the pope did not share the same views. Now, with Katherine's death, Henry's marriage was truly over in the eyes of the church. Henry and Anne both donned yellow and appeared to celebrate, Henry carrying his young daughter Elizabeth and showing her off at court.[2] It has been proposed that yellow was the colour of mourning, but it is more likely that both Henry and Anne were happy to be finally free of Katherine.

The next major event that would shock Henry VIII's world would be on 24 January. Henry VIII, a passionate lover of the joust, was to fall from his horse and, in full armour, was crushed under the weight of the animal.[3] Eustace Chapuys, Ambassador to Charles V wrote that:

> On the eve of the Conversion of St. Paul, the King being mounted on a great horse to run at the lists, both fell so heavily that every one thought it a miracle he was not killed, but he sustained no injury.[4]

The documentary *Inside the Body of Henry VIII,* presented by historians Dr Lucy Worsley and Dr Robert Hutchinson, likened Henry VIII's accident to a car crash at 40 miles per hour. The traumatic accident re-opened the ulcers in Henry's legs[5] and it has been proposed that the accident may have also caused some form of brain damage, affecting the king's mood and personality.[6]

There are no records of Brandon attending the joust, but as a fellow passionate and very skilled jouster, it is most likely that he would have done. Luckily the king survived, but he would never joust again.[7] It is unclear if Brandon ever participated in jousting events now that the king was no longer able. In 1536, Brandon was fifty-two years old and a seasoned veteran of jousting events. He and Henry VIII had been lifelong jousting partners, companions and rivals and, if the king was no longer able to participate, it is possible that Brandon chose not to as well.

The next major event was Anne Boleyn's miscarriage. On the very day that Katherine of Aragon was laid to rest at Peterborough Abbey (nowadays known as Peterborough Cathedral), Anne Boleyn tragically miscarried.[8] Chapuys once more reported:

> On the day of the interment the Concubine had an abortion which seemed to be a male child which she had not borne 3½ months, at which the King has shown great distress. The said concubine wished to lay the blame on the duke of Norfolk, whom she hates, saying he frightened her by bringing the news of the fall the King had six days before. But it is well known that is not the cause, for it was told her in a way that she should not be alarmed or attach much importance to it. Some think it was owing to her own incapacity to bear children, others to a fear that the King would treat her like the late Queen, especially considering the treatment shown to a lady of the Court, named Mistress Semel, to whom, as many say, he has lately made great presents.[9]

Whatever the reason for Anne Boleyn's miscarriage, Henry VIII's son and future heir was dead. He would have no more children with Anne.

It is interesting to note that Brandon's daughter, Eleanor, and his wife, Katherine Willoughby, Duchess of Suffolk, were the chief female mourners at Katherine of Aragon's funeral.[10] This may have been due to their high status at the time or it could be because Katherine's mother, Maria de Salinas, was a lady-in-waiting and devoted friend to the late queen, and by attending the funeral Katherine was paying respect to her mother's friend.

While these events were unfolding around him, Brandon had time to swap Suffolk Place at Southwark for Norwich Place, also known as

York House.[11] Suffolk Place was a large mansion on the High Street at Southwark. The front was ornamented with turrets and cupolas and had beautiful carved work. The rear consisted of several buildings that formed a courtyard. Suffolk Place also went by the names Duke's Palace and Brandon's House. On 18 December 1535, Brandon made an inventory of the gold and silver plate he owned at Suffolk Place. The total came to a staggering £1,457 (£580,000).[12] Once the king obtained Suffolk Place, he renamed it Southwark Place and eventually turned it into a mint.[13] It was a good exchange for Brandon as, while he already had his principal residence in the Barbican, Norwich Place *aka* York House allowed him to have a residence closer to Whitehall Palace, a frequent residence of the king.[14]

Meanwhile, things were starting to unravel for Anne Boleyn. It has been reported that she argued with Thomas Cromwell over the profits from the dissolution of the monasteries. Cromwell wished for the money to return to the king's coffers, while Anne wished for them to be put towards the founding of universities and education.[15] With her recent miscarriage and her disagreements with Thomas Cromwell, it would seem that Anne's position at court was starting to crumble.

In addition to this, the king's eye had turned to another woman. Jane Seymour was the daughter of Sir John Seymour and Margery Wentworth. Her brothers, Thomas and Edward, were also up-and-coming men of the court. Jane was a lady-in-waiting to both Katherine of Aragon and Anne Boleyn and it was probably through her time serving Anne that she caught the king's eye.[16] With Henry VIII growing ever dissatisfied with his current wife's ability to bear him a son, the Seymours, as the Boleyns and the Howards before them, saw an opportunity to further their fortunes and eagerly pushed the king's attentions with their sister.

The events that led up to Anne Boleyn's arrest and execution are far too detailed to describe here. Whole books have been dedicated to the controversy and circumstances surrounding the reasons behind Anne's fall. Whatever the reasoning behind Henry VIII turning his back on his second wife, things were moving swiftly against the queen and Charles Brandon played a major role.

On 24 April 1536, two commissions of oyer and terminer were set up at Westminster by Thomas Cromwell and Sir Thomas Audley, Henry VIII's lord chancellor. A jury of noblemen, including Charles Brandon, were presented with various offences against the king committed in both Middlesex and Kent. While examining the offences committed, the jury found enough damning evidence against Anne Boleyn and concluded that Anne had committed many illicit affairs, with Sir Henry Norris, Francis Weston, William Brereton, Mark Smeaton and her own brother, George Boleyn, Lord Rochford, as well as plotting to have her husband the King of England killed.[17]

Anne Boleyn was arrested on 2 Mary 1536 and taken to the Tower, lodged in the queen's apartments, where she had been housed on the night before her coronation.[18]

On 11 May, satisfied that enough evidence had been gathered, the jury at Westminster Hall wrote an indictment against Anne Boleyn. They determined that she had committed incest and adultery on multiple occasions as well as plotting the king's death. The indictment can be summarised as follows:

- **6 and 12 October 1533** – Anne and Sir Henry Norris slept together at Westminster
- **16 and 27 November 1533** – Anne and Sir William Brereton slept together at Greenwich
- **3 and 8 December 1533** – Anne and Sir William Brereton slept together at Hampton Court
- **12 April 1534** – Anne and Mark Smeaton slept together at Westminster
- **12 and 19 May 1534** – Anne and Mark Smeaton slept together at Greenwich
- **8 and 20 May 1534** – Anne and Sir Francis Weston slept together at Westminster
- **6 and 20 June 1534** – Anne and Sir Francis Weston slept together at Greenwich
- **26 April 1535** – Anne and Mark Smeaton slept together at Westminster
- **31 October 1535** – Anne and some of the men spoke of the king's death at Westminster
- **2 and 5 November 1535** – Anne and her brother George Boleyn slept together at Westminster
- **27 November 1535** – Anne gave gifts to the men at Westminster
- **22 and 29 December 1535** – Anne and her brother George Boleyn slept together at Eltham Palace
- **8 January 1536** – Anne compassed the king's death with Rochford, Norris, Weston and Brereton at Greenwich[19]

The next day, on 12 May, Sir Henry Norris, Sir William Brereton, Sir Francis Weston and Mark Smeaton were brought from the Tower of London to Westminster Hall to stand before a jury and face their crimes. Brandon was part of the jury that would give sentence upon each man's life.[20] The indictments of the previous two days were damning and left little room for anything but the idea that these four men were guilty.

But it was not just the false evidence that went against these men, it was the worries and fears of the men chosen to be the jurors of this case. What man could stand up and say Smeaton, Norris, Weston and Brereton were innocent when their king wanted them to be guilty? Brandon was no fool. He had challenged Henry VIII before and knew of the punishment that could be inflicted upon those defying the king's wishes. His personal thoughts on the actual guilt of each man remains unknown. However, he was currently well-positioned with Henry's good graces and would certainly not defy his king in such an important matter.

It is not surprising, then, that after each man was tried they were all found guilty. As traitors they were sentenced to be hanged, drawn and quartered, their manhoods cut off in front of their eyes before they were beheaded. Only Mark Smeaton confessed to being guilty before the grand jury. Norris, Weston and Brereton all pleaded innocent.[21]

Three days later Brandon was also amongst the jurors who were selected to try George Boleyn, Lord Rochford, and Anne Boleyn.[22] The trial was held in the king's hall at the Tower of London for fear regarding the transportation of two high profile prisoners as well as the common people's reaction.[23] Dressed in a gown of deep black with a crimson petticoat, and wearing a hat with a black and white feather on it, Queen Anne prepared to face a jury of her own peers – who were known to hold little love for her.

Hundreds of people came to the Tower to see Anne Boleyn's trial – for the very Queen of England to be tried for adultery, incest and treason was surely no light matter. Such were the number of people that a platform had to be constructed in the middle of the hall for Anne to sit on. At the other end of the hall sat her uncle, the Duke of Norfolk, who was to preside over events. Official documents of the trial have been lost over time, but word of mouth, letters and reports passed on all collaborate that Anne entered the king's hall with the poise and dignity only befitting a queen. Presenting herself to the jury, Anne showed no sign of fear or nerves. She gave a small curtsey to the jury before taking her seat in the middle of the platform.[24]

Then the charges were read to Anne. Every sordid, horrible, scandalous detail was revealed to all of those persons within the hall. It is said that throughout this indignity, Anne sat, poised and beautiful, showing no sign of disgust or guilt. Afterwards she was asked how she pleaded. The queen replied that she was not guilty of any of the charges.[25]

Those trying Anne argued staunchly of her guilt, giving the evidence presented at the Westminster and Kent indictments as examples of the horrendous crimes Anne had committed against her husband. Anne defended herself with great dignity and spirit, such was her very nature. She adamantly denied all the charges against her and argued that "she had maintained her honour and her chastity all her life long".[26] She used her famous wit, charm and intelligence to put up a such a strong defence that it was said some of those in the audience even started to doubt if the charges were real or not.

However, it was all of no avail. One by one each member of the jury gave their verdict – every man said guilty, including Brandon. Anne Boleyn, the Queen of England was found guilty of all the charges presented before her: adultery, incest and treason.[27]

The Duke of Norfolk, Anne's uncle, read out her sentence:

> Because thou hast offended against our sovereign the King's Grace in committing treason against his person, the law of the realm is this, that though hast deserved death, and thy judgement is this: that thou shalt be burnt here within the Tower of London on the Green, else to have thy head smitten off, as the King's pleasure shall be further known of the same. [28]

In response to this fateful sentence Anne is said to have replied:

> My lords, I will not say your sentence is unjust, nor presume that my reasons can prevail against your convictions. I am willing to believe that you have sufficient reasons for what you have done; but then they must be other than those which have been produced in court, for I am clear of all the offences which you then laid to my charge. I have ever been a faithful wife to the King, though I do not say I have always shown him that humility which his goodness to me, and the honours to which he raised me, merited. I confess I have

had jealous fancies and suspicions of him, which I had not discretion enough, and wisdom, to conceal at all times. But God knows, and is my witness, that I have not sinned against him in any other way. Think not I say this in the hope to prolong my life, for He who saveth from death hath taught me how to die, and He will strengthen my faith. Think not, however, that I am so bewildered in my mind as not to lay the honour of my chastity to heart now in mine extremity, when I have maintained it all my life long, much as ever queen did. I know these, my last words, will avail me nothing but for the justification of my chastity and honour. As for my brother and those others who are unjustly condemned, I would willingly suffer many deaths to deliver them, but since I see it so pleases the King, I shall willingly accompany them in death, with this assurance, that I shall lead an endless life with them in peace and joy, where I will pray to God for the King and for you, my lords.[29]

For the first time Brandon was sitting face-to-face with Anne rather than distantly removed, as he had been when the indictment was first drawn up. Did he finally see that Anne Boleyn believed herself to be innocent of the charges brought against her? Or did he, as he had always done, do his duty to his king?

After her speech, Anne curtsied again to those who had just convicted her to death, and was led out of the king's hall back to the queen's lodgings. The gaoler turned his axe inwards to show all those present that Anne had been sentenced to death.[30]

After Anne's trial, her brother George Boleyn, Lord Rochford, was led into the king's hall and his trial commenced. As with Anne, Brandon was part of the jury to judge George Boleyn on his alleged crimes. Now that Norris, Weston, Brereton, Smeaton and his own sister had been found guilty and sentenced to death, there was no hope for George. He pleaded not guilty to all the charges presented and, although he put up a brave fight and is said to have challenged the charges with great wit, he too was found guilty of incest and treason and sentenced to death. He was led out of the king's hall and back to his lodgings, where he was to await his death.[31]

It has been suggested that the charge of incest against Anne Boleyn was brought forward by Brandon himself. Previously, Anne had declared loudly that Brandon had slept with his own daughter. Was the suggestion of incest with her brother Brandon's way of getting back at Anne for her comment? Or was it simply a means to rid the court of George Boleyn, a powerful man in his own right? Either way, Brandon was no fool. He did his duty and found both Anne and George Boleyn guilty.

On the morning of 17 May, five men were led from their lodgings within the Tower to their deaths upon Tower Hill. Cromwell sent word to Sir Kingston the Tower gaoler on either the evening of the 16th or early morning of the 17th that Mark Smeaton, Sir Henry Norris, Sir Francis Weston, Sir William Brereton and George Boleyn Lord Rochford were to be beheaded rather than hanged, drawn and quartered.[32]

One by one each man was led up on to the scaffold. It has been reported that a large crowd came to watch the executions. The men were executed in order of rank and therefore George Boleyn was the first to meet his end. Next was Sir Henry Norris, Henry's master of the stool for ten years. One report states that Norris commented that no one owed more to the king than he did, nor had anyone been as ungrateful to the king as he had. He then went on to proclaim that the queen was innocent of all charges against her. He knelt at the block, laid his head down and was beheaded. After Norris's head fell, Sir Francis Weston was to face the block. Fourth was Sir William Brereton. The block and scaffold were now bloodied and holding the bodies of three men, Brereton knelt and accepted his fate. Lastly, Mark Smeaton was led up the scaffold to the block. He had been forced to watch four men beheaded in front of his eyes. Kneeling at the blood-soaked block, Smeaton met his end.[33]

It has been suggested that when Archbishop Cranmer visited Anne on 16 May, he did not go to provide her with comfort in her final hours, but to offer her a bargain. If she would agree to the annulment of her marriage with the king then perhaps the king would show leniency on her or their daughter, Elizabeth Tudor.[34] There is no way to assess if this was the purpose of Cranmer's visit to Anne as no records exist of the conversation. What we do know is that on 17 May, at Lambeth, Archbishop Cranmer declared the annulment of the marriage between Anne Boleyn and Henry VIII. Those present to hear this declaration were John de Vere, Earl of Oxford, Sir Thomas Audley and, of course, Charles Brandon. [35]

On 19 May, Anne chose to wear a dress of grey damask, which had a crimson kirtle beneath, and a mantle that was trimmed with ermine. She wore an English hood, a necklace and earrings. At 8am, Sir Kingston came to tell Anne that her hour was approaching and she should prepare herself, but Anne was already prepared. She told Sir Kingston: "Acquit yourself of your charge for I have long been prepared."[36]

At 9am, or perhaps a little before, Anne left her chambers in the queen's lodgings for the last time. She walked down the stairs to the courtyard between the Jewel House and the king's hall. Two hundred yeomen were there to lead Anne, her ladies-in-waiting, Kingston and several others to the scaffold that had been erected. She walked through the courtyard and through the twin towers of Coldharbour Gate to the scaffold that awaited her. Approximately 1,000 people surrounded the scaffold on Tower Green to watch the execution of Anne Boleyn. Of course, several of those were the men who had sought to bring the charges against her, including Thomas Cromwell, the Duke of Richmond (Anne's stepson) and Charles Brandon, Duke of Suffolk.[37]

The scaffold was draped in black cloth and had straw scattered across it. On the scaffold waited the French executioner, who was dressed like all the other men to conceal his identity. His sword was hidden under the straw to save Anne seeing the tool that would end her life. Slowly she took the four steps that led up to the scaffold and took her place in the centre. She turned and "begged leave to speak to the people, promising she would not speak a word that was not good".[38] She then asked Kingston "not to hasten the signal for her death till she had spoken that which she had mind to say".[39]

Turning back to the crowd that was staring so intently at Anne, she took a deep breath and, with a voice that wavered at first but grew stronger as she continued, Anne spoke:

> Good Christian people, I am come hither to die, according to the law, for by the law I am judged to die, and therefore I will speak nothing against it. I come here only to die, and thus to yield myself humbly to the will of the King, my lord. And if, in my life, I did ever offend the King's Grace, surely with my death I do now atone. I come hither to accuse no man, nor to speak anything of that whereof I am accused, as I know full well that aught I say in my defence doth not appertain to you. I pray and beseech you all, good friends, to pray for the life of the King, my sovereign lord and yours, who is one of the best princes on the face of the earth, who has

always treated me so well that better could not be, wherefore I submit to death with good will, humbly asking pardon of all the world. If any person will meddle with my cause, I require them to judge the best. Thus I take my leave of the world, and of you, and I heartily desire you all to pray for me. Oh Lord, have mercy on me! To God I commend my soul.[40]

After her speech, Anne's ladies helped her remove her mantle, earrings and necklace and to take off her hood. Kneeling, she was blindfolded and, as she knelt upon the straw, those around her knelt also, showing their respect for what was about to happen, all except the dukes of Richmond and Suffolk. As a thousand pairs of eyes looked at her, Anne repeated over and over the prayer: "Jesu, have pity on my soul! My God, have pity on my soul, To Jesus Christ I commend my soul."[41] It was only now in the last few minutes of her life that Anne's resolve began to falter. It is said that, nervously, she kept turning her head, trying to figure out what was happening. The executioner, seeing this, turned to his assistant and called "bring me the sword".[42] Anne turned to the sound and in this moment the executioner pulled out his sword from beneath the straw. Lifting it high above his head he swung, and with one swift blow he brought it down, severing Anne Boleyn's neck, her lips still moving in prayer.

Anne Boleyn was dead. Brandon had never seen eye-to-eye with her and they had spoken unfavourably of each other over the years. He also benefited from Anne's death because three manors formerly belonging to the de la Poles but given to Anne Boleyn, were granted to Brandon, which added around £100 (£32,210.00)[43] a year to his income.[44]

Less than twenty-four hours after Anne Boleyn's death, Henry VIII became betrothed to Jane Seymour. The king wasted little time in taking a third wife and, on 30 May, only eleven days after his second wife was executed, Henry VIII married Jane at Whitehall Palace.[45]

The king was looking to move on and to have legitimate male heirs with Jane. On 1 July 1536, Parliament proposed the Second Act of Succession, which declared that not only was Mary, Henry's daughter with his first wife Katherine of Aragon, illegitimate, but now Elizabeth, daughter of Anne Boleyn, was also.[46] Now, at forty-five years of age, Henry VIII had three known illegitimate children and no heir to succeed his throne. His hopes lay in Jane Seymour providing him with a son, but before that happened things were about to go from bad to worse for the king.

Tragically, on 23 July, the king's illegitimate son Henry Fitzroy died at St James's Palace.[47] It is unclear as of what exactly the young man died, but a strong suggestion of tuberculosis or a lung condition has been put forward. He was buried at Thetford Priory, Norfolk, but later moved to St Michael's Church, Framlingham, Suffolk, after the priory's dissolution.[48] His death came as a great shock to the king and once again his thoughts turned to the line of succession and a male heir. With Jane Seymour not yet pregnant, the king had no living male heir. In some way Brandon must have been able to sympathise with the king. Only two years previously he had lost his son and heir. One cannot help but wonder during this time if the pair turned their conversations to lost sons and thoughts of what might have been.

With the king's mind still on the line of succession and a legitimate male heir, another major trouble was to come to light. This time it would not only affect him but his entire kingdom.

The Pilgrimage of Grace rebellion was to demand a great deal of Charles Brandon's time and effort over the last three months of 1536. The rebellion initially formed as a series of revolts that originated in Lincolnshire. The people were unhappy with the dissolution of their abbey in Louth, and upset with many of the government commissions in the area that were being conducted to look at the resources that the smaller monasteries had, as well as the conduct of the clergy. There was also the widespread rumour that the government would confiscate the jewels, plate and wealth of the monasteries and also impose new taxes upon the people.[49]

On 1 October 1536, Thomas Kendall, Vicar of St James's Church, Louth, preached a sermon warning that the church was in danger. The following day, Nicholas Melton and a group of people from the city captured John Heneage, the Bishop of Lincoln's registrar, as he tried to deliver the assessment of the clergy as ordered by Thomas Cromwell. Melton ripped the papers from Heneage's hand and burned them. Melton and his followers took Heneage to Legbourne Nunnery, where several more of the king's commissioners were working and were also captured. On the 3rd, it was reported that approximately 3,000 men marched to Caistor in an attempt to capture the commissioners working there. However, the commissioners managed to escape.[50]

From here the towns of Caistor and Horncastle joined the rebellion. On 4 October, Dr John Raynes, chancellor of the Bishop of Lincoln, and Thomas Wulcey (or Wolsey), who worked for Thomas Cromwell, were captured and beaten to death by the rebels. On the same day the rebels drew up a list of articles that contained five complaints for the king. These were complaints against the suppression of the monasteries, against various taxes being imposed or rumours of taxes, and, importantly, against those people working for the king, including Thomas Cromwell. The rebels felt that these people were from a low birth and were only supporting the dissolution of the monasteries to line their own pockets with the wealth of the churches.[51]

Over the next three days more support came from Towes, Hambleton Hill and Dunholm, as well as from Horncastle and Louth. When the rebels met at Lincoln Cathedral, it is reported that they had somewhere between 10,000 and 20,000 men.[52]

Meanwhile, on 8 October, in Beverley, Yorkshire, a lawyer named Robert Aske became the leader of more rebels.[53] Then on 9 October 1536, the rebels of Horncastle dispatched their petition of grievances to the king. On the 11th, the king's reply to the commoners formally came:

> Concerning choosing of counsellors, the king wrote, "I never have read, heard nor known, that princes' counsellors and prelates should be appointed by rude and ignorant common people; nor that they were persons meet or of ability to discern and choose meet and sufficient counsellors for a prince. How presumptuous then are ye, the rude commons of one shire, and that one of the most brute and beastly of the whole realm and of least experience, to find fault with your prince for the electing of his counsellors and prelates, and to take upon you, contrary to God's law and man's law, to rule your prince whom ye are bound to obey and serve with both your lives, lands, and goods, and for no worldly cause to withstand.
>
> As to the suppression of houses and monasteries, they were granted to us by the parliament and not set forth by any counsellor or counsellors upon their mere will and fantasy, as you, full falsely, would persuade our realm to believe. And where ye alledge that the service of God is much thereby diminished, the truth thereof is contrary; for there are no

houses suppressed where God was well served, but where most vice, mischief, and abomination of living was used; and that doth well appear by their confessions, subscribed with their own hands, in the time of our visitations. And yet were suffered a great many of them, more than we by the act needed, to stand; wherein if they amend not their living, we fear we have more to answer for than for the suppression of all the rest. And as for their hospitality, for the relief of poor people, we wonder ye be not ashamed to affirm, that they have been a great relief to our people, when a great many, or the most part, hath not past 4 or 5 religious persons in them and divers but one, which spent the substance of the goods of their house in nourishing vice and abominable living. Now, what unkindness and unnaturality may we impute to you and all our subjects that be of that mind that had rather such an unthrifty sort of vicious persons should enjoy such possessions, profits and emoluments as grow of the said houses to the maintenance of their unthrifty life than we, your natural prince, sovereign lord and king, who doth and hath spent more in your defences of his own than six times they be worth.[54]

Clearly, the king was not impressed that the people of his realm would dare stand up in rebellion against him and his government. In response, he sent Brandon as his lieutenant to keep an eye on the rebels. Brandon arrived in Huntingdon on 9 October at 6am, only to find there were no men, artillery or resources for him to actually do anything.[55] From Huntingdon, Brandon moved to Stamford, arriving on the 11th. On the same day Henry VIII told Gardiner:

To repress the rising, as the duke of Suffolk has married the daughter of lord Willoughby, and is thereby become a great inheritor in those parts, the King has sent him thither as his lieutenant, and joined with him the earls of Shrewsbury, Rutland, and Huntingdon, the lord Admiral, lord Talbot, lord Borough, lord Clinton, Sir John Russell, Sir Fras. Brian, Ric. Cromwell, and all who have lands or rule thereabouts. Doubts not they will soon chastise the rebels.[56]

On the 12th, Brandon wrote to the king asking what his orders were. He asked Henry VIII if they should be allowed to pardon the traitors in Lincolnshire or if they should ride forth to suppress the rebels in the north. Brandon worried that if they should pardon the rebels and ride north, that if the rebels in Lincolnshire should decide to revolt once more, then they would be stuck between two rebelling parties.[57]

Meanwhile, the rebellion was now spreading and it was reported that all the people of Yorkshire were up in arms as well as men coming from East Riding and Marshland. It was around this time that Robert Aske began to refer to the rebellion as a pilgrimage seeking the king's support in preserving the church and the punishment of those subverting the law.[58]

On 15 October, Henry VIII wrote to Brandon again, detailing that he should instruct the rebels to surrender their weapons and give all the information they can about how the rebellion started, and if they do so they would be dismissed without any further problems. Henry also demanded that Brandon and the Earl of Shrewsbury, who was supporting the duke, should gather the leaders of the rebellion and question them. The king also stated that he was sending Brandon soldiers on foot and horseback for support.[59] Brandon began to do his duty so efficiently that by 15 October, gentry of the rebellion had already begun to come forward and surrender.[60]

From Stamford, Brandon and his men moved forward to Lincoln, arriving there on the 17th.[61] Meanwhile, the rebels marched to Pontefract Castle, where Thomas, Lord Darcy and several other leading men had gathered for safety. However, the castle fell on the 21st, and those within, including Lord Darcy, joined the rebellion as part of their leadership.[62]

On the same day a herald from Henry VIII was sent to Pontefract Castle to read a proclamation from the king. However, Robert Aske refused to let the proclamation be read.[63] Aske wanted to take the pilgrimage's petition straight to the king.

By now the two sides were vastly different in numbers. Brandon and his men only made up approximately 3,200 soldiers. The combined forces of Shrewsbury and the Duke of Norfolk only added a further 6,000 while the rebels, according to Sir Brian Hastings writing to the Earl of Shrewsbury, were reported to be "above 40,000".[64]

On 18 October, Henry VIII wrote again to Brandon stating:

> Though the gentlemen pretend "this truth and fidelity towards us," you shall try out, by examining the ringleaders of the multitude, how they really used themselves; "which you shall not well do if you shall be over hasty in the execution of such of the mean sort" as shall best know the same.

> Meanwhile you may execute as many of the common traitors in Lincoln, Horncastle, Lowth, &c. as shall seem requisite "for the terrible example of like offenders," and not execute one alone, as by your letters you intended. If any gentlemen have notably offended, you shall spare the execution of them, and either send them to us or detain them in ward.[65]

The next day Henry VIII also wrote to Brandon advising him that if he could not subdue the rebels by means of conversation:

> Then you shall, with your forces run upon them and with all extremity "destroy, burn, and kill man, woman, and child the terrible example of all others, and specially the town of Louth because to this rebellion took his beginning in the same".[66]

Brandon's job was clear. He was to stop the rebellion by means of negotiations or, if that did not work, then he was to make the king's presence known and to show no mercy upon all those who rose up against the king. While Brandon was ever the king's loyal servant, it must have been difficult to be told to kill any woman or child, no matter who they were or what they had to do, in regards to the rebellion.

Finally, on 26 October, the rebels of the Pilgrimage of Grace paused at Scawsby Leys, near Doncaster, where they met the Duke of Norfolk and his army.[67] Norfolk was not a foolish man and he knew that fighting the rebels was simply not an option. Therefore, he offered to negotiate. Despite vastly outnumbering Norfolk and his men, Robert Aske agreed to negotiate with the duke and it was decided that two representatives of the pilgrimage, Sir Robert Bowes and Sir Ralph Ellerker, would take the rebels' petition to the king. A general truce was proclaimed and Robert Aske ordered the disbanding of the pilgrimage.[68]

The king's initial response to the demands of the rebels was not positive and he wrote a harsh letter rebutting the five articles written up by the rebels:

> First we begin and make answer to the 4th and 6th articles, because upon them dependeth much of the rest. Never heard that princes' counsellors and prelates should be appointed by ignorant common people nor that they were meet persons to choose them. How presumptuous then are ye, the rude commons of one shire, and that one of

the most brute and beastly of the whole realm and of least experience, to find fault with your prince for the electing of his counsellors and prelates? Thus you take upon yourself to rule your prince. As to the suppression of religious houses we would have you know it is granted to us by Parliament and not set forth by the mere will of any counsellor. It has not diminished the service of God, for none were suppressed but where most abominable living was used, as appears by their own confessions signed by their own hands in the time of our visitations. Yet many were allowed to stand, more than we by the act needed; and if they amend not their living we fear we have much to answer for. As to the relief of poor people, we wonder you are not ashamed to affirm that they have been a great relief, when many or most have not more than four or five religious persons in them and divers but one; who spent the goods of their house in nourishing vice. As to the Act of Uses we wonder at your madness in trying to make us break the laws agreed to by the nobles, knights, and gentlemen of this realm, whom the same chiefly toucheth. Also the grounds of those uses were false and usurped upon the prince. As to the fifteenth, do you think us so faint hearted that ye of one shire, were ye a great many more, could compel us to remit the same, when the payments yet to come will not meet a tenth of the charges we must sustain for your protection? As to First Fruits, it is a thing granted by Parliament also. We know also that ye our commons have much complained in time past that most of the goods and lands of the realm were in the spiritual men's hands; yet, now pretending to be loyal subjects, you cannot endure that your prince should have part thereof. We charge you to withdraw to your houses and make no more assemblies, but deliver up the provokers of this mischief to our lieutenant's hands and submit yourselves to condign punishment, else we will not suffer this injury unavenged. We pray God give you grace to do your duties and rather deliver to our lieutenant 100 persons than by your obstinacy endanger yourselves, your wives, children, lands, goods, and chattels, besides the indignation of God.[69]

Brandon was to remain in Lincolnshire to keep the peace and to keep an eye out for any further signs of rebellion. He and his 3,600 men were spread out throughout Lincolnshire, Brandon specifically located in Lincoln with a large store of weapons and corn.[70] He could at a moment's notice sink every boat on the Trent and set his men to action.[71] He was also charged with seeking out any further stirrers of the rebellion and gaining information from them and, if needed, he was instructed to execute any who rebelled against the king. Brandon did this effectively by setting up a spy network to gather as much information as possible.[72]

In November, the pilgrimage representatives Sir Ralph Ellerker and Sir Robert Bowes met with the Duke of Norfolk and other members of council. After a great deal of discussion, the council and the Duke of Norfolk agreed that a general pardon would be given to all the rebels and that their complaints would be taken to a council meeting at York to be discussed.[73] The rebels appeared to be happy with this decision and on 3 December 1536, a general pardon was read to the rebels and those remaining dispersed and went back to their homes:

> Proclamation of the King's pardon to the rebels of the different districts, viz.: That those of Yorkshire, with the city of York, Kingston upon Hull, Marshland, Holdenshire, Hexham, Beverley, Holderness, &c., on their submission to Charles duke of Suffolk, president of the Council and lieutenant general in Lincolnshire, at Lincoln or elsewhere that he may appoint, shall have free pardons granted to them under the Great Seal without further bill or warrant or paying anything for the Great Seal. Richmond, 3 Dec., 28 Henry VIII.[74]

It was very fortunate for Henry VIII that the rebels decided to stop their march and agree to negotiate with the Duke of Norfolk. Their numbers vastly outnumbered that of the king's men and, if they marched to London, it would be quite possible that they could have taken the city. Once more Henry VIII wrote to Brandon instructing him to keep the peace in Lincoln and, if necessary, to take his men and make haste to stop any uprising that might further occur.[75]

The king took an unnaturally friendly manner with Robert Aske, talking to him and behaving in a most friendly way to a man who had dared to stand up to the king's laws. It is thought that Henry decided to take this tone with Aske in the hope of gaining more information from him about who the leaders of the rebellion were.[76] Yet despite all the king's talk, there was no meeting or parliament held to discuss the rebels complaints. This lack of action caused frustration and anger amongst some of the rebels and, in January 1537, fresh rebellions broke out in East Riding, West Riding, Lancashire, Cumberland and Westmoreland. Although these revolts were smaller than that of the previous year, the rebels had broken their promise not to riot against the king.[77] This time the king acted swiftly and he commanded that those responsible for the rebellions be tried and punished. Over the next few months between 144 and 153 people involved in the rebellions were tried and sentenced to the traitor's death of being hanged, drawn and quartered.[78]

Rebel leaders Robert Aske and Lord Darcy were taken to the Tower of London. On 15 May, Darcy was convicted of treason and executed on Tower Hill on 30 June.[79] Aske was found guilty of his crimes and sentenced to be hanged in chains from the battlement at York, where he would die a slow, painful death from exposure and starvation.[80]

Brandon's exact role in the trials and executions of the rebels remains unknown. It is likely that as the king's lieutenant he would have overseen many trials, and if those men were found guilty would have ordered their executions. There was a report in February 1537 that Brandon had promised a pardon for seven men in Lincolnshire, and yet reneged on this promise and saw that the men were hanged.[81] This information was conveyed by John Hogon, a singer who went about the country with a fiddle telling tales and singing songs, and therefore the reliability is questionable.

Despite being posted in Lincoln to ensure that there was no further rebellion or uprising, Brandon sought to return to London. In a letter to Thomas Cromwell, Richard Cromwell writes of Brandon's desire to return to court and to be with the king:

> After the dispatch of my soldiers from Newark towards London, I came this morning to Lincoln to my lord of Suffolk who has commanded me to abide with him till his coming to London and to write to your Lordship that though he is commanded to abide here with 1,000 men, he desires to see the King at "this high feast," to do his duty and declare what he knows of the late rebellion. His Grace desires your Lordship to obtain the King's letters to him to repair to his Highness; and meanwhile he will leave here sufficient men to keep the prisoners and country, and will return when the King commands.[82]

It is not known where Brandon spent Christmas 1536, but in April the next year he received a number of grants, noticeably several of them in Lincolnshire. On 4 April, Henry VIII granted Brandon:

> Grant, in tail male, of the castle, lordship, and manor of Tatishall alias Tatyrishall, Linc., with all lands, &c., in Tatishall, Conysby, Kyrkeley super Bayteyn alias Bayne, Thorp, Stratton, Langton, Marton, Roughton, Tomby, and Toftnewton, Linc.; with court leets, views of frankpledge, &c., and a ferry on the water of Withom in Tatishall.[83]

Then on the 7th, the king continued with another series of grants for Brandon:

> Charles, duke of Suffolk. Grant in tail of the site, &c., of the dissolved abbey of St. Mary, Leyston, Suff., the church messuages, &c., the manors of Leyston, Glernnyng, Culpho, Pethaugh, Darsham, and Laxfeld; and all lands, tenements, rents, &c., in Leyston, Theberton, Dersham, Middelton, Thorpe, Sisewell, Kelsall, Knottshall, Buxlowe, Billesforde, Aldryngham, Brusyard, Glarving, Colpho, Graundesburgh, Playford, Tuddenham, Witlesham, Laxfeld, Willoweby, and Corton, Suff.; the churches and rectories of Leyston, Alderyngham, Middelton, and Corton, Suff.; and all chantries, lands, glebes, &c., belonging to the premises, in as full manner as George late abbot held the same on 4 Feb., 27 Hen. VIII., in right of the monastery. Also the site, &c., of the dissolved monastery of St. Peter, Eye, Suff., the church, houses, &c., and the manors of Eye, Stoke, Laxfeld, Bedfeld, Occolt, and Fresyngfeld, with all lands, tenements, rents, &c., in Eye, Yaxley, Melles, Okeley, Stoke Thorneham, Pilcote, Thornham Magna, and Thornham Parva, Gislyngham, Laxfelde, Badyngham, Bedfeld, Occolte, Snape, Fresyngfeld, Waybrede, Stradbroke, Brome, Brisworth, Thrandeston, Thorndon, Pesenall, Dunwiche, Hollesley, Rikyngale, West Cretynge, Wynerston, Snape, Playforth, and Butley, Suff.; Colneqwynche alias Colnewake, Essex; Shelfanger and Reydon, Norf.; Sechebroke, Welbourne, and Barbeby, Linc.; also the churches and rectories of All Saints in Downewiche, and of Playford, Laxfeld, Yaxley, and Eye, Suff.; and the advowsons of the vicarages of the said churches of All Saints in Downewiche, Playford, Laxfeld, Yaxley, Eye, and Segebroke; and the chantries, lands, glebes, &c., belonging, &c., to hold at 136l. 8s. 10d. rent.[84]

Noticeably, Brandon was given Tattershall Castle, an imposing red brick castle that had been fortified over the years to create a secure base. Brandon would use Tattershall Castle as a base of operations to oversee the protection of Lincolnshire. Some time before 26 May, the king ordered that Brandon permanently position himself within Lincolnshire to make the king's presence known. Brandon wrote to Cromwell on 26 May stating:

> That the King, at his departure, allowed him six weeks to despatch his business and remove his household into Lincolnshire. Would, nevertheless, have been in Lincolnshire ere this, as the King expected, but his son fell sick of the small-pox and his wife of the ague. Will make what speed thither he can.[85]

Brandon does not make clear which of his two sons fell sick with smallpox. It is most likely to be Henry, his son born on 18 September 1535. His wife, Katherine, gave birth to a second son, named Charles, in 1537,[86] although where this son was born and exactly when has not been recorded. In regards to Katherine's health, "ague" is a sickness that involves fever and shivering.[87] It can sometimes be related to malaria, although there are no reports that Katherine suffered from malaria in the early years of her life.

After the order was given from the king, Brandon moved his family to Grimsthorpe Castle. Grimsthorpe was originally given to William Willoughby, the 11th Baron Willoughby de Eresby, father of Katherine, Brandon's wife, in 1516 to commemorate his marriage to Maria de Salinas. Brandon used his wife's family's home and set it up as his main residence in Lincolnshire. He began extensive work upon the castle over the next few years, creating a magnificent quadrangle building with a centre courtyard. Also located by the castle was a large park perfect for hunting, one of Brandon's favourite pastimes. In 1541, Henry VIII honoured Brandon with a royal visit at Grimsthorpe Castle, and the duke spent the previous eighteen months frantically upgrading and extending the castle using much of the materials of the dissolved Vaudey Abbey, which was nearby.

As well as Grimsthorpe, Brandon worked hard to purchase land throughout Lincolnshire and built up a strong presence in the area. He successfully obtained the lands held by William Willoughby and used these lands to expand his presence.[88] Meanwhile, he was bargaining with the king and Cromwell for the sale of his lands in East

Anglia. The duke, ever the opportunist, was trying to overestimate the value of his lands, parks and other properties so that he would be able to gain a decent exchange of lands and money that he could use to continue purchasing land in Lincolnshire. Ultimately, Brandon had to pass his estates at Henham and Westhorpe to the king as well as lands at Butley and Leiston. Suffolk in return would receive £3,000 (£966,300.00)[89] over a twenty year period.[90] He also received a large grant of lands in December 1538 and March 1539, many of which were former monastic lands, which saw his estates in Lincolnshire increase significantly.[91] By the end of 1538 Brandon had either handed over or sold all of his East Anglian properties, the only exceptions were the Willoughby manors, Gapton Hall and a manor at Tasburgh, which he held for sentimental reasons.[92] With the dissolution of the monasteries well underway Brandon also received estates worth £200[93] (£64,420.00)[94]. Brandon's estates in Lincolnshire were now worth around one-and-a-half-times more than the de la Pole, Percy and Willoughby estates and lands he had previously held. Towards the end of Brandon's life, his estates in Lincolnshire were bringing him more than £1,650 (£507,474.00)[95] a year.[96] In addition to this, on 1 March 1537, Brandon and his heirs were named chief stewards of the lands of Revesby Abbey for the entirety of their lives.[97]

Brandon, ever the king's loyal man, set to work on protecting and overseeing the king's country, dedicating himself to his work. Naturally, with responsibilities and duties at court, Brandon was not able to oversee the government of Lincolnshire at all times so he introduced trusted men, who had previously worked for him in East Anglia, to oversee the affairs of the country. However, Brandon still took a deep interest in the happenings of Lincolnshire and on 29 July, he wrote to Henry VIII stating that he:

> Will use diligence in pursuance of the King's letters to put in execution the commission of sewers and the statute of vagabonds in Lincolnshire. Cannot perceive but that the whole country is sorry for their offences against his Highness in times past and anxious to recover favour.[98]

Despite working together to suppress the Pilgrimage of Grace, it would appear that old tensions still simmered beneath the surface between the servants of Brandon and the Duke of Norfolk. While Norfolk was away from court, several of Brandon's followers, one in particular being Richard Cavendish, were trying to stir up trouble to discredit the duke. On 2 February 1537, Norfolk wrote to Cromwell stating that "I never knew till my first going to Doncaster he [Brandon] bare me any grudge; but, as you write, the better we agree the better the King shall be served".[99] Brandon, for his part, seems to have done little to punish Cavendish for his actions as Cavendish was still causing Norfolk trouble in August 1538.[100] How much actual resentment Brandon held towards Norfolk remains unclear. He may simply have been too busy with other business at court and in Lincolnshire to see Cavendish properly punished, or maybe he believed that it was actually Norfolk trying to seek sympathy from Cromwell.

Meanwhile, while Brandon was busy trying to secure his status within Lincolnshire, he also organised the wedding of his daughter Eleanor, his second daughter with his late wife Mary. In 1533, before Mary's death, a wedding contract between Eleanor and Henry Clifford, 2nd Earl of Cumberland, had been arranged. However, the wedding did not take place until the summer of 1537.[101] Eleanor and Henry Clifford were married at Brandon's home in London and it is reported that the king himself attended the wedding.[102] Certainly, with the king in attendance it must have been a magnificent affair. In honour of the wedding and his son marrying such a high-born woman, Henry Clifford's father, the Earl of Cumberland, built a magnificent gallery at his castle in Skipton.[103]

With the threat of rebellion finally suppressed, Henry VIII was to receive perhaps the greatest news of his life. During the beginning of 1537 Queen Jane became pregnant, and on 12 October, after a long and difficult labour, she gave birth to a son at Hampton Court.[104] At forty-seven, Henry VIII finally had a legitimate son and heir. Immediately, a grand christening was planned, overseen by the king, and Brandon was recalled to court for the celebrations.

On 15 October, a grand procession took place at Hampton Court taking the newly born prince to the Chapel Royal, where he would be christened. Henry VIII designed the procession to be the greatest that had ever taken place at Hampton Court. High ranking members of the court and clergy were required to take their place as well as foreign diplomats and ambassadors, so that they could report back to their masters what a superb event the new prince's christening had been. Brandon had the honour of participating in the royal progress:

> Then the Prince borne under the canopy by the lady
> marquis of Exeter, assisted by the duke of Suffolk and the
> marquis her husband.[105]

In addition to this, Brandon had the great honour of being appointed as godfather.[106] Edward's christening would go down in the records as one of the most prestigious and magnificent events that took place at Hampton Court. Sadly, Jane Seymour would have very little role in her son's life. She died just twelve days after the birth of what was most likely puerperal fever, an infection of the vaginal passage or womb.[107] Almost ironically the queen's body was taken on a similar procession through Hampton Court to the Chapel Royal, where she lay in state for two weeks before she was taken to St George's Chapel, Windsor Castle, for burial.

The years 1536 and 1537 were a time of great upheaval and change for Henry VIII, and for Brandon by association. The events throughout this two-year period showed just how highly the king valued Brandon and how much he trusted him to see his will implemented and his kingdom protected. The Pilgrimage of Grace alone, if successful, could have seen a drastic change in the direction of England, yet Brandon rushed to Lincolnshire to do his king's will and to help see the rebellion suppressed and order brought back to the area. Brandon would prove that he was a loyal and trustworthy man to the king and, if nothing else, these two years would show he was true to his motto *Loyaulte me oblige* (loyalty binds me).[108]

Final Years (1538 – 1545)

In 1538, Charles Brandon was fifty-three/four-years of age and was considered to be in the later stages of his life, with the average life expectancy in Tudor England a mere thirty-eight years.[1] It would not be unrealistic to think that by now Brandon would be starting to wind down his busy military and political life. He was described as "a good man and captain, sickly and half lame".[2] However, there does not appear to be any truth in this description. In fact, in his final seven years of life, Brandon attended more council meetings than he had ever done previously, and less than a year before his death he went to war against France.

Between 1538 and 1540, Brandon continued to purchase as many lands, parks and estates as possible throughout Lincolnshire, some of which he then resold for a great deal of cash. He appeared to be quite shrewd when it came to sales and in five months he made five sales worth a staggering £3,327[3] (£1,023,252.12).[4] On 24 May 1539, Brandon also sold several manors to Edward, Earl of Hertford, brother of the late Queen Jane.[5] In March 1539, Brandon was also able to lease for a period of twenty-one years lands in Somerset that had previously belonged to the king's grandmother, Lady Margaret Beaufort.[6] He felt this was a huge honour and decided to commission Hans Holbein the Younger to create a special seal for Brandon to use within these lands. The design is of a lion's head, crowned, with the motto of the Order of the Garter surrounding it: *HONI SOIT QUI MAL Y PENSE* (shame on him who thinks evil of it), which was then surrounded by a circular band inscribed: *CAROLVS DXS SVFFYCIE PRO HONORE SVO RICHEMOND.*[7] By this time Brandon was now the greatest landowner and magnate in Lincolnshire, far outdoing his previous presence in East Anglia.

In 1539, Brandon was to receive one of the greatest honours and found himself positioned in one of the most important offices in the king's household. During 1539, Thomas Cromwell sought to reform the court and council and, in December, these reforms came in the form of the Greenwich Ordinances.[8] As part of these ordinances, Brandon was appointed "the Graunde Maister or Lorde Stewarde of the Kings most honorable housholde".[9] In a bill presented to Parliament in December, Brandon was officially acknowledged as "Grande Maistre d'Hostel du Roy".[10]

This appointment was granted by the king and it declared that Brandon was the first dignitary of court and that he was responsible for the household of the court below stairs, including such things as the running of the kitchens, the provision of fuel for the household, drinks and other domestic responsibilities, as well as overseeing the maintenance of the grounds and gardens of the household.[11] Brandon was now also responsible for offences committed by the king's servants, including treason, murder or the shedding of blood. The lord grand master/lord steward was also the head of the Board of Green Cloth, so named as a deep green cloth covered the table at which the lord steward and other members of the board sat. Other members of the Board of Green Cloth included the treasurer, the comptroller and the master of the coffer. The Board of the Green Cloth was responsible for the daily expenditure of the household, to ensure payments were made to servants and other members of the household, as well as to generally oversee the servants of the household. The board met twice a week and, as head of the board, it was Brandon's responsibility to attend these meetings, [12] although how regularly he attended is unknown as from 1542 Brandon was often north on the king's business.[13]

By 1540, Henry VIII had been a single man for a little over two years.[14] With only one son and heir it was vital for the kingdom for the king to remarry and hopefully provide a spare heir for the kingdom should anything happen to his son Edward. Despite what is commonly believed, marriage negotiations began long before 1540, with Thomas Cromwell taking up the responsibility of finding the king a new wife and England a new queen. Initially, Cromwell sought a French bride for his king, as Henry VIII did not want another Spanish bride. There were a number of eligible young women in the French court and Henry asked the French ambassador, Louis de Perreau, Sieur de Castillon, if he could see the young women. At this, Castillon is reported to have said "Perhaps, Sire, you would like to try them one after the other, and keep the one you found the most agreeable".[15] Naturally, Henry was extremely embarrassed by this and quickly turned his attention for a bride elsewhere.

Christina of Denmark, Duchess of Milan, was another possible bride for the king. She was reported to have been very beautiful and is said to have resembled Lady Shelton, cousin to Anne Boleyn, in appearance. Despite Henry's initial desire to take Christina as his fourth wife, the young woman is alleged to have stated that "if she had two heads, she would happily put one of them at Henry's disposal".[16] She is also reported to have stated that "the king's Majesty was in so little space rid of the queens that she dare not trust his Council, though she durst trust his Majesty: for her council suspected that her great-aunt was poisoned, that the second was innocently put to death, and that the third lost for lack of keeping in her childbed".[17]

With no great marriage prospects and an alliance having recently been signed between France and Spain, Thomas Cromwell urged his king to look to the Protestant states of Germany for an alliance. William, Duke of Cleves, had two unmarried sisters, Anne born on 22 September 1515, and Amelia born in 1517. When the duke heard that the English king was searching for a new bride, he offered both sisters to the king.[18]

Cromwell sent Hans Holbein the Younger to paint a portrait of the Duke of Cleves' younger sisters and, seeing Anne's portrait, Henry VIII was smitten. Anne of Cleves was beautiful yet she had been raised in a closed court, learning needlework from her mother, but her education was limited and she did not know French, Latin or English. Nor could she play any musical instruments or any of the common English pastimes. Despite this the king still wished to have Anne as his fourth wife. The only limitation was the issue of negotiations of a marriage between Francis, son of Antoine, Duke of Lorraine, and Anne of Cleves. However, no actual pre-contract had been signed and Cromwell felt that Anne was eligible to marry.[19]

The Duke of Cleves signed his sister's marriage treaty on 4 September 1539, and representatives took the treaty to England, where it was officially ratified on 4 October.[20] All that was left was for Anne to come to England. It was decided that she should travel overland to Calais, but her travel was slow and she did not arrive at Calais until 11 December 1539.[21]

Finally, on 26 December, Anne set sail for England. She arrived the next day and was met at Dover Castle by Brandon and his wife Katherine. Brandon wrote to Cromwell stating that:

> The day w[as] foule and wyndye with mooch hayle and ... contynuelly in her face, her Grace was so ... and desirous to make hast to the King['s Highness] that her Grace forced for no nother, which [we] perceyvyng were very gladde to set her G[race] furthwarde.[22]

It was also reported that when Anne arrived the Mayor of Dover and the citizens were very happy to receive the future queen and they greeted her with torchlight and a display of guns. In her chambers there were around forty to fifty gentlewoman wearing velvet bonnets to greet her, and it was said that she was so joyful at the warm welcome that she completely forgot all about the horrible weather and was very merry at supper.[23] There are no records of what Brandon truly thought about Anne, her appearance or her personality, but Henry VIII's reaction towards his new wife was well-noted.

Excited to meet his future bride, the king could wait no longer and, instead of waiting for their planned meeting on 3 January the king rode ahead and met Anne at Rochester on 1 January. Believing in true love, the king and his men disguised themselves in hooded cloaks and entered Anne of Cleves' chambers while she was watching bull-baiting through a window. Henry believed that since Anne would be so madly in love with him she would recognise him immediately – however things did not go to plan. When the king attempted to kiss Anne, the young woman was utterly shocked and turned away. Unused to English traditions and masquerades, Anne was heavily reliant upon her interpreters and, unfortunately, they could not help her.

Realising his mistake Henry withdrew and, changing, returned a short time later to meet Anne. Anne now recognised the king and bowed deeply to him. The pair talked a while before Henry VIII withdrew. His grand romantic gesture had been rejected but it was Anne's appearance that had alarmed him the most. Henry decided then and there that he did not like Anne nor did he think her as attractive as he was led to believe. Leaving Rochester, the king returned to Greenwich, where he immediately informed Cromwell that he did not like Anne nor did he wish to marry her.[24]

It is unlikely that Brandon was one of the disguised men that entered Anne's chambers with the king, otherwise he would certainly have tried to alert Anne to what was happening. Nor is it clear if Brandon was aware at this early stage of his king's feelings towards Anne or his change of mind in regards to the marriage. At this stage it would appear that all Brandon could do was continue to lead Anne to London and then follow on with the events that unfolded over the next six months.

Despite his reservations, Henry went through with the marriage and he and Anne married in the Queen's Closet at Greenwich on 6 January.[25] On their wedding night, Henry was unable to consummate the marriage and soon was desperate to escape from a woman he neither loved nor felt attracted to. He ordered his council to look into the alleged pre-contract between Anne and the Duke of Lorraine's son. However, the ambassadors from Cleves assured the council that the pre-contract had never gone further than simple discussions.[26] Frustrated, Henry was desperate to get out of the marriage and he believed that since Cromwell had organised the marriage it was Cromwell who could get him out of it.

Ultimately, the failure of the Cleves marriage was laid upon Cromwell and the king's right-hand man was arrested on 10 June 1540 during a council meeting.[27] Brandon and Cromwell had always worked amicably together and Brandon had even sought Cromwell to be godfather to his son.[28] If Brandon was aware of the happenings to bring upon Cromwell's fall, it is most likely that he went along with what happened in order to appease his king. He would have gained very little from Cromwell's fall – in fact, it would most likely have been a detriment to Brandon to see Cromwell arrested as he had often worked with Cromwell to achieve the acquisitions of land or to further suits put to him by his clients.[29]

On 24 June, Anne was sent to Richmond under the illusion of avoiding an outbreak of the plague. Shortly afterwards she was visited by a number of the king's commissioners led by Brandon himself.[30] It was Brandon's responsibility to inform Anne that the king wished to submit their marriage to the judgement of convocation and to have the marriage annulled. On 6 July, Brandon wrote to the king stating that:

We have declared your Grace's commission to the Queen by an interpreter. Without alteration of countenance she answered that she was "content always with your Majest ... The whole circumstance we shall decl[are at our] coming to-morrow; and this night [according to] your Highness' appointment, we tarry a ... saving the bishop of Winchester, who r[eturns to] London this night to the intent he may t[omorrow] be at the Convocation. In our opinion ... all thing shall proceed well to th[accomplishment of] your Highness' virtuous desire."[31]

By 9 July 1540, Anne's marriage to the king had been annulled. On 7 July, Brandon was at Westminster, where he attended the commission that oversaw the annulment of the king's marriage. Brandon is reported to have given evidence against the marriage, although exactly what he reported has been lost to time. Brandon was no longer attending the king personally, so it was unlikely that he discussed the king's inability to consummate the marriage. However, it is possible that he reported to the commission of his meeting with Anne several days previously and her agreement to submit the matter to the judgement of convocation.

On 11 July, in the queen's inner chamber at Richmond, Brandon oversaw Anne signing her divorce papers.[32] Brandon, Thomas Wriothesley and William Fitzwilliam, Earl of Southampton, also advised Anne on how she should write to her brother informing him of her annulment and her new position.[33] It would also seem that Brandon had men that worked for him placed in Anne's residence, who reported back to the duke on the happenings of the former queen and any letters that she received from her brother.[34] It may be that the king himself had some involvement in this, wishing to know what passed between Anne and her brother the Duke of Cleves, or simply that Brandon wished to keep himself informed of what was happening in Anne's residence so that he could inform his king if there were any grumblings from the Duke of Cleves.

Yet Brandon need not have been alarmed as, despite Anne's initial distress, which was duly understandable as one of her predecessors had been executed and another cast off and left to die in poor conditions, Anne finally came to accept her new position. Henry VIII would refer to Anne as his "sister" and allotted her an allowance of £4,000 a year as well as a number of residences including Richmond Palace and Hever Castle.[35]

While Henry VIII was seeking an annulment from his fourth marriage, the king had fallen in love and was seeking to marry for a fifth time. The woman in question was Catherine Howard, niece of the Duke of Norfolk and cousin to the late Anne Boleyn. Young, English, beautiful, small of stature, Catherine Howard was everything that Anne of Cleves was not and Henry VIII was smitten.[36]

At around ten or twelve, Catherine was sent to live in her step-grandmother's home, the Dowager Duchess of Norfolk. One of the richest women outside of the royal household, it was common for her to keep a large household, a dormitory of sorts, which included a number of young women who would, it was hoped, learn the skills required to position themselves into good marriages. Catherine learned quickly and it was soon discovered that her music teacher, Henry Manox, who was hired to teach Catherine the virginals, was madly in love with the young woman. Catherine kept him at bay, however her heart quickly turned to another. Francis Dereham was a gentleman server and a distant Howard cousin. He was very handsome and had some money behind him and gave Catherine small gifts. Soon the young Catherine had fallen for Dereham.[37]

The girls under the Dowager Duchess of Norfolk's care would sleep together in a large room, normally two to a bed and it was well-known that Dereham would sneak into the dorm and share Catherine's bed with her. Witnesses reported that Catherine and Dereham would hang together by their bellies like sparrows, which left little doubt that the pair were sexually active together.[38]

Yet when Catherine came to the king's attention Henry VIII thought the young, beautiful Catherine to be a virgin and her past was kept from him. Henry and Catherine were married on 28 July 1540 at Oatlands Palace in Surrey, and the king wasted little time lavishing expensive gifts and presents upon his new queen.[39]

Ironically, on the same day that Henry VIII and Catherine married, Thomas Cromwell was executed on Tower Hill. His head was placed on a spike on London Bridge,[40] a clear sign that he was considered a traitor. We have no record of where Brandon was on this fateful day. It is possible that he attended the king at his fifth wedding, or perhaps he was on Tower Hill to witness the execution of his one-time friend. Wherever Brandon was on the 28th, his working relationship with Cromwell was at an end.

On 1 July 1541, Henry VIII set off on his yearly summer progress with his new wife. Despite his initial desire for the young and beautiful Catherine, there were already strains on their marriage. During the early months of 1541, the king was often ill and avoided his new wife, perhaps due to being sick or maybe because he was embarrassed that he could not keep up with Catherine's youth and vigour. Perhaps he was even disappointed that after a year of being married, Catherine was not yet pregnant. Whatever the reason, the couple set off on progress throughout the north as a means of displaying the royal power and supremacy to the northerners who had rebelled several years earlier.[41]

On 7 August, Brandon had the great honour of hosting the king and new queen at his home at Grimsthorpe.[42] Brandon wrote to the Earl of Shrewsbury asking him to "send him a fat stag by the 5th Aug., at which time the King intends to visit him at Grymsthorpe".[43]

Before Henry and his new queen arrived, Brandon had ordered a renovation of Grimsthorpe, seeing a new courtyard built in addition to a new, lavish hall. It was the duke's intention to display as much wealth as possible and this included having a vast number of tapestries, plate and carpets on show.[44] Brandon was fully aware that he was not only trying to impress his king and display his wealth as an extension of the king, but he was also trying to impress the other members of the council. Brandon was, after all, the king's oldest friend and his position only remained while he kept this close relationship with him.

While a royal visit from the king was a great honour, it was also extremely expensive and Brandon had to lay out a great deal for additional food and entertainment on top of the expenses he had already paid to have Grimsthorpe extended.[45] Figures for having the king visit no longer exist, but one can assume that Brandon had to either borrow money or draw heavily upon his income to see the king thoroughly entertained and impressed.

It seemed as though the king only stayed for one or two nights before moving on with the rest of his royal summer progress. The king and queen returned to Hampton Court on 29 October. The next day the king would find out about his supposedly innocent wife's past.

Mary Hall, née Lascelles, informed her brother John of Queen Catherine's past with her music teacher Henry Manox and of her sexual liaisons with Francis Dereham. John Lascelles went to Archbishop Thomas Cranmer, who informed the king via a letter left on his seat during mass.[46] From here the rest of Queen Catherine's past unravelled as well as a more recent and extremely damming affair she had conducted right under the king's nose. Henry Manox was called in for questioning and admitted to his past desire for Catherine. Francis Dereham was also called in and he too admitted to having a sexual relationship with Catherine while she was living with the Dowager Duchess of Norfolk. Devastated at this news, the king left Hampton Court for Whitehall on 6 November, never to see his wife again. [47]

It was Dereham who implicated Thomas Culpeper, a handsome young gentleman of the privy chamber who attended the king's most personal needs, as having a relationship with the queen. There has been a great deal of debate over the centuries as to the exact nature of the relationship between Catherine and Culpeper. Some suggest that it was sexual, others propose that it was nothing more than flirtation. Whatever the exact nature of the relationship, there was no denying that Catherine had spent time alone with Culpeper behind the king's back. Their affair continued while the king and queen were on their summer progress, although it is reported that Grimsthorpe was one of the only places where the queen had not misbehaved.[48]

Brandon played a leading role in the examination of Catherine Howard, Francis Dereham, Thomas Culpeper and the Dowager Duchess of Norfolk.[49] Catherine admitted to her past and to having met with Culpeper at Lincoln, Pontefract and York, but denied having a sexual affair with Culpeper. Catherine laid the blame on Jane Boleyn, Lady Rochford, sister-in-law to the late Anne Boleyn, for having organised the pair's meetings. On 1 December 1541, Dereham and Culpeper were tried at Guildhall and both were found guilty of treason. On 13 December, at Tyburn, Dereham was hanged, quartered and disembowelled, while Culpeper was beheaded. Both of their heads were placed on spikes on London Bridge.[50]

On 10 February, Catherine was taken via barge down the Thames to the Tower of London. It would appear that the responsibility of escorting Catherine to the Tower fell to Brandon, and he organised three barges to escort the queen to the Tower. Members of the privy council and guards were escorted in the first barge; Catherine followed in a second barge, with four ladies-in-waiting; and behind in a third came Brandon and a number of soldiers.[51] Horrifically, as the barges passed under London Bridge, Catherine would have seen the heads of her former lovers Francis Dereham and Thomas Culpeper on the spikes.[52]

Catherine Howard was beheaded at the Tower of London on 13 February 1542. Eustace Chapuys wrote to Charles V of Catherine's death stating that at:

> About 7, those of the Council except Suffolk, who was ill, and Norfolk, were at the Tower, accompanied by various lords and gentlemen, such as Surrey (Norfolk's son and the Queen's cousin), and she was beheaded in the same spot where Anne Boleyn had been executed.[53]

Chapuys notes that Brandon was ill and thus did not attend Catherine's execution. The reason behind Brandon's illness is never stated. It may have been that he was genuinely sick or perhaps having witnessed Anne Boleyn's execution Brandon made the excuse of illness to excuse himself from witnessing another of Henry VIII's queens being sent to her death.

As well as dealing with the king's marital problems and securing his position in Lincolnshire, Brandon would suffer the loss of his second oldest daughter. By 1544, Brandon had lost three of his eight children. Previously, both of his sons by his third wife Mary Tudor had died and then between 1540 and 1544, his daughter Mary Brandon, by his first wife Anne, also passed away. The exact date of Mary's death is unknown, as is the location of her grave.[54] Luckily, Mary sat for a sketch in the later years of her life, by the incredibly talented Flemish painter Hans Holbein the Younger. The image is simply titled *The Lady Monteagle*, and shows a very beautiful woman with big eyes, jewels around her neck and a French hood. Since it is known that Holbein was in England between 1526 and his death in 1543, we can assume that the sketch of Mary was done some time during this period. Interestingly, Holbein also painted miniatures of Brandon's two sons, Henry and Charles, with his fourth wife Katherine Willoughby, when both were just young boys.[55] Clearly Brandon was a regular patron of Hans Holbein.

In the early 1540s, relations between England and Scotland were breaking down. There had been many "hit and run" attacks conducted by the English into Scottish towns just across the border where English forces had burned villages and stolen livestock.[56] The king needed someone he could trust to guard the English/Scottish borders and once more he turned to Brandon. [57]

Figure 5. The Lady Monteagle after Holbein
Engraved by Franchesco Bartolozzi.
Published 1796 by I Chamberlaine

Brandon was appointed as royal lieutenant of the north and sent to the border in January 1543, and stayed there overseeing the defences until March 1544. His duties did not just include protecting the border from Scottish invasion, piracy or insurrection by the local Scots, he was also entrusted with overseeing trials, administering punishments accordingly, as well as following the directions given to him by the king and council.[58]

By cementing his presence in the north for over a year, many turned to Brandon for patronage. An example of this was in July 1543 when not just one person but multiple fishermen on the Yorkshire coast turned to Brandon for help as they were being harassed by French ships.[59]

Brandon was one of the men responsible for brokering a treaty between England and Scotland. Throughout the early months of 1543, he was one of several men who wrote directly to Sir George Douglas and the Earl of Angus in the hope of organising a peace treaty that would see the infant Mary Queen of Scots married to Henry VIII's young son Prince Edward.[60] A tentative treaty with Scotland was signed on 1 July 1543 at Greenwich,[61] and on 7 July, Brandon was ordered by the privy council "to take hostages and agree with prisoners of Scotland for their ransoms".[62]

Brandon was also responsible for proclaiming the truce in the north.[63] However, he had little time for dealing with prisoners and ransoms as only seven days later the peace treaty was broken by the Scots.[64] It would seem that Brandon was furious at the breakdown of the treaty he had worked so hard to broker, and perhaps he was even insulted that those to whom he had written and dealt with would turn against him and break his trust. Brandon was eager for war with Scotland and on 21 September 1543, he wrote to the privy council stating that:

> I dowt not to sustaigne not oonly that jomaye, but I trust many worse then that, as well as they that arr more yonger then I. Wherefore I most humble beseche the Kinges Mghnes that his majeste woll graunt me that I may not only serve his majestie in that jorney, but in all other suche lyke; trustinge to do his highnes suche service as shalbe to his majeste contentacione. For I ensewer you, that and I shuld

be lefte behynde in suche jornaye, it shuld not be a lytle to
my discomeforthe for the lacke that shold be reputide in me;
whiche men wold thinke either my taryeenge was for lacke of
good will to serve in suche jorneys, or ells for lacke of harte,
whiche I wold be very sorye shuld be reputide in me.[65]

While an invasion was indeed being planned against Scotland, it
would not be one Brandon would have the honour of leading. On
29 January 1543, Henry replied to Brandon's letter deciding that:

> Fynally, albeit we have determined to revoque youe
> shortly from thens, to thintent youe might prepare yourself
> to passe over with us to Fraunce, and to send our right trusty
> and right wel- biloved cousin thErle of Hertford down thither
> to supplie your place, yet for asmuche as youe have ben there
> nowe a greate while, and taken moche payn in our service,
> if youe shall thinke this entreprise, faisible, and that there is
> honour to be gotten by the same, we wold be loth but that
> youe shuld have thonour thereof recompense of your former
> travail, being nethertheles contented.[66]

It would seem that the king was turning his sights against his old
enemy, France, and he would have his trusted military advisor and old
friend by his side. Meanwhile, an invasion was led against Scotland by
the Earl of Hertford. He was ordered by the privy council to:

> Burn Edinburgh town, and so deface it as to leave a
> memory for ever of the vengeance of God upon "their
> falsehood and disloyalty," do his best without long tarrying
> to beat down the castle, sack Holyrood House, and sack,
> burn and subvert Lythe and all the towns and villages round,
> putting man, woman and child to fire and sword where
> resistance is made; then pass over to Fifeland and extend like
> destruction there, not forgetting to turn upside down the
> Cardinal's town of St. Andrews, so "as th'upper stone may be
> the nether and not one stick stand by another," sparing no
> creature alive, especially such as be allied to the Cardinal, and,
> if the castle can be won destroying it piecemeal.[67]

The Earl of Hertford followed his orders and on 4 May, the
English forces landed near the port of Leith. After blasting open the
gates of Edinburgh they entered the city three days later, successfully
burning much of the city to the ground.[68]

With Scotland successfully subdued, the king turned his full
attention to a war against France. This would be Henry VIII's

final hurrah against his old enemy, and he sought to align with Charles V once more in an attempt to capture Paris. A peace treaty between the Holy Roman Emperor and England had been signed in February 1543, but at the time Scotland was causing difficulties and the king's attention had been turned to his northern borders.[69] Now that Scotland was no longer an issue, Henry returned his sights to invading France.

Brandon was called to action and at the age of fifty-nine/sixty he went to war once more. While Henry VIII's initial plan was to take Paris, he abandoned this idea and decided a more strategical town to take was Boulogne, as it could be used as ransom.[70] Brandon was appointed lieutenant and captain general of the army[71] and tasked with the taking of Boulogne, and it would seem that he was excited about what lay ahead as he made jokes with other members of the council about the upcoming war.[72] Meanwhile, the Duke of Norfolk was ordered to besiege Montreuil.[73]

It is interesting to note that Brandon wrote his will on 20 June 1544,[74] only days before he travelled across the Channel to wage war against France. It was most likely written to ensure that should anything happen to Brandon while he was in France there would be no contesting or arguments regarding the happenings of his wealth. It may be that Brandon knew his time was coming to an end, or perhaps he realised that he was not as young and fit as he had been when he first went to war against France. Either way, Brandon's will is a fascinating read. His will starts off stating:

> I CHARLES DUKE OF SUFFOLK, being of hole and perfite memory, considering the greate ambiguities, doubts, and questions that dayly do ryse and growe in last willes, the twentie day of June, in the yere of oure Lord God a thousande five hundredth xliiij., make this my last testament of all my goodes, catalles, and my will of my lands, teements, and hereditaments, according to the lawes of the realme.[75]

In his will Brandon first and foremost bequeaths his soul to God and requests that his body be buried "without any pompe or outward pryde of the worlde".[76] Brandon also requests that masses and "diriges" are said for his soul according to the Church of England. It is interesting to note that Brandon asks for these to be said as this was a Catholic belief that people could fast-track their time in Purgatory by the amount of prayers said for them by people on Earth. Brandon also requests that no black gowns or black coats be worn for him by those that mourn his death save for his servants and torch-bearers that attend his burial.[77]

The next thing Brandon requests is that the executors of his will, his wife Katherine Willoughby; Lord Wriothesley, the lord chancellor of England; Sir Anthony Browne; and William Paulet, Lord St John, lord chamberlain of the king's household, pay off all his outstanding debts. Brandon also asks that his executors immediately after his death give £100 to the poorest households "next unto my houses of Tatteshall, Eresham, Ellowe and Grymsthorp".[78] Clearly Brandon was concerned for his soul and wished to do all that he could to see his time in Purgatory shortened by seeing his debts paid off, masses be said for his soul and good deeds be done in his name.

The first person that Brandon grants property to is his king and he gives Henry VIII a cup of gold valued at £100. Interestingly, he requests that the cup be made from the gold from his Order of the Garter chain. This would signify that Brandon held great value in the chain and the honour awarded to him and wished to pass this to his king and long-time friend. He also asks that a gold cup worth 100 marks be given to Prince Edward.[79] And he begs the king to bring up his sons:

> In lernyng and other vertuose educacion, and most especially of Henry my eldest sonne, wherby he might the rather atteyn to be able to so to serve his most excellent Majestie and my Lorde Prince his master.[80]

This is interesting as Brandon spends a great deal of time praising the king and beseeching him to take his oldest son Henry into his service so that he may be educated and serve alongside Prince Edward. Certainly Brandon was very aware of the benefits of growing up with and being close friends with the king, and he was hoping to set up the same situation for his son.

To his wife, Brandon bequeaths 500 marks, plate worth the same amount, all her own plate to be returned to her, Brandon's jewels and pearls to the value of 500 marks, household goods valued at the same, and all the sheep and land in Lincoln.[81] He does note that if Katherine marries after his death before his son's coming of age, or refuses to follow the will then the executors of Brandon's will have the right to keep all of the goods Brandon bequeathed until his son comes of age.[82]

To his daughters Frances and Eleanor by his third wife Mary Tudor, Brandon provides the value of £200-worth of plate to each. He also bequeaths cattle to both women.[83]

To his son and heir Henry, Brandon provides the largest portion of his land, money and property. He bequeaths all his horses, mares and geldings, of which Brandon had many, all his remaining gold, silver and gilded plate, his remaining jewels, clothing and household belongings. He does make a note that all these belongings are to be given to Henry Brandon only when he reaches eighteen or twenty-one, depending on what the executors of the will decide. Brandon then states that if Henry should die before he reaches eighteen years of age, all the above mentioned shall go to Charles, his second son with Katherine Willoughby.[84]

Interestingly Brandon makes provision should both of his sons die before they are twenty-one years of age. If both Henry and Charles die before this age then all the goods Brandon had provided for his sons should be divided between his wife Katherine and his daughters Eleanor and Frances, or the heirs of Eleanor and Frances.[85]

Brandon also makes provision for his grandson, William Stanley, son of Brandon's daughter Mary to her husband Thomas Stanley, Lord Monteagle. Brandon provides the marriage of Anne Howard for William and the yearly rents, issues and profits of the manors, lands and tenements in the county of Lancaster to the yearly value of £100 sterling.[86] It should be noted at this stage that while Brandon provides for his grandson, he does not provide for his daughter Mary. During her marriage to Thomas Stanley, Mary had conducted an affair[87] and perhaps because of this Brandon chose not to include his daughter in his will.

Brandon did not forget his servants. To those who did not continue under the service of his wife or sons he granted two years' wages and a black coat each, and to those who continued in the service of his wife or sons he granted a year's wage.[88]

To his executors (besides his wife) he grants plate to the value of £40 sterling as well as fifteen years' worth of rent from a large number of houses, tenancies and lands that Brandon owned throughout England.[89] He asked that his executors use 8,000 marks from these incomes to purchase lands for his son Charles.[90] Brandon also grants the custody and marriage of Agnes Woodhall, daughter and heir of Anthony Woodhall of Thenford, to his son Charles.[91] Brandon asks that the king hold Tattershall Castle and a number of other important manors and lands mostly in Lincoln for his oldest son until Henry Brandon came of age.[92]

Brandon ends his will simply stating "In wytnes wherof to thiese my present will and testament I have subscribed my name and put to my seal the day and year abovesaied".[93]

With his will written, Brandon could leave for Calais knowing that his property and possessions would be granted to his wife and children accordingly. By the end of June 1544, Brandon and his men were in France and shortly afterwards they began the great siege against Boulogne.[94] Brandon was firmly in control of his men and the campaign, working with his council to ensure that not only his men but also the horses that had been brought across had enough food and water for the campaign.[95] Brandon saw that no mercy was shown to Boulogne and over a period of six weeks he oversaw around 100,000 gun-stones fired into the town. In addition to this, tunnels and trenches were dug in order to assault the outer layers of the city.[96]

Brandon even took an active, front line role in the fighting. Lord Lisle wrote that Brandon:

> Has been as far as any gunner in the field. Yesternight after supper I went with him to the trenches, in one of which three pioneers were killed a little before. "He passeth so little upon shot of artillery that he enforceth others to be hardy whether they will or not."[97]

Even when the king himself arrived on the battlefront, albeit at a safe distance, much of the organisation of the siege was left to Brandon.[98] Boulogne finally surrendered on 14 September 1544 at 10am, and a treaty was organised between Brandon and Jacques de Coucy, seigneur de Vervins, the captain of Boulogne. [99] This was a huge honour granted to Brandon as it was he who rode into Boulogne on the 14th to signal the surrender of the city.

Satisfied with this victory, the king returned home, but not before ordering Brandon to provide aid to Norfolk at Montreuil. However, before Brandon could provide this aid, on 18 September, France and Charles V signed a secret peace treaty leaving England alone in the war.[100] Poor weather and lack of supplies saw Brandon, Norfolk and their men retreat to Calais.[101] In distress, on 7 October, Brandon wrote to the king:

> As the King showed him special favour and credit, he had
> rather spend his life than be driven to make any excuse why
> he did not as commanded. Nothing has grieved him more
> than this departure from Boleyne and he saw none here but
> were ready to tarry at Boleyne if the case would have suffered
> it. Begs Henry to accept the doings here, and not to show
> displeasure to the rest, whereby people and captains might be
> discouraged hereafter.[102]

The king did not seem to take any great offence at Brandon's
retreat, however he did ask him to stay at Calais so that he and his
men could provide support to Boulogne if needed. On 26 October,
Henry wrote to Brandon with favour:

> For his acceptable service in winning Bulloyn, and for a
> special confidence in him, has resolved to have him remain on
> that side (as the Council's letters to him and others will show)
> until affairs there are more perfectly established. Requires him
> to have a good respect to his own health, and, if the danger
> of infection at Calais be such as is reported, to remain with
> his attendants at Guisnes or some other place within the
> marches.[103]

However, the French withdrew their attack upon Boulogne
and Brandon was soon playing a small role in the peace negotiations
with the French. Unfortunately, these negotiations were not
going anywhere and by 22 November, Brandon was back in
England.[104] Despite being forced to retreat, the recent war with France
brought Brandon several interesting rewards. He was able to purchase
Tattershall College for only £2,666 (£819,954.96)[105], less than eight
times its annual worth,[106] and then in May 1545, Brandon was
granted the distinct honour of being able to retain 100 men as part of
his guard.[107] This was a huge reward considering how suspicious the
king was growing in his final years of personal threats to himself and
to his son's claim to the throne.

On 12 July 1543, in the Queen's Closet at Hampton Court,
Henry VIII married his sixth and final wife, Catherine Parr. Catherine
was the daughter of Sir Thomas Parr, a favourite of King Henry VIII
during his early reign, and Maud (née Green), who served as a lady-
in-waiting to Henry VIII's first wife Katherine of Aragon, and was
most probably named after Henry VIII's first wife.[108] While Brandon
did not attend the wedding, as he was positioned as royal lieutenant

of the north, his wife, Katherine Willoughby did. She was also appointed as a lady-in-waiting to the new queen and would become close friends with Catherine and come to share a love of the new learnings that were spreading across Europe.[109]

It has recently been speculated by one leading historian that Henry VIII had romantic feelings for Katherine Willoughby and sought to make her his wife after Brandon's death. Katherine was regularly at court, by her husband's side when he was attending the king or in service to Anne of Cleves and Catherine Howard before she moved on to become a lady-in-waiting to Catherine Parr.[110]

On 23 March 1538, Chapuys, the imperial ambassador at the English court, had written to the Queen of Hungary explaining that:

> On the same day, the 18th, the painter returned with the Duchess' likeness, which has pleased the King much, and put him in much better humour. He has been masking and visiting the duchess of Suffolk.[111]

The fact that the king visited and entertained Katherine Willoughby has been used to suggest that he was romantically interested in her even from as early as 1538. However, it should be pointed out that in the previous sentence, Chapuys informs the Queen of Hungary that the painter (Hans Holbein) returned with the "duchess's likeness which has pleased the king much". The duchess in question here was Christina of Denmark, Duchess of Milan, who Henry VIII was investigating as a potential fourth wife. Even Chapuys states that the king liked the appearance of the duchess, confirming his further interest in her for a bride, so it makes little sense that he would then go and romantically pursue Katherine Willoughby.

Imperial ambassador Francois van der Delft wrote to Charles V telling him of rumours he had heard about the king and Katherine Willoughby:

> Sire, I am confused and apprehensive to have to inform your Majesty that there are rumours here of a new Queen, although I do not know why, or how true it may be. Some people attribute to it the sterility of the present Queen, whilst others say that there will be no change whilst the present war lasts.

Madame Suffolk is much talked about, and is in great
favour; but the King shows no alteration in his demeanour
towards the Queen, though the latter, as I am informed, is
somewhat annoyed at the rumours.[112]

It must be noted that this letter was written on 27 September 1546,
over a year after Brandon's death. The letter also states that the king is
annoyed by these rumours, which certainly goes a long way to suggest
that he was not romantically interested in Katherine Willoughby, or
at least he was not seeking to cast off his sixth wife and replace her
with a seventh.

There is very little to suggest that Henry VIII was romantically
interested in Brandon's wife or that he was seeking to make her his
own wife after his friend's death. Perhaps the king simply sought
to spend time with Katherine as a means to reminisce and remind
himself of happier memories after Brandon's death.

There are few records of Brandon's health over the last few years of
his life and so it is extremely difficult to piece together what may have
caused his death. In January 1542, Brandon was allowed to sit during
the opening of Parliament and in October of the same year he wrote
to Thomas Wriothesley of a sore leg that immobilised him for a short
period of time. If the two incidences are related it remains unknown,
but a pain in the leg or a leg injury is a valid reason to be unable to
stand in Parliament.[113]

In March 1545, Brandon suffered another bout of ill health.
On 18 November 1547, Henry, Lord Neville, son of the Earl of
Westmoreland, wrote to Sir William Paget about an incident that
had happened in March 1545. He stated that he had been tricked
by a man named Wisdom into purchasing a ring that would bring
him money and fortune. Neville caught the man and brought him
to Brandon's home at the Barbican in hopes to declare the matter
to the duke, but was unable to see Brandon as he had been ill the
night before and had only just fallen asleep.[114] Another source states
that Brandon was indeed ill, but not so much that he could not
receive visitors.[115] Whatever the true story, Brandon was clearly ill in
March 1545. However, the extent or severity of this illness remains
unknown, but it is clear that soon after he was able to attend council
meetings and travel with the king.

On 15 August 1545, the privy council, which included Brandon,
moved from Petworth to Guildford, Surrey. Brandon and the privy

council met daily from the 15th to the 21st, where they discussed issues such the licence of a shipment of woad and the granting of licences and warrants.[116] However, on 19 August, Cornelius Scepperus, an ambassador to Charles V, arrived at Guildford to see the king. Scepperus wrote to Charles V stating that Brandon was ill and unable to take him to the king and instead he was conducted by Winchester and Paget.[117] Brandon is recorded as attending the council meeting on the 19th as well as on the 20th and 21st,[118] but Scepperus's letter indicates that Brandon's health must have been in serious decline in the latter days of his life.

On 21 August, Henry VIII moved to Woking and a privy council meeting was held there on the same day, but Brandon is not recorded as attending.[119] It is most likely that Brandon was seriously ill at this time and unable to travel, and therefore remained at Guildford. Perhaps he hoped he could rest for a time and join the king later. Whatever his thoughts, Brandon would never see his king and friend again.

Charles Brandon, Duke of Suffolk, died on 22 August at four o'clock in the afternoon.[120] Despite wishing to be buried in the collegiate church of Tattershall in Lincoln without any pomp or display, he was buried at St George's Chapel in Windsor near the south door of the choir at the king's expense. Charles Wriothesley wrote:

> This moneth also died at Gilford the excelent Prince Charles Brandon, Duke of Suffolke, and Lord Great Master of the Kinges Household, whose death all true Englishment maie greatlie lament, which had been so valiant a captaine in the Kinges warres, booth in Scotland, Fraunce, and Irelande, to the great damage and losse of the Kinges enemies, whose bodie was honorably buried at Windsor at the Kinges costs.[121]

In his *Chronicle*, Edward Hall wrote:

> In thys moneth died Charles, the noble and valiaunt duke of Suffolke a hardye gentleman, and yet not so hardy, as almoste of all estates and degrees of menne high and lowe, rych and poore, hartely beloued and hys death of theme muche lamented, he was buryed at Wyndsore.[122]

On 8 September 1545, the day of Our Lady, in the afternoon Brandon's body was taken to the great chamber at Guildford, where it was laid upon a trestle. Brandon's body was then covered in a rich pall of gold cloth of issue, bearing images of his coat of arms. A cross was laid over him and on the trestle were two silver candlesticks that held burning candles. The great chamber was hung with black cloth and images of Brandon's coat of arms, and the floor was also laid with black cloth. At the end of the trestle was a stool covered in black cloth for mourners to kneel. The Lord Marquis of Dorset was present and dirges were said for Brandon's soul. The room is reported to have been full of gentleman and lords who mourned the loss of the duke.[123]

The next day, 9 September, at 7am, Brandon's body was removed from Guildford and taken to Windsor Castle. Brandon's body was laid upon a chariot that was painted black and drawn by five horses. Brandon's body was covered in a pall of cloth of gold and the chariot was covered in black cloth with white crosses. Upon the black cloth were images representing Brandon's family history. There was one that represented Brandon alone, one for his grandparents' marriage, one for his parents' marriage, one for his marriage to Anne Browne, one for his marriage to Mary Tudor, and one for his marriage to Katherine Willoughby. At either end of the chariot sat a gentleman usher wearing a hood upon his head.[124]

Brandon's funeral procession was long, consisting of John Osborne and Thomas Tooby, who led the procession dressed in black, carrying black staves as they rode. Next came the cross of St Mary Church of Guildford. Then followed the priests and clerks and a large number of other men, including William Clifton, John Parker, John Swaynsland, Thomas Darcy, John Rous, Henry Neville, Anthony Seckford, Nicholas Bayly, John Dynon, John Drury, John Gedge and George St Poll, to name just a few.[125]

Following these men rode three officers of Brandon's household, treasurer Sir William Naunton, steward John Wingfield, and comptroller Mr John Marbury. After this followed Francis Seckford, who carried Brandon's banner of arms. Following Seckford came men wearing Brandon's coat of arms, his helm and crest as well as his sword.[126]

On the right side of the corpse rode Sir Christopher Baynham, who distributed alms to the poor along the journey. Also on the left side of the chariot rode men carrying the banner of St Barbara, the banner of Our Lady, and on the right side men carried the banner of St George and the banner of the Holy Trinity.[127]

At 3pm, the procession rode into the town of Windsor, where they were met by poor men dressed in black gowns and hoods holding torches, and the Mayor of Windsor. The procession then entered Windsor Castle before Brandon's corpse was taken out of the chariot and carried by John and Anthony Seckford, Thomas Darcy (son of Arthur Darcy), who had been with Brandon when he commanded in the north, and John Porter, who was bailiff in the town of Tattershall. A rich canopy of cloth of gold covered Brandon's body while it was carried into St George's Chapel.[128]

The inside of St George's Chapel was hung with black cloth and covered with images of Brandon's coat of arms. Brandon's body was once more placed upon a trestle covered in cloth of gold. Once this was done, the gentlemen and lords departed to put on their gowns for the funeral. They returned at 4pm, where the funeral service was started with the announcement "For the sol of the Right Noble high and mighty Prince Charles Duke of Suff Lord Presidente of the Kinges Ma[jesties] most honourable Counnsell & great M[aster] of his household k[night] and Companyon of the Noble Order of the Gartier". The funeral service was conducted jointly by Stephen Gardiner, Bishop of Winchester, and Henry Holbeach, Bishop of Rochester.[129]

After the service Brandon was buried close to the quire near the south door of the choir. After a handful of dirt was thrown into the grave, the officers of Brandon's household, Sir William Naunton, John Wingfield, John Marbury and Thomas Seckford broke their staves and threw them into the grave as a sign of respect.[130]

The next morning, 10 September, another mass was held and a sermon conducted by Stephen Gardiner and Henry Holbeach, before the requiem mass was sung. After this one-by-one the mourners approached. One of these men was William Parr, Earl of Essex, brother of Queen Catherine Parr, and close friend of Brandon.[131] The pair had been friends, having raced greyhounds together in May 1543[132] and having communicated regularly while Brandon guarded the northern border.[133] The Earl of Essex along with the Earl of Arundel brought up Brandon's coat of arms while the Earl of Huntington and Lord William Howard brought the targe. Sir Anthony Browne and Sir Anthony Wingfield brought up Brandon's helm and crest. Once the service was finished, banners were set up around where Brandon was buried. It is reported that there was great weeping at Brandon's funeral and that many lamented his death.[134]

It is said that the king was struck with grief at the loss of his longest and most loyal friend and upon hearing the news of Brandon's death declared that Brandon had been one of his best friends. He went on to say that Brandon had always been loyal and generous and that he had never taken unfair advantage of a friend or enemy and was truly fair towards all his political enemies.[135]

In 1749, Joseph Pote wrote *The History and Antiquities of Windsor Castle, and the Royal College, and Chapel of St. George*. In his book he stated that:

> In this Arch, close to the Choire lyes buried, the most noble Prince Charles Brandon, Duke of Suffolk, He married Mary Queen Dowager of France, and Sister to K. Henry VIII. His Grace died Anno 1545 and was buried at the Royal Expence, and probably with some honourable Memorial, tho' now nothing remains to distinguish the Grave of this noble Duke, but a rude brick pavement, and the remainder of his Atcheivements affixed to the Pillar above.[136]

It appears that there must have been some sort of memorial or monument to commemorate the place of Brandon's burial, but over the decades this fell into ruin. An entry in the 1787 Chapter Acts reads:

> Ordered that leave be given to lay a stone above the grave of Charles Brandon Duke of Suffolk, according to His Majesties directions.[137]

When Henry Emlyn began his repaving work of the quire aisle and nave, he oversaw the laying of a black marble stone that can still be seen to this day near the south door of the choir at St George's Chapel. Upon the stone is written:

> Charles Brandon Duke of Suffolk KG Died 24 August 1545 Married Mary Daughter of Henry VII Widow of Louis XII King of France.

Frustratingly the date on the marble stone is inaccurate, stating Brandon's death on 24 rather than 22 August. Still, it is almost poetic that Henry VIII chose to see his long-time friend buried at St George's Chapel as he himself would be buried there almost eighteen months later alongside his third wife Jane Seymour. It would seem that in death as in life, Brandon would remain the king's man.

Figure 6. Detail of the grave marble on the tomb of Charles
Brandon, Chapel of St. George, Windsor.
Photo Copyright © Charlie Fenton, 2015

Legacy

After Brandon's death, John Dymmock, who had sold lead for Brandon in Antwerp, wrote to Thomas Wriothesley that "My lord's Grace owes a good deal of money".[1] However, this was not quite the case. Upon his death, Brandon's estates combined with the Willoughby estates brought in around £3,400 (£1,045,704.00)[2] a year minus £413 (£127,022.28),[3] which was part of Norfolk's pension. In 1553, Brandon's debts to the king were estimated to be around £3,059 (£940,826.04),[4] for which, in his will, he had left £620 (£190,687.20)[5] a year to pay off.[6] By the time of his death Brandon had come a long way from the mere son of a knight. He had paid off a great deal of his debt and through shrewd purchases, clever haggling and an advantageous marriage had managed to increase his yearly income to quite an impressive amount. He had also become the largest magnate in Lincolnshire, leaving much of his lands, manors and wealth to his sons. He also impressively extended Grimsthorpe and Tattershall castles.

At the time of his death Brandon left his fourth wife, Katherine Willoughby, and five surviving children, three daughters and two sons. His surviving daughters were Anne (aged thirty-eight), born from Brandon's first marriage to Anne Browne, Frances (aged twenty-eight), and Eleanor (aged twenty-four to twenty-seven), from his marriage to Mary Tudor. Brandon's surviving sons were Henry and Charles Brandon (aged ten and eight respectively), from his marriage to Katherine Willoughby.

Upon Brandon's death it was to his oldest surviving son Henry that the majority of Brandon's estates and wealth would go when the boy reached his majority. Young Henry's wardship and the right to organise his marriage were granted to his mother Katherine Willoughby in May 1546 for the sum of £1,500[7] (£461,340.00),[8] which was to be paid off in seven instalments.[9]

Until he reached his majority, Henry Brandon was sent to be educated with Prince Edward, Henry VIII's son and heir. He was taught by Richard Coxe, John Cheke and Roger Ascham. In January 1547, upon Henry VIII's death, Edward succeeded his father and became King Edward VI. During the young king's coronation, both Henry and Charles Brandon were knighted and Henry Brandon had the great honour of carrying the king's orb.[10]

After Edward VI's coronation, Henry Brandon continued to remain in the new king's household. He participated in various courtly events including revelling with the king in March 1547, running at the ring in May 1550, and dressing up as a nun in a masque in June of the same year.[11]

In 1549, Henry Brandon went to France for a brief period as a hostage to fulfil the Treaty of Boulogne. In essence, the treaty granted France the return of the city of Boulogne, and France in return had to pay 400,000 crowns and withdraw their troops from Scotland.[12] In France, young Henry impressed the French nobility with his ability to ride while wearing armour and also his skills in Latin. Upon his return to England, Henry returned to Edward's household until the autumn of 1549, where he began his education. Katherine Willoughby decided that both of her children should attend St John's College, Cambridge, and thus Henry Brandon and his younger brother Charles started their education at fourteen and twelve years respectively.[13]

At St John's College, both boys would have participated in a strict and gruelling regime of education, which saw them wake up at around four or five in the morning before they attended church. Afterwards they would start their studies, which lasted twelve hours a day with little time for leisure or entertainment. After their studies they had a simple dinner and went to bed.[14] This must have been quite a shock to them, especially to Henry who had spent the last several years with Edward VI. However the boy's education would only last two years before tragedy struck.

In the summer of 1551, another case of the dreaded sweating sickness broke out in Cambridge.[15] The sweating sickness had first struck in the fifteenth century and appeared on and off between 1485 and 1551. The symptoms appeared to be something like influenza or pneumonia, with the patient having pains and aches all over the body, headaches, and a great thirst, and also breaking out in a horrible sweat. Many people that caught the sweat were dead within twenty-four hours.[16]

Hearing of the outbreak, Katherine ordered that her sons and their cousin George Stanley move to Kingston, several miles from St John's. However, George Stanley soon died and both Brandon boys were moved to Buckden. On 14 July 1551, both Henry and Charles died of sweating sickness within half-an-hour of one another.[17] Thomas Wilson, who had been a tutor to both boys, described Henry and Charles's deaths:

> They both were together in one house, lodged in two separate chambers, and almost at one time both sickened, and both departed. They died both dukes, both well learned, both wise, and both right Godly. They both gave strange tokens of death to come. The elder, sitting at supper and very merry, said suddenly to that right honest matron and godly gentlewoman [probably Mrs Margaret Blakborn, who had acted as their governess and who would later share Katherine's exile], "O Lord, where shall we sup tomorrow at night?" Whereupon, she being troubled, and yet saying comfortably, "I trust, my Lord, either here, or elsewhere at some of your friends' houses." "Nay," said he, "we shall never sup together again in this world, be you well assured," and with that, seeing the gentlewoman discomfited, turned it unto mirth, and passed the rest of his supper with much joy, and the same night after twelve of the clock, being the fourteenth of July, sickened, and so was taken the next morning, about seven of the clock, to the mercy of God. When the eldest was gone, the younger would not tarry, but told before (having no knowledge thereof by anybody living) of his brother's death, to the great wondering of all that were there, declaring what it was to lose so dear a friend, but comforting himself in that passion, said, "Well, my brother is gone, but it makes no matter for I will go straight after him," and so did within the space of half an hour.[18]

It is reported that Katherine Willoughby was at Kingston when she heard of her sons falling ill. Despite being sick herself, Katherine hurried to Buckden, but Henry died before she arrived. It is unclear if she was there to be with her youngest, Charles, before he too passed, but if she was one can only hope she provided him some comfort in his final hour. Henry and Charles Brandon were buried in the church at Buckden.[19]

Henry and Charles Brandon were both praised by author Thomas Wilson and he describes a little of their personalities and love of learning in his book *Art of Rhetoric*: (1560):

> The elder, waiting on the King's Majesty that now is, was generally well esteemed, and such hope was conceived of his towardness, both for learning and all other things, that few were like unto him in all the court. The other, keeping his book among the Cambridge men, profited (as they well know) both in virtue and learning, to their great admiration. For the Greek, the Latin, and the Italian, I know he could do more than would be thought true by my report. I leave to speak of his skill in pleasant instruments, neither will I utter his aptness in music, and his toward nature to all exercises of the body. But his elder brother in this time – besides the other gifts of the mind, which passed all others and were almost incredible, – following his father's nature was so delighted with riding and running in armor upon horseback, and was so comely for that feat, and could do so well in charging his staff, being but fourteen years of age, that men-of-war even at this hour moan much the want of such a worthy gentleman. Yeah, the Frenchman that first wondered at his learning when he was there among them and made a notable oration in Latin were much more astonied when they saw his comely riding, and little thought to find these two ornaments joined both in one, his years especially being so tender and his practice of so small time.
>
> Afteward, coming from the court, as one that was desirious to be among the learned, he lay in Cambridge together with his brother, they were both so profited and so gently used themselves, that all Cambridge did reverence both him and his brother as two jewles sent from God. The elder's nature was such that he thought himself best when he was among the wisest, and yet contemned none, but thankfully used all, gentle in behaviour without childishness, stout of stomach without all pride, bold without all wariness and friendly with good advisement. The younger, being not so ripe in years, was not so grave in look, rather cheerful than sad, rather quick than ancient; but yet if his brother were set aside, not one that went beyond him. A child that by his own inclination that so much yielded to his ruler as few by chastement have done the like, pleasant of speech, prompt of wit, sitting by nature,

haught without hate, kind without craft, liberal of heart,
gentle in behaviour, forward in all things, greedy of learning,
and loath to take a foil in any open assembly. They both in
all attempts sought to have the victory, and in excersise of wit
not only the one with the other did oft stand in contention,
but also they both would match with the best, and thought
themselves most happy when they might have any occasion to
put their wits to trial.[20]

Even putting any boasting aside it is clear that both Henry and
Charles Brandon were very bright young men with a great deal of
promise. They appeared to have had a great love for learning and
enjoyed sharing their learning and having their own thoughts and
ideas challenged. It also seems that Henry shared his father's skill and
ability in horse-riding and jousting. Losing her two sons at such a
tender age must have been devastating for Katherine Willoughby.

With the death of Henry and Charles Brandon on
14 July 1551, Brandon's direct name and bloodline ceased. The
title of Duke of Suffolk went to Brandon's son-in-law, Henry Grey,
husband of Frances Brandon.

Brandon's first-born child, Anne, who was born in 1507, outlived
her father but had caused such a scandal that Brandon excluded her
from his will. Relations between Anne and her husband Edward Grey,
Lord Powis, were not good and on 30 June 1537, Brandon wrote
to Cromwell from his residence at Grimsthorpe, interceding for his
daughter. Brandon begged Cromwell:

> To continue his goodwill to his daughter Powes, to whom
> he will be good lord and father if she will follow Cromwell's
> advice and live after such an honest sort "as shall be to your
> honour and mine."[21]

Anne, it seems, did not take her father's nor Cromwell's advice
and took a lover. It is reported that one night Anne's husband Edward
stormed into her chambers and removed her lover. Anne's lover was
Randal Haworth, and while this caused quite a stir, nothing was
openly done to see her marriage reunited. In fact, Thomas Cromwell
had to step in and negotiate an agreement between the couple that
allowed them to separate.

In 1537, Brandon petitioned the court to make Anne's husband
pay an annuity of £100 (£30,756.00)[22] to help support his wife. With
Thomas Cromwell's help, Brandon proved successful in his petition.

However, three years later Grey petitioned the privy council, of which Brandon was a member, asking the council to punish Anne for adultery and also stating that Anne and her lover were trying to kill him. Not surprisingly nothing came from this.[23] Anne continued to enjoy court life, however, she had to borrow money from Cromwell and her father and was ultimately left out of Brandon's will, most probably for the great scandal that she had caused by openly taking a lover while she was a married woman.[24]

Between 1545 and 1551, Anne used forged documents (supposedly written by her late father) to obtain lands that she then sold to John Beaumont, a judge in Chancery. This action defrauded her brother-in-law Henry Grey, Marquis of Dorset (husband of Frances, Brandon's oldest daughter with his third wife Mary Tudor). The illegal actions came to light in 1552, and John Beaumont was arrested. However, Anne does not seem to have faced any punishment.[25]

After the death of her husband on 2 July 1551, Anne married her lover. From 1556 until her death, Anne and her husband brought suit against Frances and her then second husband Adrian Stokes regarding lands in Warwickshire, which had previously belonged to their father. There does not seem to be an outcome from this suit as Anne died childless in early January 1557/58. She was buried on 13 January 1557/58 in St Margaret's, Westminster, Middlesex. [26]

Eleanor Brandon, Brandon's second daughter with his wife Mary Tudor, would only survive her father by a little over two years. Despite being eighth in line for the English throne, upon her father's death there does not seem to be any record of any great happening in her life. She seems to have continued to live with her husband Henry Clifford, 2nd Earl of Cumberland, after their marriage in 1537. Clifford was a busy courtier acting as sheriff of Westmoreland, constable and steward of the castle, and honour of Knaresborough in 1542, as well as being councillor of the north in the same year. He was also captain of the West Marches in 1544.[27] Eleanor's whereabouts during this time remain unknown but it is likely that she spent some of her time at her husband's castle in Skipton, where lavish extensions were added for the celebrations of her marriage. With her husband, Eleanor had three children, a daughter named Margaret born in 1540, and two sons, Henry and Charles, who both died in infancy.[28] Eleanor died on 27 September 1547, at Brougham Castle, Westmoreland, and was buried at Skipton, Yorkshire.[29]

Of all Brandon's children it is probably his daughter Frances, also by his wife Mary Tudor, who is most remembered. Born on 16 July 1517, Frances was just sixteen when she married Henry Grey, Marquis of Dorset.[30] Frances had three surviving daughters, Jane born in 1537, Katherine born in August 1540, and Mary born in 1545.[31] Frances would be a regular member at court, attending the funeral of Henry VIII's third wife Jane Seymour. She was also present at the festivities to celebrate the arrival of the king's fourth wife, Anne of Cleves. It has been suggested that Frances was with her father at Guildford when he died on 22 August, but there does not seem to be any firm evidence to support this.[32]

Brandon left Frances £200-worth (£61,512.00)[33] of plate in his will and should both her half-brothers die before her she would inherit the lands and property that Brandon left to them. As both boys died in 1551, Frances inherited a great deal of her late father's possessions and property.[34] In addition to this, after the death of her half-brothers, her father's title of Duke of Suffolk passed to Frances's husband Henry Grey on 11 October 1551.[35]

Frances's oldest daughter, Jane, would become the famous Lady Jane Grey, the Nine-Day Queen. Whole books have been dedicated to Jane and her tragic journey to becoming queen and then her ultimate fall, therefore only a simple summary shall be provided to outline the context of Frances's role within her daughter's rise and fall. In 1553 Jane married Guildford Dudley, son of John Dudley, Duke of Northumberland and protector of the realm while King Edward VI was under-age. It was soon clear that Edward was sick and would not live long and he died on 6 July 1553.

Before his death, the boy-king wrote his will entitled *my Device for the Succession*, in which he overlooked his half-sisters Mary and Elizabeth in favour of Lady Jane Grey, his cousin's daughter and the granddaughter of Mary Tudor, younger sister of Henry VIII. Edward was a staunch Protestant and wished for England to continue to follow the Protestant faith. Mary, Edward's half-sister, was a devout Catholic and had been her whole life. Therefore, he did not wish for her to succeed to the throne and return England to Rome. But if the boy-king overlooked Mary, then he would also have to overlook his other half-sister Elizabeth. He did this on the grounds that she was illegitimate.[36]

Lady Jane Grey, like her mother, was a firm Protestant and in her Edward saw a way to pass the line of succession while keeping England a Protestant nation. What he did not anticipate was the support that Mary Tudor would receive. Upon Jane's coronation, Frances carried her daughter's train. Frances was now mother to the Queen of England. However, things would not be as Edward VI desired. While Jane was proclaimed queen in London, Mary was proclaimed queen in Norfolk and parts of Suffolk.[37] Mary soon gained huge numbers of the common and gentry as well as nobility who supported her claim. One-by-one members of the council turned their back on Jane. On 19 July 1553, soldiers arrived at the Tower to inform Jane that she was no longer queen.[38]

As well as Jane, Frances and her husband Henry Grey were arrested for their roles in putting Jane on the throne. However, after a personal plea from Frances to the new Queen Mary, Frances and her husband were released from the Tower. Henry Grey, Duke of Suffolk, returned to his house in Richmond while Frances attended court.[39] It is interesting to note that Frances became a regular member of court after her role in attempting to see her daughter rather than Mary become queen.

In early 1554, Thomas Wyatt the Younger, son of the famous poet and courtier Thomas Wyatt who had been romantically linked to Anne Boleyn, led a rebellion against Mary. The rebels wished to stop Mary's marriage to the Spanish Philip and the legalisation of Catholic masses. Frances's husband Henry Grey attempted to raise men in the Midlands while Wyatt raised rebels in Kent.[40] Ultimately the revolt was a failure, and while there had never been any intention to return Jane Grey to the throne it was simply too late for Jane. She was caught up in the revolt and many saw her as a figurehead and she would continue to be dangerous to Mary while she lived. Jane was executed at the Tower of London on 12 February 1554.[41] On 23 February, Frances's husband Henry Grey was also executed for his role in the rebellion.[42]

On 1 March 1555, Frances married Adrian Stokes, a firm Protestant and her master of the horse.[43] Frances married far beneath her station but there may have been good reason for this. It may simply be that Frances married for love, yet a marriage so soon after her husband's own death and to a man of such low standing certainly put Frances out of contention for the throne and distanced herself from any thought or idea of challenging Mary for her title as queen.

For the short remainder of her life, it is reported that despite the loss of her first husband and her daughter, Frances remained on good terms with Mary I. After Mary's death, Frances's cousin, Elizabeth came to the throne. After her remarriage, Frances spent little time at court and in the last years of her life she was reported as suffering from poor health. Frances died in London on 21 November 1559, with her two surviving daughters by her side. She was buried in St Edmund's Chapel in Westminster Abbey. Her funeral was paid for by Elizabeth I.[44]

In the end it would be the children of Brandon's daughters that would see his bloodline continued.

As well as being a father to eight children, and one possible illegitimate son, history has often left Charles Brandon with the legacy as a womaniser.[45] Certainly Brandon was no stranger to women. He had four wives and at least one pre-contract that was eventually called off. Yet does this make him a womaniser or are we viewing the man's life through a modern lens?

According to the Merriam Webster dictionary, a womaniser is a person that pursues "casual sexual relationships with multiple women".[46] It is clear that there were two marriages and one proposal of marriage that Brandon went into for the sole reason of furthering his financial prospects, but he did not enter them for the singular purpose of casual sexual relationships as the definition of a womaniser describes. His behaviour with regards to women needs to be considered according to the beliefs and behaviours of the time period in which he lived. It was a common belief that sexual intercourse during pregnancy could damage the child and that a man needed sex to remain healthy and strong,[47] so it was not unthinkable, nor was it unusual, for a man to seek a mistress while his wife was pregnant. Certainly Henry VIII was known to have several mistresses in addition to his six wives. William Compton, courtier and close friend of the king, took the Duke of Buckingham's sister to be his mistress for many years.[48] Thomas Howard, Duke of Norfolk, put aside his wife and took one of his servants, Bess Holland, as his mistress. Henry VIII's sister, Margaret of Scotland, had an annulment of her second marriage. Even Cardinal Thomas Wolsey, a dedicated man of the church, was living with his mistress, with whom he had children.[49]

When considering Brandon's actions compared to those around him it does not seem as though he was out of the ordinary, or behaving in a manner that was not common of the time. Certainly he knew how to play the game of courtly love. His very public flirtation with Margaret of Austria[50] is testament to that. He knew how to woo women and there is no denying that he was an extremely handsome man. And in his younger years, Brandon used Margaret Neville, Dame Mortimer, to further his financial position and gained the wardship of Elizabeth Grey to claim her land and wealth. Yet his marriage to Anne Browne was made due to love, as was his marriage to Mary Tudor.

Brandon did have a chequered marital and romantic life but to call him a womaniser would be judging him through the lenses of modern standards. It does not appear that he entered his relationships with the sole purpose of having "casual sexual relationships"[51]. Yes he had a way with women, that is quite obvious. But he also loved deeply and had two long lasting marriages.

Despite some accusations that clouded his marital life, Brandon's greatest legacy, and one for which he should be remembered, was his unwavering loyalty and dedication to his friend and King.

In 1520 Henry VIII, ever fearful of treason, wrote a secret letter to Thomas Wolsey stating:

> To this that followeth I thought not best to make [the messenger] privy, nor none other but you and I, which is that I would you should make good watch on the Duke of Suffolk, on the Duke of Buckingham, on my Lord of Northumberland, on my Lord of Derby, on my Lord of Wiltshire and on others which you think suspect.[52]

Despite what the king might have thought at the time, Brandon went on to prove that he was always a faithful and loyal servant. Unlike the Duke of Buckingham, who was executed for treason in 1521, or Thomas Boleyn, Lord Wiltshire, who faced an uphill battle to regain the king's trust after the fall of his daughter Anne Boleyn, Brandon remained loyal to his king.

There were times throughout his life that Brandon would step out of line and dare to challenge the king, for example when he married Henry VIII's sister Mary without his permission, or when he dared to stand up to the king against his marriage to Anne Boleyn. But the king always seemed to forgive Brandon these discrepancies and their friendship remained strong. For the times that Brandon defied the king there were countless more where he served Henry VIII faithfully.

Throughout his life Brandon showed time and time again that he was a loyal servant and devoted friend. He never openly challenged the king on religious or political decisions. Despite not having a great love for Anne Boleyn, Brandon publicly supported her at her coronation and banquet, as well as signing the oath of succession, which stated that only the children of Henry VIII's marriage to Anne were lawful. He did not challenge the king in regards to the dissolution of the monasteries nor Henry VIII's wavering religious beliefs. Nor did he publicly disagree with Henry VIII on military matters. In fact, Brandon dutifully went to war for his king and proved himself to be an expert military leader as well as defending the king against the biggest rebellion faced during Henry VIII's reign.

Even after his death, Henry VIII publicly recognised his long-time friend's loyalty. He told his courtiers that Brandon had been one of his greatest friends and that he had always been loyal to him.[53]

Brandon was able to walk the fine line between furthering his own career and remaining loyal to his king. As author and historian G W Bernard states, Brandon was:

> Very much the King's friend and King's man. Whatever his private thoughts – and there are some hints that he was not altogether enthusiastic – there is nothing to suggest he would go against Henry.[54]

Brandon was, until the day he died, loyal to his king.

Appearance

Four portraits of Charles Brandon are known to exist in some form today, each one depicting Brandon at a different stage of his life. Three of these portraits have authentically been identified as Charles Brandon painted during his lifetime. A fourth, thought to be Brandon, is an engraving based on what is believed to be a lost portrait painted by Hans Holbein the Younger.

The first known portrait of Charles Brandon is the famous wedding portrait. This portrait, painted by an unknown artist, depicts Charles Brandon with his third wife Mary Tudor. Sadly, it would seem that the original version of this portrait has been lost over time. However, there are four separate copies of this version all depicting the couple in a similar pose wearing very similar clothing.[1] It has been proposed that the original portrait was painted by either Jean Clouet or Jean Perreal. Both were well-known artists and were employed by Francis I, King of France. It is interesting to know that Perreal painted a portrait of Mary Tudor in 1514 prior to her becoming Queen of France.[2]

The sitters in the portrait are dressed in rich apparel, holding hands in an intimate manner. Their bodies seemed to be tilted inward, as though expressing their love and union. Mary appears to be tucked under Brandon's broad shoulder, as though he is protecting her as a mighty leader and military man. Brandon wears thick fur and richly decorated clothing, his eyes appear to be blue and he has a strong nose and think lips as well as thick brown hair and a square-cut beard. Brandon also seems to stare out of the portrait, as though looking at something just out of range of the viewer. He wears his Knight of the Garter chain. The fact that the chain is so bright and prominent in the portrait suggests that Brandon was proud of his place in the highest order of chivalry in England. Upon Brandon's hat is a medallion of a woman in flowing robes. She holds a rope or

Figure 7. Etching of the wedding portrait of Charles Brandon and
Mary Tudor from *Henry VIII* by A F Pollard, 1902.
Goupil and Co, London, Paris, New York

cord that points downwards and there is a motto inscribed, *Je tiens en sa cord* [I'm holding onto her cord]. This may make reference to the cord device and the motto "who can hold that will away" that Brandon adopted during his time visiting Margaret of Austria, where he famously flirted with the archduchess and stole a ring from her finger.[3] The cord in the medallion may signify the princess giving her favour to St George, the patron saint of England, or it may signify the princess leading the dragon away from St George. If the motto is accompanied with the latter description of the princess, it may signify that Mary Tudor is leading Brandon into marriage.[4] There is an air of pride about Brandon in the portrait and that is understandable as, after all, he just married the Dowager Queen of France, a princess and the most beautiful woman in England.

There are two lines of thought as to when exactly this double portrait was painted. The first is that it was painted shortly after Brandon and Mary's wedding and was most likely done in France during the time that the couple awaited nervously the news if King Henry VIII would accept their union. Finding a moment of peace and quiet amongst the hustle and bustle of the French court, the newly married couple may have sought Perreal or another French artist to paint a portrait representing the couple's wedding.[5] This suggestion is supported by the fact that Mary holds an artichoke, a vegetable strongly associated with France. The artichoke also had close associations with sexuality and seduction.[6] But in relation to Mary Tudor, it may have meant her triumph over love, marrying a man of her own choosing who she loved, rather than being forced into a marriage. The shape of the artichoke and the way it is held in Mary's hand could also make reference to the globe held by royalty, thus reminding those that viewed the portrait that she was once Queen of France. It is also interesting to note that atop the artichoke is a caduceus which makes reference to the union of opposites, of which Mary, a member of royalty, and Brandon, the son of a mere knight, certainly were.[7]

Another train of thought suggests that the wedding portrait was not in fact painted until around twenty years after the couple were married, and may have been painted as late as the mid-1530s after Mary Tudor's death. This has been suggested as when studying the clothing that Mary wears it is proposed that the style of the French gown she wears was not popular until the mid-1520s – 1530s.

Also, the sleeves that she wears show the lace of her chemise at the wrists and also up along the sleeve. This is very similar to the style of clothing that Katherine of Aragon wears in a portrait painted in the mid- to late-1520s. It has also been suggested that the French hood Mary is wearing in the wedding portrait is more elaborate and decorated on two levels while French hoods in 1515 were more simple with one layer of decoration rather than two.[8] If the wedding portrait was indeed painted in retrospect, it may have been done as a celebration of Mary's life and a commemoration of her death. It may also be possible that Brandon had the double portrait painted to remind people that he was once married to the king's sister and was the king's brother-in-law.

Whether painted shortly after their marriage in 1515 or several decades later, after Mary's death in 1533, the wedding portrait of Charles Brandon and Mary Tudor is a magnificent piece of work that depicts Brandon in his most distinguished image.

The second known portrait of Brandon is the *Master of the Brandon Portrait*, believed to be painted around 1530 when Brandon was approximately forty-five/forty-six years of age. There has been some confusion surrounding this portrait and initially it was believed to be a portrait of Edward Stafford, Duke of Buckingham. In the 1930s, Paul Ganz identified the sitter in the portrait as Charles Brandon, basing this on the resemblance between the wedding portrait and a line engraving done by Wenceslaus Hollar in 1647. Also, the sitter in the *Master of the Brandon Portrait* wears the same Knight of the Garter chain and medallion on his hat as Brandon does in his wedding portrait.[9]

Max J Friedländer proposed three separate artists as the man behind the *Master of the Brandon Portrait*. He suggested that it may have been Gerard Horenbout, or his son Lucas Horenbout, who was appointed as the king's painter in 1534, or possibly Jan Rav, also known by the Latinised name Johannes Corvus. Gerard Horenbout was mostly known for his religious paintings and his son Lucas predominantly worked in miniature form therefore it is strongly suggested that the artist behind the *Master of the Brandon Portrait* is Jan Rav. Rav was living in England around 1530 when the portrait was believed to be painted and he is also suggested as having been connected to Brandon's household.[10]

Figure 8. Master of the Brandon Portrait
by an unknown artist.
From a private American collection

In the *Master of the Brandon Portrait* Brandon wears a silk shirt, a magnificent doublet made from cloth of gold and a rich fur-lined coat. Once more Brandon wears a medallion on his hat with the inscription *Je tiens en sa cord* as well as his Knight of the Garter chain, which is prominent in the centre of the painting. Brandon's right hand rests upon the hilt of his sword, which may signify his military knowledge and strength. Again, Brandon looks out of the portrait as though his eyes are locked on something the viewer cannot quite see. With his square beard, thin lips and broad shoulders filling the entire frame, Brandon's image depicts one of strength and importance.

The third portrait of Brandon shows the man clearly in the later years of his life and is painted by an unknown artist. One copy of this portrait was owned by the Earl of Huntingdon in the eighteenth century and was credited as being painted in 1544, a year before Brandon's death. Underneath the portrait an inscription is included: "Charles Brandon, Dvke of Svffolke, Lord Great Master to K. Henrye VIII. The Fayrest man at armes in his tyme, Leftenant to the Kyng in his grettest warres, voyd of despite, most fortvnate to the ende, never to displeasvre with his Kynge." [11]

The portrait shows a distinguished but stern looking man with a white beard and wrinkles on a face that has clearly seen many years. Brandon's famous beard remains, covering a square jaw, but is wispy and white. A black cap covers his head, probably hiding hair the same colour as the beard. Thin lips are pressed together as almond-shaped eyes stare out from the painting. Brandon is sitting in a large, lavishly decorated chair. He is wearing a thick, rich brown fur coat, intricately designed sleeves and, of course, his famous Knight of the Garter chain. Brandon also wears a single leather glove and is holding what appears to be a bunch of posies. Although now in the final years of his life, Brandon is still shown to be a distinguished and imposing member of the court.

The fourth image associated with Charles Brandon is located at the National Portrait Gallery London. It is a line engraving done by Wenceslaus Hollar in 1647. This engraving is thought to be based on the lost portrait by famous Tudor painter Hans Holbein the Younger.[12] Hollar was born in Prague and relocated to London in 1637.[13] There is no age given for the sitter although he is depicted in the prime of his life staring straight out of the picture. He wears a dark coloured cap, rich clothing and a full dark beard. The nose

Figure 9. Charles Brandon 1ˢᵗ Duke of Suffolk
by an unknown artist c.1540 - 1545
NPG516 Copyright National Portrait Gallery, London

and thin lips, however, do depict a striking resemblance to a known portrait of Charles Brandon which shows the duke with his third wife Mary Tudor.

It is interesting to note that in the other three portraits identified as Charles Brandon the duke proudly wears his Knight of the Garter chain. Brandon was installed as a Knight of the Garter in 1513.[14] It would appear that Brandon was proud to be a Knight of the Garter, the highest order of chivalry in England at the time. In the engraving by Hollar there is no chain. It can be assumed that if this is indeed Charles Brandon, then the painting must have been done before he was invested in 1513. However, the engraving is said to be based on a Holbein portrait and Hans Holbein did not come to England until 1526,[15] well after Brandon was invested as a Knight of the Garter. Of course it is possible that Brandon had an early portrait painted of him without his chain, but it does seem unlikely as all three of his following portraits show him wearing his chain, something he appeared to be immensely proud of.

It should be noted that there is a similar drawing by Francesco Bartolozzi (1727 – 1815)[16] which depicts a man of similar facial features and wearing similar clothing as the Hollar engraving. It has been proposed that Bartolozzi's portrait is also based on a portrait by Holbein. If this is the case then it could be that Brandon sat for a portrait by Holbein, who was officially appointed as court painter in 1535 and paid the sum of £30 (£9,663.00)[17] a year.[18] This lost portrait by Holbein may be the same portrait that Wenceslaus Hollar used to base his sketching of Brandon on. Or it could simply be that Bartolozzi's drawing is based on Wenceslaus Hollar's. Unfortunately, without finding the lost original portrait we may never know if either Wenceslaus Hollar's or Francesco Bartolozzi's sketches are the true face of Charles Brandon.

Brandon is also associated with the magnificent *The Field of Cloth of Gold* painting. The stunningly detailed picture depicts Henry VIII with his entourage riding from Guînes in France towards Val d'Or on 7 June 1520. On the very bottom left of the painting, behind the king is a man on a white horse. He is wearing an orange-coloured cloak, a black hat and a Knight of the Garter chain. This man is believed to be Charles Brandon, although since the image is so small, the likeness is hard to identify.[19]

Figure 10. Charles Brandon by Wenceslaus Hollar
after Hans Holbein The Younger.
Line engraving possibly 1647
D24200 Copyright National Portrait Gallery, London

Figure 11. Engraving of Charles Brandon
by Francesco Bartolozzi 1798

Figure 12. Etching of the Field of Cloth of Gold from a large print published by the Royal Society of Antiquaries, after the original picture preserved in Hampton Court

Figure 13. Detail of Charles Brandon
(on the white horse, left hand side) from the Field of Cloth of
Gold Painting

In addition to portraits of Brandon there have been many descriptions of him recorded and written both during his lifetime and afterwards. These descriptions help to build a greater understanding and image of what Brandon looked like and how he presented himself during his lifetime. Richard Davey in his book *The sisters of Lady Jane Grey and their wicked Grandfather* describes Brandon as:

> In person, he bore so striking a resemblance to Henry, that the French, when on bad terms with us, were wont to say that he was his master's bastard brother. The two men were of the same towering height, but Charles was, perhaps, the more powerful... Both king and duke were exceedingly fair, and had the same curly, golden hair, the same steel-grey eyes, planted on either side of an aquiline nose, somewhat too small for the breadth of a very large face. In youth and early manhood, owing to the brilliancy of their pink-and-white complexions, they were universally considered extremely handsome.[20]

Davey also goes on to state that a French chronicler saw Brandon in Paris in 1514, when the duke was there for the marriage of Mary Tudor to King Louis XII, and he stated that:

> He had never seen so handsome a man, or one of such manly power who possessed so delicate a complexion – rose et hlanc tout comme une fille. And yet he was not the least effeminate, for of all the men of his day, he was the most splendid sportsman, the most skilful in the tilt-yard, and the surest with the arrow. He danced so lightly and so gracefully that to see him was a sight in which even Henry VIII, himself an elegant dancer, delighted.[21]

Even the ambassador Philippe De Bregilles writing to Margaret of Austria in August 1513 stated that Charles Brandon was like a "second King".[22]

In *Memoirs of the Life of Anne Boleyn* by Elizabeth Benger, the author describes Brandon as "confessedly one of the most handsome and accomplished cavaliers of the age".[23]

And in her book Henry VIII: King & Court, Alison Weir describes Brandon as "the perfect companion for the King who he so resembled in looks and built that some people thought he was Henry's bastard brother".[24]

In August 1519, Sebastian Giustinian, the Venetian ambassador, described Henry VIII as "much handsomer than any sovereign in

Christendom, a good deal handsomer than the king of France; very fair, and well proportioned".[25]

By all accounts Charles Brandon was an extremely attractive man for his time. In an age where men strived to recreate the Arthurian code of chivalry and appearance, Brandon was the perfect example. He presented himself well, always dressing in the finest clothing and apparel, even if he could not always afford to do so. Tall, broad-shouldered, handsome, and active in extreme physical sports such as jousting, Brandon would have been one of the most notable and striking figures at court. The fact that he resembled the king so closely would have only added to his attraction.

Why was Charles Brandon so Successful?

While other men in Henry VIII's life came and went, Charles Brandon remained. Cardinal Thomas Wolsey, one of Henry VIII's most trusted advisors, ever loyal to his king, eventually met his end by thinking himself too grand and failing to gain the king's desire of the annulment of his marriage to Katherine of Aragon. Thomas Cromwell, hard-working servant of the king, able to bend the rules to get what the king wanted also fell from grace and met his end at the executioner's block when he too faced a coup at court. Anne Boleyn, second wife of the king, who Henry had fought so hard to marry and turned a country upside down for, was beheaded in 1536. Thomas More, Bishop Fisher, Edward Stafford, all men who had once been friends with the king, met horrible ends, and yet Charles Brandon remained. Throughout the years as the king grew older and his worries and tyrannical behaviour increased, Brandon remained at his side. In fact not only did Brandon stay a close friend to the king, he also flourished. Why then did so many men fall around Henry VIII but Brandon remained?

It was no mystery to anyone at the Tudor court that Henry VIII greatly loved his closest friend and brother-in-law.[1] Anyone who knew the king or saw Brandon and Henry VIII together recognised the close bond between the pair.

Philippe De Bregilles writing to Margaret of Austria in August 1513 referred to Brandon as the "second King".[2]

The preface to the first volume of *Letters and Papers* describes Charles Brandon, quoting Sebastian Giustinian, Venetian ambassador at the English court between 1515 and 1519:

Charles Brandon Duke of Suffolk, nearer than any other to the King in age, tastes, and love of martial exercises, shared much of his confidence, although he was infinitely inferior to Henry in all literary and intellectual qualifications. "He is associated with his Majesty," says Giustinian, "tanquam intelligentiam assistentem orbi, which governs, commands, and acts with authority scarcely inferior to the King himself."[3]

It goes on to describe Brandon's relationship with the king:

For the affection which the King entertained for Charles Brandon, afterwards Duke of Suffolk. Henry's partiality to this brilliant nobleman exceeded the bounds of ordinary friendship. He pushed Brandon's fortunes with the affection and assiduity of a brother. But Suffolk managed a war-horse much better than he wielded a pen. He took but little interest in politics [...][4]

While Brandon was neither a great politician nor a lover of letter-writing or academic pursuits, he still possessed many talents and skills that greatly endeared him to the king. Elizabeth Benger in *Memoirs of the Life of Anne Boleyn* describes Brandon as "endeared to his master by sympathy in tastes, habits and amusements".[5] As stated earlier, Brandon was one of the best, perhaps even the best, jousters of his time.

Jousting has a long and rich history that stretches back several hundred years before the Tudor period. Starting around the early 1100s jousting was initially used as a means for knights to train for warfare. In the latter half of the eleventh century, warfare included mounted cavalrymen with heavy lances who would charge at their enemy in formation. Due to this new strategy, more practice was required to undertake such large-scale attacks. Initially, jousting tournaments consisted of mock-battles with dozens or even hundreds of men all riding horses and carrying lances. They would attack one another with their lances, swords and maces across a large area such as the countryside. Then, from around the mid-1300s, the more formalised style of jousting began where one man charged at another. Jousting was now used more as a means to practice and refine fighting skills.[6]

Jousting became popular events to which hundreds of people would flock and knights and noblemen would fight for the honour of their king or queen. Henry VIII loved jousting and during his reign jousting events were more than competitors charging at one another. Jousting celebrations became huge spectacles designed to impress and overwhelm spectators. Men would dress up in disguises, and magnificent and intricate floats and decorations were designed and developed. In addition, lavish prizes were also granted to the winner.

The joust became a highly formalised event and Brandon was put in charge of the 1514 jousting tournament to celebrate Mary Tudor's marriage to King Louis XII. There was a great deal involved in organising a joust. A suitable area needed to be found and then set-up, and men had to be chosen to represent various members of royalty. The area designated to hold the joust was called the list, a roped-off area where the two competitors challenged one another. Down the centre of the list a barrier was erected to create two lanes for the jousters to ride down. This barrier was initially known as the tilt and was first made out of cloth and then, in the early sixteenth century, was made out of wood. The tilt also allowed riders to focus more on their opponent rather than steering their horse. Over time, the tilt became known as the tilt barrier and the act of riding down the list was called tilting.[7]

The rules surrounding jousting are complicated, but it was the aim of a participant to strike his opponent upon the shield or armour, or to wield such strength that using his lance he could dismount his opponent.[8] Specialised armour was created for jousters and in many tournaments the participant rather than the king would have to supply his own armour, horses and weaponry. Lances were often blunted, but this did not stop an array of injuries or even deaths occurring during a joust. Bone fractures from the blow of the lance or falling from the horse were common and bones could even be broken. While not frequent, death could also be the final result of a joust. For example, King Henry II of France died in 1559 from wounds he received while jousting. Henry VIII suffered several injuries while jousting, one of these being when he was hit in the brow by Charles Brandon's lance.[9] There are few records of Brandon suffering any injuries as a result of jousting but it is known that in the 1514 jousting celebrations he did injure his hand, although there are no records of this being a long term injury.[10]

With his physical size and muscular body structure, Brandon was perfect for the joust.[11] From the beginning of Henry VIII's reign, Brandon was making a name for himself as one of the best jousters in England, yet the man was not so smart as to think he was better than the king. Brandon knew when he could win and when he needed to lose. By beating every other opponent and then falling to the king, he ensured that the king was the greatest opponent upon the field.[12]

Derek Wilson in his book *Henry VIII Reformer and Tyrant* writes:

> In the February 1511 tournament Charles Brandon, a talented performer, excelled in all his bouts, until he came up against the king. At the hallway-way point the scores were close but in the last three courses Brandon was careful to miss his target and to allow Henry to break his lance against him and, thus, to emerge as the victor in a "hard fought" contest.[13]

Not only was Brandon allowing Henry VIII to beat him but he was also displaying his own masculinity, a quality greatly admired by the king.[14] Henry VIII lived by the code of chivalry and aimed to achieve great success such as King Arthur of the Round Table and the crushing defeats King Henry V achieved in Europe.[15] Warfare, jousting and other physical pursuits were closely tied with the code of chivalry and Brandon, an excellent jouster, was able to display his masculinity and his ties to the code of chivalry through his jousting skills.[16] Being such a skilled jouster and yet always falling at the last hurdle to Henry VIII helped to deeply endear Brandon to his king.

In relation to the codes of chivalry, Henry VIII also expected the nobility around him to act and dress according to their status and Brandon worked hard to do this. Unlike the dukes of Norfolk[17] and Buckingham,[18] who inherited titles, land and wealth, Brandon did not come from such prosperous beginnings. He had to work for what he had and was lucky enough to be granted a great deal of land and married well to gain property and coin. Brandon was also extremely smart and a cunning agent, purchasing and exchanging lands and properties to build up his estates.[19] It was clear that Brandon worked hard to maintain his public image. He presented himself not as a man from humble beginnings but as the powerful and influential Duke of Suffolk, who was not only the president of the council but also a close friend of the king. Looks and image were extremely important to Henry VIII and Brandon was able to successfully present himself as the perfect image of a loyal, faithful courtier.

Brandon also possessed the ability to be friends, or at least to have a working relationship, with almost everyone at court. Naturally he was very close to the king, but he also appears to have an easy relationship with many of the other members at court. There is only one case when it appears that Brandon had fallen out with those on the council and that was when he married Mary Tudor. Brandon wrote that those on the council were against him but this could have been the working of Thomas Howard, Duke of Norfolk:

> All the Council, except my Lord of York [Thomas Wolsey], are determined to have Suffolk put to death or imprisoned. This is hard; for none of them ever were in trouble but he was glad to help them to the best of his power, and now in this little trouble they are ready to destroy him.[20]

Brandon and Norfolk seemed to have had an uneasy working relationship throughout their lives. Norfolk was from an old line of nobility and had inherited his title from his father, although re-granted to him by Henry VIII. Brandon's title of duke was gifted to him from the king.[21] It is possible that Norfolk thought of Brandon as an upstart and lacking in political skills and knowledge. However, they were able to work together when required. Both men were on the privy council and both men helped to put down the Pilgrimage of Grace in 1536.

Other than the Duke of Norfolk, Brandon seems to have been a well-respected and greatly admired member of the council and court.[22] He did clash with Cardinal Wolsey towards the end of the man's life but that appears to be only when Wolsey was unable to obtain Henry VIII's annulment. Before this, Brandon sought Wolsey's help after he had married Mary Tudor, and appears to have had a close relationship with him. He also had a good working relationship with Thomas Cromwell, even asking if the man could be godfather to his son.[23] Brandon was petitioned regularly by those of lesser classes throughout his life for help and support.[24] After Brandon's death Henry VIII stated that: "For as long as Suffolk had served him, he had never betrayed a friend or knowingly taken unfair advantage of an enemy"[25] and that Brandon was "truly magnanimous towards his political enemies".[26]

Brandon clearly had the talent and ability to manoeuvre himself at court, being able to further his own desires and career while retaining friendships and working relationships with those around him, especially that of the king.

Henry VIII had a good eye for using people who possessed skills he required. For example, he could see the many administrative skills that both Thomas Wolsey and Thomas Cromwell held, and used both men to do a great deal of the paperwork involved with the running of government. Henry VIII saw the military skills and abilities that Brandon possessed, and put these to use. Brandon's military efforts in 1513, 1523 and 1544 not only showed the king that he was an effective, skilled and trustworthy military commander, but also that the king trusted Brandon to lead his army into war.

As well as all these qualities, Brandon was extremely loyal to his king and worked hard to maintain that loyalty and friendship. His father died defending Henry VII at the Battle of Bosworth[27] and Brandon continued this family loyalty with Henry VIII. Brandon did not appear to try and influence Henry VIII in his decision-making in religious or state matters. Instead he followed his king's lead and rarely stepped out of line. He was a loyal servant and courtier, and this was a quality that Henry VIII seemed to value within his friend.

In the 19th century, Charles Knight wrote of Brandon that:

> It was proof of is sagacity to have adopted by choice the character of mere courtier; but he moved in it with rare dignity; and envy, malice, and duplicity seemed to have been unknown to him. Possessing a fine person, an agreeable address, and a sparkling wit, which he knew well how to temper with discretion – skilled at all courtly exercises of the day, and honoured with the confidence of the King, Charles Brandon rapidly rose to distinction; and by avoiding all interference with religion and politics; the rocks on which so many so many in that hazardous reign ruined their fortunes, he contrived to maintain his place in the King's friendship to the last.[28]

Brandon's greatest quality was not his skill in jousting, nor was it his success in military campaigns, it was his ability to read his king and know how to respond appropriately. James Granger wrote of Brandon in 1824:

> Charles Brandon was remarkable for the dignity and gracefulness of his person, and his robust and athletic constitution. He distinguished himself in the tilts and tournaments, the favourite exercises of Henry. He was brought up with that Prince, studied his disposition, and exactly conformed to it. The conformity gradually brought on a stricter intimacy; and the King, to bring him nearer to himself, raised him from a private person to a duke.[29]

Brandon "studied his disposition, and exactly conformed to it", this very quality, the ability to read his king and friend and to be able to conform to the king's wishes and desires, is ultimately what made Charles Brandon, Duke of Suffolk, the success that he was. He knew what angered the king, what he liked, what he did not like, he knew what made him happy and what he despised. Even when Henry VIII was constantly changing his mind regarding religious views, Brandon was able to understand the king's beliefs and conform to them. This did not mean that Brandon did not hold his own beliefs and opinions. Brandon showed in his life that he did not always privately agree with Henry. He did not agree with Henry's treatment of his wife Katherine of Aragon when he banished her from court, he did not agree with Henry's romantic interest in Anne Boleyn. And yet, despite speaking against these matters, Brandon knew how far he could push his own personal thoughts and opinions and when he had to conform to the king's wishes.

Brandon was careful not to speak publicly about his personal thoughts and religious beliefs. While a reasonably conservative Catholic, Brandon knew the king wanted reform and change and he went along with it. He was careful to keep his political views to himself and only moved against others, such as the Boleyn faction, when he believed it was important for his own standing with the king.

Through a friendship that lasted almost all of his life, Charles Brandon came to know his king and friend possibly better than any other at court. He was able to keep him happy and ultimately keep his head.

Places of Interest

Grimsthorpe Castle

Figure 14. Grimsthorpe Castle
Copyright © Ray Biggs

Grimsthorpe Castle is located in Lincolnshire and was first thought to be built in the thirteenth century by Gilbert de Grant. However, since de Grant died in 1156, the origins of the castle are much older and most likely date to around 1140. While called Grimsthorpe Castle, the building is actually more of a large manor house than a castle. De Grant's original building consisted of a square-shaped building around a large courtyard with four varying sized towers located on each corner. The south-east tower of the castle is known as "King John's Tower", and this name may have led to the confusion that the castle was built during the reign of King John rather than a century earlier.

Charles Brandon used Grimsthorpe and set it up as his main residence in Lincolnshire. The castle was built on a rise that affords a magnificent view of the surrounding area. Brandon began extensive work on the castle over the next few years, creating a magnificent quadrangle building with a centre courtyard. The castle is made of warm grey stone and slate roofing. Also located by the castle was a large park perfect for hunting, one of Brandon's favourite pastimes. In 1541, Henry VIII honoured Brandon with a royal visit at Grimsthorpe Castle, and the duke spent the previous eighteen months frantically upgrading and extending the castle, using much of the materials of the dissolved Vaudey Abbey, which was nearby.

After Charles Brandon's death on 22 August 1545, Katherine married Richard Bertie, her gentleman usher. They had two children, a daughter name Susan and a son named Peregrine. After Katherine's death the Willoughby title and the castle of Grimsthorpe passed to her son. Grimsthorpe Castle has been in the hands of the Barons/Baronesses Willoughby de Eresby ever since.

By 1707, the north front of Grimsthorpe had been rebuilt in the classic style. However, in 1715, Robert Bertie, 16th Baron Willoughby de Eresby, employed Sir John Vanbrugh to rebuild the front of Grimsthorpe in the baroque style to celebrate Bertie's elevation to the title of Duke of Ancaster and Kesteven. The front of Grimsthorpe was subsequently redesigned and there were plans to complete the other three facings of the castle in the same style, but these were never carried out.

The south façade of the castle remains similar to that which Charles Brandon extended during his time at Grimsthorpe, and which he would have been familiar with. The south-west tower of Grimsthorpe Castle is known as the "Brandon Tower".

Visitor Information

April and May: Sundays, Thursdays and Bank Holiday Mondays 12:00pm – 3:00pm

June to September: Sunday to Thursday (inclusive): 12:00pm – 3:00pm

Closed: October to March and Fridays and Saturdays.

Website: http://www.grimsthorpe.co.uk/

Figure 15. The Brandon Tower
Copyright © Ray Biggs

Hampton Court Palace

Figure 16. Hampton Court Palace
Copyright © 2012 Tim Ridgway

Beneath the grand estate of Hampton Court Palace are the remains of a house built for the Knights Hospitallers of St John some time in 1236. The house of Hampton was used to manage the knights' agricultural estates. In 1494, a courtier of Henry VII's named Giles Daubeny leased Hampton Court. Thomas Wolsey, who would become a cardinal and Henry VIII's right-hand man, acquired Hampton Court in 1514 and began massive and lavish construction work on the palace. Millions of pounds (in today's money) was spent on the palace, fitting it out with the finest and most exquisite architecture, furniture and tapestries. Wolsey also oversaw the building of private rooms for himself, King Henry VIII, Katherine of Aragon and their daughter Princess Mary. He also ordered the construction of the huge and magnificently impressive base court. Truly it would become a palace fit for a king and in 1528, when Cardinal Wolsey fell from grace, he gave Hampton Court (as well as York Place) to Henry VIII in an attempt to please his king.

Henry VIII continued to build on Hampton Court Palace, and he added bowling alleys, tennis courts, hot and cold running water to the king's chambers, the breathtaking chapel royal and magnificent gardens. He also oversaw the building of a massive hall known as the great hall. The great hall is a spectacular hall in which up to 600 people could dine twice a day. The hall is by far the largest room in the palace and measures 32 metres long, 12 metres wide and over 18 metres high. The roof is intricately decorated with miniatures of people, who seem to look down at the diners, and other beautiful emblems. There are also massive and beautiful tapestries, which in today's money are priceless.

The watching chamber is a large room just off of the great hall and its name is derived from the guards who were positioned within the room to watch over Henry VIII. From this chamber are a series of rooms in which Henry VIII lived and conducted his day-to-day business.

Another magnificent part of Hampton Court is the chapel royal. The chapel, a place of worship, has a stunning vaulted ceiling painted blue and decorated with thousands of golden stars. The architecture in this room is breathtaking.

Hampton Court also holds Henry VIII's impressive astronomical clock. Designed by Nicholas Crazter and made by Nicholas Oursian for Henry VIII in approximately 1540, this magnificent clock has three separate copper dials that are operated by a series of very complex gears and dials. The clock tells the hour, month and day of the year. It tells the position of the sun and the zodiac and the phases of the moon. It can also tell the time of high tide at London Bridge, which was very important for travel up and down the Thames River during Henry VIII's reign.

The impressive Tudor kitchens must not be forgotten. With the need to feed up to 600 people, twice a day, the kitchens of Hampton Court needed to be large. They are a series of huge rooms that contained areas for receiving food, preparing food, keeping food cool, serving food and, of course, an area that contained massive fires that were used to cook food, especially meats.

With Hampton Court being one of Henry VIII's favourite residences, Charles Brandon was often at this magnificent palace. One of the most well-known times that Brandon was at Hampton Court was for the christening of Henry VIII's son Edward.

Visitor Information

Palace and Maze: 29 March – 25 October (Summer Season)
   Monday – Sunday: 10:00am – 6:00pm
   Last Tickets Sold: 5:00pm
   Last Entry into Maze: 5:15pm
Palace and Maze: 25 October – 26 March (Winter Season)
   Monday – Sunday: 10:00am – 4:30pm
   Last Tickets Sold: 3:30pm
   Last Entry into Maze: 3:45pm
Formal Gardens
   Summer: 10:00am – 6:00pm
   Winter: 10:00am – 5:30pm
Informal Gardens
   Summer: 7:00am – 8:00am
   Winter: 7:00am – 6:00pm
Closed: 24, 25 and 26 December.
Website: http://www.hrp.org.uk/HamptonCourtPalace/

St George's Chapel, Windsor Castle

Figure 17. St George's Chapel, Windsor
Copyright Lewis Clarke, licensed for reuse under
Creative Commons Licence

Windsor Castle has a long and rich history dating back to the time of William the Conqueror in the late eleventh century. William the Conqueror started building Windsor Castle in 1070 and work was completed in 1086. The castle was built as a means to defend and secure the western path towards London. It was built on an earth mound that supported a keep. The castle has an upper and a lower ward. Initially the walls around the castle were made of timber, but King Henry II changed this and rebuilt the outer walls using stone.

Over the next several hundred years the castle was rebuilt and developed. The initial keep built by William the Conqueror was replaced with the round tower in 1170. Edward III transformed Windsor Castle from a defence castle to a grand Gothic palace. Under the guidance of Edward III, William of Wykeham, Bishop of Winchester, oversaw the building of many new structures within the castle, including an inner gatehouse with cylindrical towers and the building of royal apartments on the north side of the quadrangle.

Edward III also founded the Order of the Garter, the oldest surviving order of chivalry in the world. In addition to this he founded the College of St George, St George being the patron saint of the Garter. Edward IV, great-great-grandson of Edward III, began the building of St George's Chapel in 1475 and it was within this chapel that he was buried. Henry VII continued the work that Edward IV had begun and also rebuilt the Albert Memorial Chapel. Henry VIII added a large stone gate at the bottom of the lower ward, which to this day bears his name. He also oversaw the building of a wooden oriel window within the quire of St George's Chapel so that his first wife and queen, Katherine of Aragon could view the church services. In 1533/34 he also added the terrace, which was made of wood, along the north side of the external wall in the upper ward. From this terrace Henry VIII could watch men hunting in the forest or practise shooting. By the time Henry VIII's daughter Elizabeth was Queen of England, the terrace was in great ruin and was rebuilt with stone.

Charles Brandon's legacy is permanently cemented within St George's Chapel as it is here that the Duke of Suffolk is buried. Despite wanting a quiet funeral, the duke was buried at St George's Chapel near the south door of the choir at the king's expense. On the marble slab marking the duke's final resting place is written "Charles Brandon Duke of Suffolk KG Died 24 August 1545 Married Mary Daughter of Henry VII Widow of Louis XII King of France".

In addition to this, Charles Brandon was elected to the Order of the Garter on 23 April 1513. A requirement of the order is that each knight's banner of arms, helmet, crest and sword, as well as a stall plate, are displayed within the stalls of St George's Chapel. Upon a knight's death, their banner of arms, helmet, crest and sword are removed, leaving only the stall plate. The stalls at St George's Chapel contain stall plates of previous knights dating back over 600 years, including that of Charles Brandon.

Visitor Information

March – October: 9:45pm – 5:15pm
    (last admission 4:00pm)
November – February: 9:45pm – 6:15pm
    (last admission 3:00pm)
Windsor Castle Closed: 25 and 26 December
St George's Chapel Closed: Sundays
Windsor Castle Website:
    https://www.royalcollection.org.uk/visit/
    windsorcastle/ plan-your-visit
St George's Chapel website:
    http://www.stgeorges-windsor.org/

Tattershall Castle

Figure 18. Tattershall Castle
Photo © 2016 Sophie Carter, Forget Me Not Tudor Designs

Tattershall Castle, the magnificent deep red tower that can be seen many miles away, has a relatively short history compared to some of England's other castles. Located in Lincolnshire around 250 yards from Tattershall, the castle was built by lord treasurer Ralph Cromwell between 1434 and 1447. Born in 1393, Cromwell was a self-made man who served the Duke of Clarence and notably Henry V in France. He married Margaret Deincourt, a wealthy heiress who brought his income to a staggering £5,000 a year. Between 1433 and 1443, he was the lord treasurer of England and needed a dwelling to suit such an important and illustrious position.

There has been a building at Tattershall since 1231 when Robert de Tattershall built on the land. However, between 1434 and 1447, Lord Cromwell extended on these original buildings and then built an imposing red brick tower on the edge of the bailey. This tower is what we know today as Tattershall Castle.

The castle at Tattershall is more than the huge imposing brick structure that can be seen from a great distance away. Originally to gain entrance into the castle a person had to first pass through a gatehouse and then over the outer moat so they could enter the outer bailey. From there they then passed through another gatehouse and crossed over a second inner moat to get to the inner bailey, the keep, castle and other buildings including a series of kitchens. Unfortunately these protective gatehouses no longer exist.

It is clear from the design of the surrounding moats that the castle was built for military defence The castle stands at over 100 feet high and has thick, imposing walls built from deep red brick. It is estimated that over a million bricks were made for the building of the castle, which were all made locally but by foreign craftsmen. The castle was designed as a rectangular brick tower five storeys high with a basement and four imposing octagonal towers at each corner. The first floor of the castle consisted of a magnificent hall, which was designed not only to welcome visitors but to impress them and lavish upon them the wealth and power that Lord Cromwell held. The height and location of the castle allow for an uninterrupted view of the surrounding area. Over several of the fireplaces within the castle Lord Treasurer Cromwell had his personal motto and crest added.

Lord Cromwell died on 4 January 1455 without a male heir, leaving his two nieces, daughters of his sister, as his heiresses. It is unclear as to who was granted the castle at Tattershall. It is possible that the castle reverted to the crown because in 1487 King Henry VII granted it to his mother, Lady Margaret Beaufort. Upon Lady Beaufort's death it appears the castle reverted once more to the crown until 4 April 1537.

In October 1536, rebellion had broken out in Lincolnshire. In an attempt to secure Lincolnshire and to ensure no further rebellions broke out Henry VIII granted Tattershall Castle to Charles Brandon,

Duke of Suffolk, on 4 April 1537. The king ordered the duke to set-up his main place of residence in Lincolnshire, and Brandon used Tattershall Castle as a base of operations to oversee the protection of Lincolnshire. After the duke's death he bequeathed Tattershall Castle to his son and heir Henry Brandon, however both of Brandon's sons died in July 1551 of the sweating sickness. Without any heirs of their own, Tattershall Castle once more reverted to the crown.

Visitor Information

Castle Open: 11:00am – 5:00pm on selected days of the year. Please check the website for further information on which days the castle is open.
Website:
http://www.nationaltrust.org.uk/tattershall-castle/

Tower of London

Figure 19. The Tower of London
Copyright © 2012 Tim Ridgway

The Tower of London has a long and rich history filled with celebration, joy, tragedy and bloodshed. The Tower's history began with William the Conqueror (1066 – 87) who believed that he had a claim to the English throne after the death of his relative Edward the Confessor. William was the Duke of Normandy and he sailed across to England and defeated King Harold Godwinson, brother-in-law to Edward the Confessor, at the Battle of Hastings. William the Conqueror recognised the need to fortify London and create strongholds that would help to protect against threats against his rule. It is believed that one of these strongholds was the first construction at the Tower of London – the White Tower. There are little details about the building of the famous White Tower, but it was believed to have been completed by 1100.

Over the centuries additions were made to the Tower of London, with separate buildings being built close to the White Tower. In 1238, Henry III began the building of the massive walls around the north, east and western sides of the Tower, which were reinforced by nine towers and the whole structure being surrounded by a great moat.

The Tower of London was used as a fortress and stronghold for protection, but it was also at various times a place in which the king and his court could reside. It also acted as a prison and the first prisoner to be held in the Tower of London was Ranulf Flambard in 1100. In addition to a prison and a place to stay, the Tower held many various and exotic animals over the centuries, including lions, a polar bear, an elephant and ostriches.

The Tudors have a rich and long history with the Tower of London and two of Henry VIII's wives lost their lives (and their heads) within the tower walls: Anne Boleyn and Catherine Howard. Many other famous people lost their lives at the Tower, including Jane Boleyn, Lady Rochford, sister-in-law to Anne Boleyn and lady-in-waiting to Catherine Howard; Margaret Pole, Countess of Salisbury; Lady Jane Grey, who was queen for just nine days, and Robert Devereux, Earl of Essex, courtier and favourite of Elizabeth I. The Tower also held many famous and important prisoners including John Dudley, 1st Duke of Northumberland and Henry Percy, 9th Earl of Northumberland; four dukes of Norfolk; Sir Thomas More; John Fisher, Bishop of Rochester, Sir Walter Ralegh and even Elizabeth I.

Charles Brandon has strong ties with the Tower of London and visited many times during his life. It was here that he watched the execution of Anne Boleyn and he also escorted Henry VIII's fifth wife Catherine Howard to the Tower for her imprisonment before her execution.

Visitor Information

1 March – 31 October (Summer Season)
    Tuesday – Saturday: 9:00am – 5:30pm
    Sunday – Monday: 10:00am – 5:30pm
    Last Admission: 5:00pm
1 November – 28 February (Winter Season)
    Tuesday – Saturday: 9:00am – 4:30pm
    Sunday – Monday: 10:00am – 4:30pm
    Last Admission: 4:00pm
Closed: 24, 25 and 26 December and 1 January.
Website: http://www.hrp.org.uk/TowerOfLondon/

Westminster Abbey

Figure 20. Westminster Abbey
Copyright Peter Langsdale, licensed for reuse under
Creative Commons Licence

Westminster has a rich and detailed history and is perhaps one of the most well-known and most beautiful abbeys in England. It has played a huge part in English history throughout the centuries and some of England's most famous kings, queens and people lie forever within the magnificent tombs contained inside.

Westminster Abbey, or as it is officially called since 1560 "The Collegiate Church of St Peter, Westminster", is more than 1,000 years old. In 960 AD, the Bishop of London and twelve monks created a small church in which to come together and worship. This small church was known as Thorney Island, as it was built along the banks of the Thames, which at the time was a very isolated and marshy area.

During the reign of Edward the Confessor, the monks were given extra land and the king and monks began to build a stone church. The church was dedicated in December 1065 and became known as West Minster. It was named such to distinguish this church from St Paul's Cathedral, which was then known as East Minster. Unfortunately, nothing remains of this stone church except for some of its foundations that rest below the present day abbey.

Edward the Confessor died in 1066 and was buried within the church. Almost a hundred years later Edward was canonised and given the title of St Edward the Confessor. Due to this, Westminster Church quickly became a place of pilgrimage.

The abbey we see today was mostly build by King Henry III between 1245 and 1272. It was the king's intention to build a new and marvellous place to celebrate and worship St Edward the Confessor. The abbey was built using French and English design. More work was done on the abbey, focusing on rebuilding the nave during 1376 to 1498.

King Henry VII continued work on Westminster Abbey and in 1503 oversaw work on the building of the Lady Chapel, otherwise known as King Henry VII's Chapel. It is within this beautiful chapel, in a large and stunning tomb, that Henry VII and his wife Elizabeth of York are buried. Also within the chapel are the tombs of Henry VII's granddaughters, Elizabeth I and Mary I, buried together on the north side of the chapel. The Tudor monarchs certainly left their mark as it is littered with the emblem of the Tudor rose.

Due to the connection between the church and the monarchy over the centuries, Westminster Abbey grew to become one of the most magnificent and wealthiest monasteries within England. Westminster

Abbey would also continue to be closely linked with the monarchy as many kings and queens lie at rest within its walls, including Henry III, Eleanor of Castile, Henry V, Edward III, Richard II, Anne of Bohemia, King Henry VII and his wife Elizabeth of York, their granddaughters Elizabeth I and Mary I, as well as James I, Charles II, William and Mary, Queen Anne and George II. Other notable figures buried within Westminster are Mary, Queen of Scots, Margaret Douglas, Countess of Lennox, and Margaret Beaufort, Countess of Richmond, mother of Henry VII. It is estimated that there are around 600 tombs within the abbey and perhaps around 3,000 people buried within the abbey walls.

Also within Westminster Abbey is the famous coronation chair which was first used in 1308 by Edward II. This chair holds a great deal of importance to the British monarchy as kings and queens have sat upon the same chair for their coronations for hundreds of years.

It was at Westminster Abbey that Anne Boleyn's coronation was held on 1 June 1533. Brandon's role during the coronation was to carry Anne's royal crown into Westminster Abbey and then during the coronation he stood close to the queen holding a white staff of office.

Visitor Information

Opening Times: Check website as the opening times may change due to various events being held at the abbey.
Website: http://www.westminster-abbey.org/

Westminster Hall

Figure 21. Westminster Hall
Copyright Christine Matthews, licensed for reuse under
Creative Commons Licence

Westminster Hall has a long and rich history dating back almost 1,000 years. The oldest building in Parliament, Westminster Hall was built under instruction from William II (otherwise known as William Rufus), son of William the Conqueror. The king wanted a magnificent building that would not only impress but amaze his subjects. Building of Westminster Hall began in 1097 and was completed in only two years. When it was finished, Westminster Hall was the biggest hall in England at the time, although according to William II it was not big enough. The hall measured 73 meters by 20 metres and had a floor space of 1,547 square metres. The stone walls of Westminster Hall are two metres thick and remain relatively intact to this day. There has been some controversy surrounding the roof of Westminster Hall. It was not believed that carpenters of the time could create a roof with wooden beams larger than the original piece of timber. However, it is now believed that the roof was actually supported by pillars that created three aisles within the hall.

In 1393, Richard II commissioned a new hammerbeam roof for Westminster Hall. Measuring a staggering 20.7 metres by 73.2 metres, the new roof was designed and created by Richard II's chief mason Henry Yevel and carpenter Hugh Herland. The roof of Westminster Hall is the largest medieval timber roof in all of Europe. The wood for the roof came from near Farnham, Surrey and was transported to Westminster by a series of wagons and barges. Around 660 tonnes of wood was used. The new hammerbeam roof eliminated any aisles and created a massive, wide open space inside Westminster Hall.

In the early nineteenth century, Westminster Hall fell into disrepair. In 1818, the north façade was in a serious state of decay and was rebuilt by John Soane between 1819 and 1822. Then in 1834 and 1837, Sir Robert Smirke had to remove all the wall refacings inside the hall and he replaced them with a layer of Huddlestone stone, which can still be seen today. At this time Smirke also lowered the level of the floor to what is believed to be the floor level during Richard II's time.

In 1834 a fire broke out at Westminster Palace and the flames came close to threatening the wooden roof of Westminster Hall. Luckily the prime minister at the time, Lord Melbourne, ordered the roof to be covered with water and the hall was spared while much of the palace was lost due to the fire.

Over the centuries Westminster Hall has been used regularly by the kings and queens of the time, as well as other administrative positions of the court. Before the twelfth century, justice was administered from wherever the king was. Then, under the rule of King Henry II, it was declared that five judges should sit in a single place together to administer the king's laws. The three main courts – the Court of the King's Bench, the Court of Chancery and the Court of Common Pleas – were held at Westminster Hall. The Court of the King's Bench was held at the southern end of the Hall in one corner, the Court of the Chancery in the other corner, while the Court of Common Pleas was held on the northern end. In the early thirteenth century the royal exchequer was located in a building that adjoined Westminster Hall.

These courts were not permanently standing. The judges sat at raised benches and the senior clerks on smaller benches below. These benches could be dismantled to hold feasts, coronations, trials or other major events.

There have been several infamous trials held at Westminster Hall over the years, these include William Wallace in 1305, who led the Scottish rebellion against King Edward I; Sir Thomas More, former lord high chancellor to King Henry VIII who was tried for treason in 1535; Cardinal Fisher who was also tried for treason in 1535; and most famously Charles I, who was tried at Westminster Hall on 20 January 1649. The Earl of Essex was also tried in 1600 for his rebellion against Elizabeth I, as well as Guy Fawkes and those involved in the Gunpowder Plot in 1606.

Coronation banquets were held at Westminster Hall and one of the most famous was the coronation banquet of Anne Boleyn on 1 June 1533. Anne Boleyn walked barefoot from Westminster Hall to Westminster Abbey where she was crowned Queen of England. Afterwards, a great banquet was held at Westminster Hall, which consisted of about 800 people and approximately thirty-two dishes. Charles Brandon was appointed as lord high steward and constable for the coronation and banquet. During the banquet Brandon wore a doublet covered in pearls and rode a charger covered in crimson velvet up and down the great hall.

Visitor Information

Opening Times
Monday – Friday 9:00am – 5:00pm*
Please check website for further details as Westminster Hall may be closed due to public events
Website: http://www.parliament.uk/

Timeline

1425: Approximate birth-date of Charles Brandon's grandfather Sir William Brandon of Wangford and Southwark.

1458: Probable birth-date of William Brandon, Charles Brandon's father.

c.1473 – 1476: William Brandon, son of Sir William Brandon, marries Elizabeth Bruyn of South Ockendon.

1478: Allegations are made against William Brandon for forcing himself upon an older woman and also making an attempt to have some sort of relationship with the woman's daughters.

1484: Both William Brandon and his younger brother Thomas Brandon flee to Europe to join forces with Henry Tudor, who is in exile. During this year a general pardon is offered to both William and Thomas by Richard III, although neither accepts.

1484: Charles Brandon is born to William Brandon and Elizabeth Bruyn sometime during 1484. The exact date is not known nor the location although it is strongly believed that Brandon was born in France while his parents were in exile there with Henry Tudor.

1485: On 7 August, Henry Tudor and his men, including William Brandon land at Mill Bay, 6 miles west of Milford Haven located along the Pembrokeshire coastline, on Henry Tudor's quest to claim the English throne.

1485: On 22 August 1485, the Battle of Bosworth at Bosworth Field takes place between the forces of Henry Tudor and Richard III. William Brandon, Henry Tudor's standard-bearer, is killed by Richard III.

1486: In September, Thomas Brandon is appointed an esquire of the body for King Henry VII.

1487: Thomas Brandon is commander of a naval force.

1490s: Death of Charles Brandon's older brother William – exact date and year remains unknown.

1491: Birth of Henry Tudor, future Henry VIII.

1491: Death of Brandon's grandfather Sir William Brandon.

1493/4: Death of Elizabeth Bruyn in March.

1497: Death of Brandon's grandmother Elizabeth Wingfield on 28 April.

1497: Thomas Brandon is knighted after the Battle of Blackheath.

1499: Sir Thomas Brandon is firmly established in Henry VII's court, participating in council meetings, acting as a diplomat and being appointed master of the horse.

1501: Sir Thomas Brandon participates in the wedding of Prince Arthur and Katherine of Aragon, reportedly wearing a gold chain worth around £1,400.

1501: Charles Brandon waits upon Prince Arthur the morning after his wedding. He also participates in the jousting events to celebrate the wedding of Arthur Tudor and Katherine of Aragon.

1502: Death of Arthur Tudor at Ludlow Castle.

1503: Charles Brandon waits upon King Henry VII at his table.

1505/06: Brandon is appointed to the king's spears, a group of men who are active in participating in jousting and courtly displays.

1505/06: Brandon writes to Walter Devereux stating that he is in love with Anne Browne.

1506: Birth of Anne Brandon, daughter of Charles Brandon and Anne Browne.

1507: In April, Sir Thomas Brandon is elected as a Knight of the Garter.

1507: Brandon marries Margaret Neville, Dame Mortimer. On 7 February 1507, Brandon has licence of Dame Margaret's lands and begins to sell them off in quick succession, profiting over £1,000.

1507: Brandon is appointed as an esquire of the body to Henry VIII.

1508: Brandon marries Anne Browne at Stepney church. They later repeat the marriage in a public ceremony at St Michael Cornhill.

1509: On 2 June, Sir Thomas Brandon is created warden and chief justice of the royal forests south of Trent.

1509: Death of King Henry VII on 21 April at Richmond Palace.

1509: On 11 June, Henry Tudor marries Katherine of Aragon, his brother's widow. On 24 June, the coronation of King Henry VIII and Katherine of Aragon takes place at Westminster Abbey. Charles Brandon is selected to be one of the six challengers in the grand tournaments that is held to celebrate the king and queen's coronation.

1509: Charles Brandon is granted the position of chamberlain of the principality of North Wales in November.

1510: On 27 January, Sir Thomas Brandon passes away at Blackfriars. He is buried on 29th at London Blackfriars.

1510: Birth of Mary Brandon and the death of Anne Browne shortly after.

1510: Brandon is appointed as marshal of the King's Bench.

1511: Brandon participates in the jousting events organised to celebrate the birth of Henry VIII's son. He wears a long robe of russet satin and appears to be in the form of a recluse or a religious person. His horse is also draped in the same colour cloth. Once the queen grants permission for him to joust, Brandon throws off his disguise to reveal a rich suit of armour.

1511: In January, Brandon is named a justice of the peace for Surrey.

1511: Henry VIII joins the holy league against France.

1512: In April, Brandon is granted for life the office of ranger of the New Forest. In May he is also made keeper of Wanstead in Essex. On 6 October, he is created master of the horse, of which title had once been held by his uncle, and is granted £60 13s from the chamber and an additional £40 from the exchequer.

1512: Brandon is granted joint captaincy of the sovereign in the naval campaign against France.

1513: On 23 April, Brandon is elected to the Order of the Garter.

1513: Brandon is contracted to marry Elizabeth Grey, Viscountess Lisle, daughter of John Grey, 2nd Baron. On 15 May, Brandon is created Viscount Lisle and receives a number of grants to signify his new position.

1513: Once more at war with France, Henry VIII appoints Brandon high marshal and lieutenant of the army, in which he is responsible for discipline, including dispensing the death penalty, selecting campsites, and creating knights. Brandon also leads the vanguard of the king's ward, which consists of around 3,000 men. Brandon and his men lead the assault against Tournai.

1513: Charles Brandon is knighted on 30 March.

1513: Brandon flirts with Margaret of Austria, Duchess of Savoy, causing a scandal by stealing a ring from her finger. Rumours spread that Brandon and the duchess will marry, which Henry VIII has to strongly deny.

1514: On Candlemas day, 2 February 1514, Charles Brandon, Viscount Lisle, is formally invested as the Duke of Suffolk. The ceremony takes place at Lambeth and is conducted by the king.

1514: In January, Brandon is granted the custody of the lands and marriage of Roger, son and heir of Sir Robert Corbett. In February, the king grants Brandon the manor, castle and park of Donnington, Berkshire, and an annuity of £40.

1514: On 13 August, Mary Tudor is married via proxy to King Louis XII. The Duke of Longueville, who had been captured in the 1513 campaign of France, acts as proxy for the French king. On 9 October, Mary is married to Louis XII at nine o'clock in the great hall of the Hotel de la Gruthose.

1514: On 25 or 26 October, Brandon enters into talks with King Louis XII about a possible alliance between France and England against Ferdinand of Spain, as well as to discuss the jousts organised to celebrate the king's marriage to Mary Tudor.

1514: On 5 November, Mary is crowned Queen of France in Paris. On 9 November, Brandon receives a French pension of 1,000 crowns. On 13 November, Brandon participates in the jousting events organised to celebrate the marriage of Mary Tudor and King Louis XII. He outshines all his opponents and is reported to be the best jouster in all of Europe.

1515: 1 January, King Louis dies. Brandon returns to France on 31 January to bring Mary home. However, while there he marries Mary Tudor without the king's permission some time between 15 and 20 February. The newly married couple return to Dover on 2 May, and are married again on 13 May at Greenwich in front of the king and queen. In February, the king grants Brandon many of the former de la Pole estates in East Anglia.

1515/1516: Brandon borrows £12,000 from the crown.

1516: On 11 March 1516, between ten and eleven o'clock at night, Mary gives birth to a healthy baby boy at Bath Place, London, named Henry after the king. The christening ceremony takes place in the hall at Suffolk Place and is attended by the king, who stands as one of the godfathers alongside Cardinal Thomas Wolsey.

1516: On 19 and 20 May 1516, a magnificent jousting event is held where Brandon jousts alongside his king. Brandon scores far better than the king and Henry VIII vows never to joust against someone unless they are as good as himself. In the future Brandon jousts against the king and not alongside him.

1516: During the king's summer progress he stops at Donnington to visit Brandon and Mary.

1517: On 16 July, between two and three o'clock in the morning, Mary gives birth to a healthy baby girl. The little girl is named Frances.

1518: The Treaty of London is signed between the major European nations including France, England, Spain, the Holy Roman Empire, the papacy, Burgundy and the Netherlands. The treaty states that none of the signatories should attack one another and if they do the others will come to their aid.

1518 – 1521: Birth of Eleanor Brandon, third child of Charles Brandon and Mary Tudor. Eleanor's exact birth-date is unknown.

1520: Between 7 June and 24 June, a meeting known as the Field of Cloth of Gold is held on a piece of land between the English stronghold of Guînes and the French town of Ardres. The purpose of the meeting between Henry VIII and Francis I of France is to solidify the Treaty of London and strengthen relations between the two countries. However, before Henry VIII returns home to England, he goes to Gravelines to meet with the Holy Roman Emperor, Charles V, to discuss a possible alliance.

1522: Death of Henry Brandon, the exact date of death and reason is unknown.

1522: Birth of Henry Brandon (second son named after the first).

1522: On 25 August, the secret Treaty of Bruges is signed between Charles V and Thomas Wolsey on behalf of Henry VIII, declaring that Henry will support Charles V in the war against France.

1523: In May, England declares war on France. In August, Brandon is appointed lieutenant-general and is sent to Calais at the head of an army of 10,000 men.

1524: Brandon's uncle, Sir Robert, dies, leaving Brandon the manor of Henham, which the duke incorporates into his East Anglian estates

1524: Second military expedition led by Brandon against France is aborted.

1524: On 10 March, Brandon jousts against the king. The king forgets to lower his headpiece and Brandon strikes the king, sending splinters from his lance flying into the king's helmet. Luckily the king is not seriously hurt and lays no blame on Brandon.

1525: Cardinal Thomas Wolsey proposes an "amicable grant", hoping to gain an estimated £800,000 for the purpose of war against France. Widespread rumblings in Essex, Kent, Norfolk, Warwickshire and Huntingdonshire break out. However, the greatest protests are in Lavenham, where around 4,000 people gather to protest against the grant. The king quickly sends Brandon and the Duke of Norfolk to try and deal with the protesters.

1525: In March, Anne, Brandon's daughter with his first wife Anne Browne, marries Edward Grey, Lord Powis. Brandon had purchased Grey's wardship in 1517 for the sum of £1,000.

1525: On 18 June, at Bridewell Palace, Henry Brandon is created Earl of Lincoln.

1525: Brandon loses his position as chief justice of North Wales under a new scheme by Thomas Wolsey where the council in the marshes is incorporated into the council of Princess Mary. Brandon's position is granted to his deputy. Brandon is compensated with the castle of Ewelme.

1527: Brandon decides to build a lavish manor in East Anglia, which becomes his main country residence. This manor becomes known as Westhorpe Hall. Total building costs are £12,000.

1527/28: Marriage of Mary Brandon, Brandon's second daughter by Anne Browne, to Thomas Stanley, Lord Monteagle.

1528: Brandon purchases the wardship of Katherine Willoughby, daughter and heiress of the late Lord Willoughby de Eresby, from the king for a staggering £2,266 13s 4d.

1529: On 29 August, Pope Clement VII issues a bull stating the legitimacy of Brandon's marriage to Mary Tudor and in turn the legitimacy of their children.

1529: In May, Charles Brandon and Sir William Fitzwilliam are sent to France in an attempt to attend a possible meeting between Francis I and Charles V at Cambrai. Brandon is also tasked with seeking Francis I's thoughts on Thomas Wolsey and his opinion towards the annulment of the king's marriage.

1529: A legatine court is held at Blackfriars by Cardinal Campeggio and Cardinal Thomas Wolsey to hear the case for an annulment of Henry VIII's marriage to Katherine of Aragon. On 23 July, Cardinal Campeggio announces that he cannot give a final judgement until he has discussed the matter further with Pope Clement VII. Brandon is furious and openly argues with Thomas Wolsey over the matter.

1530: Brandon questions the king about his relationship with Anne Boleyn and is banned from court for a short period.

1531: Henry VIII publicly separates from Queen Katherine of Aragon.

1532: On 23 April, a quarrel breaks out between some of the Duke of Norfolk's men and Brandon's men regarding the king's separation from Katherine of Aragon and his desire to marry Anne Boleyn. This quarrel results in the death of Sir William Pennington, one of Brandon's men.

1532: On 24 October, Brandon is elected to the Order of St Michel, the French equivalent of the Order of the Garter.

1533: On 25 January, just before dawn, Henry VIII marries his second wife Anne Boleyn at Whitehall Palace. On 9 April, Brandon and the Duke of Norfolk inform Katherine of Aragon that she is no longer Queen of England, but from that day forward has to style herself as the Dowager Princess of Wales. In December, Brandon is sent once more to try and convince Katherine that she is no longer to style herself Queen of England and that she must be moved from her present lodgings to Somersham.

1533: The Duke of Norfolk demands that Brandon relinquish the office of earl marshal to Norfolk, in turn the king grants Brandon the offices of warden and chief justice of the royal forests south of the Trent, a post formerly belonging to Brandon's uncle, Sir Thomas.

1533: In May, Frances Brandon marries Henry Grey, Marquis of Dorset, at Suffolk Place in a spectacular wedding attended by the king.

1533: On Sunday 1 June, Anne Boleyn is crowned queen at Westminster Abbey. Brandon's duty is to walk before the queen carrying her royal crown, and then during the coronation he stands close to the queen holding a white staff of office. Brandon acts as lord high steward and constable at Anne Boleyn's coronation feast at Westminster Hall. He wears a doublet covered in pearls, and rides a charger covered in crimson velvet up and down the hall.

1533: Charles Brandon is forced to intervene in his son-in-law Thomas Stanley's financial business, having to pay the sum of £1,452 to pay off his debts, of which over half were owed to Brandon. Fifteen days later Monteagle asks to borrow another £300 from Brandon. Clearly Monteagle cannot cope and thus Brandon takes charge of Stanley's finances. He declares that Monteagle's debts are to be paid in regular instalments and that he will oversee his son-in-law's expenditures.

1533: On 25 June, Mary Tudor dies at Westhorpe Hall between seven and eight o'clock in the morning.

1533: On 7 September, Charles Brandon marries Katherine Willoughby. Brandon is forty-nine and Katherine fourteen. Birth of Elizabeth Tudor, daughter of Henry VIII and Anne Boleyn.

1533: On 10 September, at the Chapel of the Observant Friars, Brandon attends the christening of Elizabeth Tudor. Brandon has the honour of escorting the princess, along with the Duke of Norfolk.

1534: Brandon signs the oath of succession.

1534: On the morning of 1 March, Brandon's son, Henry Brandon, Earl of Lincoln dies, aged just eleven.

1535: On 19 July, the late Mary Tudor, Dowager Queen of France's debts are cancelled. But Brandon still has to pay a staggering sum of £6,700.

1535: On 18 September, Katherine Willoughby gives birth to a boy named Henry after the king. Henry VIII stands as one of the godfathers at the baby's christening and even gives the midwife and nurse £4 for their efforts.

1535: On 18 December, Brandon makes an inventory of the gold and silver plate he owns at Suffolk Place. The total comes to £1,457 (£580,000 in modern times).

1536: On 7 January, Katherine of Aragon dies. On 24 January, Henry VIII falls from his horse during a joust wearing his full armour and is crushed under the weight of the animal. It is reported that the king lies unconscious for two hours. On 29 January, Katherine of Aragon is buried at Peterborough Abbey (nowadays known as Peterborough Cathedral). On the same day Anne Boleyn miscarries a male foetus at around three-and-a-half months into her pregnancy.

1536: 24 April 1536, two commissions of oyer and terminer are set-up at Westminster by Thomas Cromwell and Sir Thomas Audley.

1536: On 2 May, Anne Boleyn is arrested and taken to the Tower of London. A jury of noblemen, including Charles Brandon, are presented with various offences against the king committed in both Middlesex and Kent. Anne is charged with committing incest and adultery on multiple occasions as well as plotting the king's death. On 19 May, Anne is beheaded by a French swordsman within the Tower of London, Brandon attends Anne Boleyn's execution. Upon Anne's death three manors formally belonging to the de la Poles and previously in the possession of Anne Boleyn are granted to Brandon, which adds around £100 a year to his income.

1536: On 30 May, only eleven days after his second wife was executed, Henry VIII marries his third wife, Jane Seymour, at Whitehall Palace. On 23 July, the king's illegitimate son Henry Fitzroy dies at St James's Palace.

1536: Brandon swaps with the king Suffolk Place at Southwark for Norwich Place, also known as York House.

1536: On 1 October, the Pilgrimage of Grace rebellion begins. Over the coming weeks it is reported that the rebels have gathered 40,000 men to support their cause. On 9 October, the rebels dispatch their petition of grievances to the king. Brandon is chosen by the king as his lieutenant to keep an eye on the rebels. Brandon arrives in Huntingdon on 9 October at 6am, then on the 15 October, Henry VIII writes to Brandon detailing that he should instruct the rebels to surrender their weapons and give all the information they can about how the rebellion started, and if they do so they will be dismissed without any further problems. By early 1537, the rebellion is finally subdued and the rebels dispersed.

1537: On 1 March, Brandon and his heirs are named chief stewards of the lands of Revesby Abbey for the entirety of their lives. Then on 4 and 7 April, Brandon receives a number of grants from the king, including the formidable Tattershall Castle. In May, Brandon is ordered by the king to permanently locate himself in Lincolnshire to make the king's presence known.

1537: Birth of Charles Brandon, Brandon's second son with his fourth wife Katherine Willoughby.

1537: In the summer, Eleanor Brandon and Henry Clifford are married at Brandon's home in Southwark and it is reported that the king himself attends the wedding.

1537: On 12 October, Jane Seymour gives birth to a son named Edward. On the 15th, a grand procession takes place at Hampton Court Palace taking the newly born prince to the chapel royal where he is christened. Brandon has the great honour of being appointed as godfather. Jane Seymour dies twelve days after the birth of her son.

1539: In March, Brandon is able to lease for a period of twenty-one years lands in Somerset that had previously belonged to the king's grandmother, Lady Margaret Beaufort. This is a huge honour for Brandon and he decides to commission Hans Holbein the Younger to create a special seal for him to use within these lands.

1539: Brandon is appointed the lord grand master/lord steward of the household.

1539: On 4 September, the Duke of Cleves signs his sister Anne's marriage treaty and representatives take the treaty to England, where it is officially ratified on 4 October. On 27 December, Anne of Cleves arrives at Dover Castle and is formally met by Brandon and his wife.

1540: Henry VIII and Anne of Cleves marry in the Queen's Closet at Greenwich on 6 January. On 24 June, Anne is removed to Richmond under the illusion of avoiding an outbreak of the plague. A short time afterwards she is visited by Brandon and a number of the king's representatives, where Anne is informed that the king wishes to submit their marriage to the judgement of convocation and to have the marriage annulled. On 7 July, Brandon is at Westminster to attend the commission that oversees the annulment of the king's marriage. On 11 July, in the queen's inner chamber at Richmond, Brandon oversees Anne signing her divorce papers.

1540: On 28 July, at Oatlands Palace in Surrey, Henry VIII marries his fifth wife, Catherine Howard.

1541: Henry VIII honours Brandon with a royal visit at Grimsthorpe Castle during his summer progress on 7 August. Brandon has spent the previous eighteen months frantically upgrading and extending the castle using much of the materials of the dissolved nearby Vaudey Abbey.

1541 On 30 October, Henry VIII discovers Catherine Howard's scandalous past and then her relationship with Thomas Culpeper.

1541: On 1 December, Dereham and Culpeper are tried at Guildhall and both are found guilty of treason for their relationships with Catherine Howard. On 13 December, at Tyburn, Dereham is hanged, drawn, quartered and disembowelled while Culpeper is beheaded. Both of their heads are placed on spikes on London Bridge.

1542: On 10 February, Brandon escorts Catherine Howard to the Tower of London. On 13 February, the former queen is beheaded. Brandon is reported as being ill and, thus, does not attended Catherine's execution.

1540/44: Death of Mary Brandon. The exact date and location of her burial remain unknown.

1543: In January, Brandon is appointed royal lieutenant of the north and sent to the Scottish border. He is there overseeing the defences in the north until March 1544. Brandon also attempts to broker a treaty between Scotland and England. A tentative peace treaty with Scotland is signed on 1 July, at Greenwich. However, it is broken seven days later by the Scots.

1543: A peace treaty between the Holy Roman Emperor and England is signed.

1543: On 12 July, in the Queen's Closet at Hampton Court, Henry VIII marries his sixth wife Catherine Parr.

1544: On 20 June, Brandon writes his will.

1544: Brandon is appointed lieutenant and captain general of the army in the war against France. He is tasked with the taking of Boulogne. Over a period of six weeks he oversees around 100,000 gun-stones fired into the town. In addition to this, tunnels and trenches are dug in order to assault the outer layers of the city. Boulogne finally surrenders on 14 September at 10am, and a treaty is organised between Brandon and Messire Jacques de Coucy, seigneur de Vervins, the Captain of Boulogne. Brandon rides into Boulogne on the 14th to signal the surrender of the city.

1545: In March, Brandon suffers a bout of ill health. In May, Brandon is granted the great honour of being able to retain 100 men as part of his guard.

1545: On 22 August at 4 o'clock in the afternoon, Charles Brandon dies at Grimsthorpe, wishing to be buried in the collegiate church of Tattershall in Lincoln without any pomp or display. On 9 September, Brandon is buried at St George's Chapel in Windsor near the south door of the choir at the king's expense.

1547: On 27 September, Eleanor Brandon dies at Brougham Castle, Westmoreland, and is buried at Skipton, Yorkshire.

1551: On 14 July, Henry and Charles Brandon die of the sweating sickness at Buckden.

1554: On 12 February, Lady Jane Grey, granddaughter of Charles Brandon and Mary Tudor, is executed at the Tower of London.

1557/58: In January 1557/58, Anne Brandon dies. She is buried on 13 January in St Margaret's, Westminster, Middlesex.

1559: On 21 November, Frances Brandon dies in London with her two surviving daughters by her side. She is buried in St Edmund's Chapel in Westminster Abbey. Her funeral is paid for by Elizabeth I.

1580: Katherine Willoughby dies on 19 September. It is not known where Katherine died but her funeral took place at Spilsby on 22 October.

Bibliography

1525: Amicable Grant 2014, All Kinds of History, viewed 28 June 2015,
https://tudorrebellions.wordpress.com/2014/11/23/1525-amicable-
grant.

A Topographical Account of Tattershall in the County of Lincoln, viewed 30
July 2015,
https://books.google.com.au/
books?id=zQ4HAAAAQAAJ&source=gbs_navlinks_s.

Ackroyd, P 2012, *The History of England, Volume II : Tudors,*
Macmillan, London.

Arthur Bulkeley, World Heritage Encyclopaedia, viewed 21 June
2015, http://self.gutenberg.org/articles/arthur_bulkeley.

Bain, J 1980, *The Hamilton Papers. Letters and papers illustrating the political
relations of England and Scotland in the XVIth century*, Edinburgh, HM
General Register House, Scotland.

Baldwin, D 2015, *Henry VIII's Last Love The Extraordinary Life of
KatherineWilloughby, Lady-in-Waiting to the Tudors,*
Amberley Publishing, Gloucestershire.

Baldwin Smith, L 2008, *Catherine Howard,* Amberley
Publishing, Gloucestershire.

Battlefields Resource Centre 2015, *Battle of Bosworth,* The Battlefield Trust,
viewed 16 January 2015,
http://www.battlefieldstrust.com/resource-centre/warsoftheroses/
battleview.asp?BattleFieldId=8.

Bayani, D 2014, *Jasper Tudor Godfather of the Tudor Dynasty,* Self-
Published, USA.

Benger, E 1822, *Memoirs of the Life of Anne Boleyn, Queen of Henry VIII,*
Abraham Small, Available from the collections of New York
Public Library.

Bernard, G W 2007, *The King's Reformation Henry VIII and the Remarking
of the English Church,* Yale University Press, UK.

Betteridge, T & Freeman, T 2012, *Henry VIII and History,* Ashgate Publishing Limited, England.

Bilyeau, N 2014, *Who Was the Real Charles Brandon?,* viewed 8 June 2015, http://englishhistoryauthors.blogspot.com.au/2014/10/who-was-real-charles-brandon.html.

Binyon, L 1900, *Catalogue of Drawings by British Artists and Artists of Foreign Origin Working in Great Britain,* Printed by the order of the Trustees, London.

Brady, M 1876, *The episcopal succession in England, Scotland and Ireland, A.D. 1400 to 1875: with appointments to monasteries and extracts from consistorial acts taken from mss. in public and private libraries in Rome, Florence, Bologna, Ravenna and Paris,* Tipografia della Pace, Rome.

Breverton, T 2014, *Jasper Tudor Dynasty Maker,* Amberley Publishing, Gloucestershire.

Brewer, Gairdner and Brodie (ed) 1862–1910, *Letters and Papers Foreign and Domestic of the Reign of Henry VIII, 1509–47,* London.

Brigden, S 2001, *The Penguin History of Britain: New Worlds, Lost Worlds: The Rule of the Tudors 1485-1630,* Penguin, UK.

Brimacombe, P 2004, *Tudor England,* Jarrold Publishing, UK.

Britain's Tudor Treasure: A Night at Hampton Court 2015, Documentary, BBC, United Kingdom, Presented by Dr Lucy Worsley and Dr David Starkey.

Bunbury, S 1844, *Star of the court; or, The maid of honour & queen of England, Anne Boleyn,* Grant, Available from the collections of Harvard University.

Burke, J 1833, *The Portrait Gallery of Distinguished Females Including Beauties of the Courts of George IV. and William IV.,* Bull and Churton, London.

Calendar of State Papers, Spain, Her Majesty's Stationery Office, London, 1877.

Calendar of State Papers Relating To English Affairs in the Archives of Venice, Volume 4, 1527-1533, Her Majesty's Stationery Office, London, 1871.

Chapman, H W 1974, *Anne Boleyn,* Jonathan Cape, London.

Charles Brandon, 1ˢᵗ Duke of Suffolk, National Portrait Gallery London, viewed 27 June 2015, http://www.npg.org.uk/collections/search/person/mp04365/charles-brandon-1st-duke-of-suffolk.

Charles Brandon, 1st Duke of Suffolk, World Public Library, viewed 25 April 2015, http://www.worldlibrary.org/articles/Charles_Brandon,_1st_Duke_of_Suffolk.

Charles Brandon, Duke of Suffolk. Art Institute of Chicago, viewed 27 June 2015, http://www.artic.edu/aic/collections/artwork/133344.

Cherry, C & Ridgway, C 2014, *George Boleyn: Tudor Poet, Courtier & Diplomat,* MadeGlobal Publishing, UK.

Chilvers, A 2010, *The Berties of Grimsthorpe Castle,* Author House, Bloomington Indiana.

Christie & Masson 1838, *Catalogue of the Entire Collection of Portraits of the Most Illustrious Persons of British History: Consisting of the Drawings Made (with Permission) from the Original Pictures in the Royal Collection, the Galleries of the Nobility & Gentry, and the Public Collections Throughout the Kingdom,* The Firm, UK.

Chronicles of England, Scotland, and Ireland 2015, The Holinshed Project, viewed 16 January 2015, http://www.cems.ox.ac.uk/holinshed/index.shtml.

Correspondance du Cardinal Jean du Bellay, Tome Premier 1529-1535, 1969, Paris Librairie C Klincksieck.

Currency Converter, The National Archives, viewed 10 October 2015, http://www.nationalarchives.gov.uk/currency/default0.asp#mid.

Davey, R 1848, *The sisters of Lady Jane Grey and their wicked grandfather; being the true stories of the strange lives of Charles Brandon, duke of Suffolk, and of the ladies Katherine and Mary Grey, sisters of Lady Jane Grey, "the nine-days' queen,",* Chapman and Hall, London.

De Lisle, L 2013, *Tudor The Family Story,* Chatto & Windus, London.

De Worde, W 1884, *The Maner of the tryumphe of Caleys and Bulleyn and The noble tryumphaunt coronacyon of Quene Anne, wyfe unto the most noble kynge Henry VIII,* Edinburgh, https://archive.org/stream/maneroftryumpheo00goldiala#page/n3/mode/2up.

Denny, J 2007, *Anne Boleyn A New Life of England's Tragic Queen,* Da Capo Press, Great Britain.

Dolman, B, Holmes, S, Impey, E and Spooner, J. 2009, *Historic Royal Palaces Experience the Tower of London,* Historic Royal Palaces, Surrey.

Dolman, B, Edwards, S, Groom, S and Meltonville, M 2009, *Historic Royal Palaces Explore Hampton Court Palace,* Historic Royal Palaces, Surrey.

Doran, S 2008, *The Tudor Chronicles,* Quercus Publishing, London.

Emerson, K L 2015, *A Who's Who of Tudor Women,* viewed 20 June 2015, http://www.kateemersonhistoricals.com/TudorWomenIndex.htm.

Encyclopaedia Britannica, Inc. 2015, *Jean Clouet French Painter,* viewed 27 June 2015, http://www.britannica.com/biography/Jean-Clouet.

Encyclopaedia Britannica, Inc. 2015, *Jean Perreal French Artist*, viewed 27 June 2015, http://www.britannica.com/biography/Jean-Perreal.

Encyclopaedia Britannica, Inc. 2015, *The Most Noble Order of the Garter*, viewed 7 January 2015, http://www.britannica.com/EBchecked/topic/226255/The-Most-Noble-Order-of-the-Garter.

Fraser, A 2002, *The Six Wives of Henry VIII*, Phoenix Press, London.

Francesco Bartolozzi (Italian, 1727-1815) after Hans Holbein the younger (German, 1497-1543) 2015, Art Institute of Chicago, viewed 29 September 2015, http://www.artic.edu/aic/collections/artwork/133344.

Franklin-Harkrider, M 2008, *Women, Reform and Community in Early Modern England: Katherine Willoughby, Duchess of Suffolk, and Lincolnshire's Godly* Aristocracy, 1519-1580, The Boydell Press, Woodbridge.

Fisher, C 2002, "The Queen and the artichoke: A study of the portraits of Mary Tudor and Charles Brandon", *The British Art Journal*, Vol. 3, No. 2, pp. 20-27.

Gairdner, J 1904, *The Paston Letters 1422 – 1509*, London, Chatto & Windus, viewed 6 June 2015, http://www.archive.org/stream/pastonlettersad06gairuoft#page/230/mode/2up/search/Brandon.

Granger, J 1824, *A Biographical History of England, from Egbert the Great to the Revolution, Volume 1*, W. Baynes and Son, London.

Gunn, S 2015, *Charles Brandon*, Amberley Publishing, Gloucestershire, UK.

Hall, E 1809, *Hall's chronicle: containing the history of England, during the reign of Henry the Fourth, and the succeeding monarchs, to the end of the reign of Henry the Eighth, in which are particularly described the manners and customs of those periods. Carefully collated with the editions of 1548 and 1550*, J. Johnson, London.

Hall, E 1904, *Henry VIII*, London, T C & E C Jack, Available from the collections of Cornell University Library.

Hans, the Younger Holbein: The Complete Works 2015, viewed 27 February 2015, http://www.hans-holbein.org.

Hanson, Marilee. "*Charles Brandon, duke of Suffolk and Princess Mary Tudor*" viewed January 31, 2015, http://englishhistory.net/tudor/relative/charles-brandon-mary-tudor.

Harris, B 2002, *English Aristocratic Women, 1450-1550: Marriage and Family, Property and Careers*, Oxford University Press, New York.

Harbison, C 2014, *Hans Holbein the Younger,* Encyclopaedia Britannica, viewed 27 February 2015, http://www.britannica.com/EBchecked/topic/269121/Hans-Holbein-the-Younger.

Harris, B 1989, "Power, Profit, and Passion: Mary Tudor, Charles Brandon, and the Arranged Marriage in Early Tudor England", *Feminist Studies,* Vol. 15, No. 1, pp. 59-88.

Hart, K 2009, *The Mistresses of Henry VIII,* The History Press, Gloucestershire.

Herbert, E 1649, *The Life and Raigne of King Henry the Eighth,* E G for T Whitaker, London.

Herbert, H W 1855, *Memoirs of Henry the Eighth of England: with the fortunes, fates, and characters of his six wives,* Auburn, Miller, Orton, & Mulligan, New York.

Historic Royal Palaces 2015, *A Building History: Hampton Court,* viewed 25 July 2015, Available from Internet http://www.hrp.org.uk/HamptonCourtPalace/sightsandstories/buildinghistoryHamptonCourtPalace.

Historic Royal Palaces 2011, "Tower of London", viewed 25 September 2015, http://www.hrp.org.uk/TowerOfLondon

History of Jousting, History, viewed 7 June 2015, http://www.history.co.uk/shows/full-metal-jousting/articles/history-of-jousting.

Holbein: Eye of the Tudors 2015, British Broadcasting Company, United Kingdom. Presented and Directed by Waldemar Januszczak.

House of Lords Precedence Act 153, Legislation, The National Archives, viewed 14 September 2015, http://www.legislation.gov.uk/aep/Hen8/31/10.

Hui, R 2013, *New Impressions On The Brandon Wedding Portrait,* viewed 27 June 2015, http://tudorfaces.blogspot.com.au/2013/07/the-brandon-wedding-portrait-some-new.html.

Hume, M 1905, *The Wives of Henry the Eighth and the Parts They Played in History,* Eveleigh Nash, London.

Hutchinson R 2006, *The Last Days of Henry VIII,* Phoenix, London.

Hutchinson, R 2009, *House of Treason The Rise & Fall of a Tudor Dynasty,* Phoenix, London.

Hutchinson, R 2011, *Young Henry The Rise of Henry VIII,* Orion Books, London.

Hutton, W 1813, *The Battle of Bosworth Field, Between Richard the Third and Henry Earl of Richmond, August 22, 1485,* Nichols, Son, and Bentley, Fleet Street.

Ingram, M 2015, "Bosworth The Day The Tudors Came", *Tudor Life*, vol. 5, pp. 2-7.

Inside The Body of Henry VIII 2009, documentary presented by Robert Hutchinson, historian Dr Lucy Worsley and Dr Catherine Hood, *National Geographic*.

Ives, E 2005, *The Life and Death of Anne Boleyn*, Blackwell Publishing, Oxford.

Jokinen, A 2002, *The Act of Succession, 1534*, Luminarium, Encyclopaedia Project, viewed 7 June 2015, http://www.luminarium.org/encyclopedia/firstsuccession.htm.

Jokinen A 2010, *The Battle of Bosworth Field*, Luminarium Encyclopaedia Project, viewed 16 January 2014, http://www.luminarium.org/encyclopedia/bosworth.htm.

Johnson, B 2015, *The Red Dragon of Wales*, Historic UK, viewed 16 January 1015, http://www.historic-uk.com/HistoryUK/HistoryofWales/The-Red-Dragon-of-Wales.

Johnson, D 1969, *Southwark and the City*, Oxford UP, UK.

Johnson, M 2013, *Behind the Castle Gate: From the Middles Ages to the Renaissance*, Routledge, London.

Kadouchkine, O 2014, *The Amicable Grant, 1525*, viewed 28 June 2015, http://jwsmrscott.weebly.com/tudorpedia/the-amicable-grant-1525.

Kesselring, K 2002, *Reviewed Work: The Defeat of the Pilgrimage of Grace. A Study of the Postpardon Revolts of December 1536 to March 1537 and Their Effect* by Michael Bush, David Bownes, *The Sixteenth Century Journal*, vol. 33, no. 2, pp. 600–602.

Keys, D 2015, "Inside the bloody world of the medieval tournament", *History Magazine*, February, pp. 11-12.

Knapton, S 2014, "Jousting secret explains how Charles Brandon rose in the court of Henry VIII", *The Telegraph*, viewed 7 June 2015, http://www.telegraph.co.uk/history/11196723/Jousting-secret-explains-how-Charles-Brandon-rose-in-the-court-of-Henry-VIII.html.

Knight, C 1840, *The Penny Magazine of the Society for the Diffusion of Useful Knowledge, Volume 9*, C Knight & Company, London.

Langley, P & Jones, M 2013, *The King's Grave: The Search for Richard III*, Hachette, United Kingdom.

Lehmberg, S E 1977, *The Later Parliaments of Henry VIII, 1536-1547*, Cambridge University Press, UK.

Letters and Papers, Foreign and Domestic, of the Reign of Henry VIII, 1509-47, ed. J S Brewer, James Gairdner and R H Brodie, His Majesty's Stationery Office, 1862-1932.

Levitt, E 2014, *A second king: chivalric masculinity and the meteoric rise of Charles Brandon, duke of Suffolk* (c. 1484 – 1545), University of Winchester – Gender and Medieval Studies.

Licence, A 2012, *In Bed with the Tudors: The sex lives of a dynasty from Elizabeth of York to Elizabeth I*, Amberley Publishing, Gloucestershire.

Licence, A 2013, *Bessie Blount: Mistress to Henry VIII*, Amberley Publishing, Gloucestershire.

Licence, A 2014, *The Six Wives & Many Mistresses of Henry VIII*, Amberley Publishing, Gloucestershire.

Lipscomb, S 2009, *1536: The Year that Changed Henry VIII*, Lion Hudson plc, Oxford.

Lipscomb, S 2012, *A Visitor's Companion to Tudor England,* Ebury Press, Croydon, UK.

Living Heritage 2015, *Westminster Hall,* Parliament.uk, viewed 1 August 2015
http://www.parliament.uk/about/living-heritage/building/palace/westminsterhall.

Loades, D 2010, *The Six Wives of Henry VIII,* Amberley Publishing, Gloucestershire.

Loades, D 2011, *Henry VIII,* Amberley Publishing, Gloucestershire.

Loades, D 2012, *The Tudors: History of a Dynasty,* Continuum International Publishing Group, London.

Loades, D 2012, *Mary Rose,* Amberley, Gloucestershire.

Lord Charles Brandon, Our Family Genealogy Pages, viewed 25 April 2015, http://www.familyrecord.net/getperson. php?personID=I46126&tree=CorlissOrdway.

Master of the Brandon Portrait, Sothebys, viewed 27 June 2015, http:// www.sothebys.com/en/auctions/ecatalogue/2013/old-master-british-paintings-evening-l13033/lot.1.lotnum.html.

Mackay, L 2014, *Inside the Tudor Court,* Amberley Publishing, Gloucestershire.

MacCulloch, D 1995, *The Reign of Henry VIII: Politics, Policy and Piety,* St Martin's Press, New York.

Marsden, J and Winterbottom, M 2009, *Windsor Castle Official Souvenir Guide,* Royal Collection Enterprises Ltd, St James's Palace, London.

Medieval Lives: Birth, Marriage and Death 2013, BBC Scotland.

Medieval Jousting Tournaments, 2014, viewed 17 October 2015, http://www.medieval-life-and-times.info/medieval-knights/medieval-jousting-tournaments.htm.

Medieval Rules for Jousting, 2015, Medievalist.Net, viewed 17 October 2015, http://www.medievalists.net/2015/01/07/medieval-rules-jousting.

ed. Medine, P, 2010, *Art of Rhetoric:* (1560) Thomas Wilson, Penn State Press, USA.

Merriam-Webster Incorporated 2015, *Standard-bearer,* An Encyclopaedia Britannica Company, viewed 11 January 2015, http://www.merriam-webster.com/dictionary/standard-bearer.

Meyer, G J 2010, *The Tudors The Complete Story of England's Most Notorious Dynasty,* Delacorte Press, New York.

Morrill, J S, *Charles Brandon, 1st Duke of Suffolk*, Encyclopaedia Britannica, viewed 8 June 2015, http://www.usq.edu.au/library/referencing/harvard-agps-referencing-guide.

Nichols, J G (ed.) 1846, *The chronicle of Calais, in the reigns of Henry VII and Henry VIII to the year 1540*, Ed. From mss. In the British Museum, The Camden Society, London.

Nichols, J G & Bruce J 1863, *Wills from Doctors' Commons. A selection from the Wills of Eminent Persons Proved in the Prerogative Court of Canterbury, 1495 – 1695,* Camden Society, UK.

Norton, E 2013, *The Boleyn Women The Tudor femmes fatales who changed English history,* Amberley Publishing, Gloucestershire.

Norton, E 2013, *Bessie Blount: Mistress to Henry VIII,* Amberley Publishing, Gloucestershire.

Oxford Bodleian Library, *The Interment of Charles Brandon, Duke of Suffolk,* MS Ashmole 1109, ff. 142-6.

Oxford Dictionary of National Biography: Brandon, Charles, first duke of Suffolk (c.1484–1545), 2015, Oxford University Press, viewed 14 March 2015, http://www.oxforddnb.com.

Oxford Dictionary of National Biography: Brandon, Sir Thomas (d. 1510), 2015, Oxford University Press, viewed 14 September 2015, http://www.oxforddnb.com.

Oxford Dictionary of National Biography: Fitzroy, Henry, duke of Richmond and Somerset (1519–1536), 2015, Oxford University Press, viewed 14 March 2015, http://www.oxforddnb.com.

Oxford Dictionary of National Biography: Grey [other married name Stokes], Frances [née Lady Frances Brandon], 2015, Oxford University Press, viewed 14 September 2015, http://www.oxforddnb.com.

Oxford Dictionary of National Biography: Katherine [Kateryn, Catherine; née Katherine Parr], 2015, Oxford University Press, viewed 14 September 2015, http://www.oxforddnb.com.

Paston letters and papers of the fifteenth century, Part I, viewed 15 June 2015, http://quod.lib.umich.edu/c/cme/ Paston/1:9.82?rgn=div2;view=fulltext

Penn, T 2011, *Winter King: The Dawn of Tudor England*, Penguin Group, London.

Pennington, R 1982, *A Descriptive Catalogue of the Etched Work of Wenceslaus Hollar 1607-1677*, Cambridge University Press, Cambridge.

Perry, M 2002, *Sisters to the King*, Andre Deutsh, London.

Pettifer, A 2002, *English Castles: A Guide by Counties*, Boydell & Brewer, Suffolk.

Pevsner, N & Harris J, 2002, *Lincolnshire: The Buildings of England*, Yale University Press, London.

Pisano, S 2008, *St George's Chapel, Windsor Castle*, Scala Publishers Ltd., London.

Pote, J & Leake, S M 1749, *The History and Antiquities of Windsor Castle, and the Royal College, and Chapel of St. George*, Joseph Pote Bookfeller.

Rabon, J 2015, *A Brief Overview of What Life Was Like in Medieval London*, Londontopia, viewed 1 August 2015, http://londontopia.net/site-news/featured/life-medieval-london.

Records of the Lord Steward, the Board of Green Cloth and other officers of the Royal Household, The National Archives, viewed 14 September 2015, http://discovery.nationalarchives.gov.uk/details/r/C202.

Report on the manuscripts of the Earl of Ancaster, preserved at Grimsthorpe 1907, John Falconer, Dublin.

Richardson, D 2011, *Plantagenet Ancestry: A Study In Colonial And Medieval Families, 2nd Edition*, CreateSpace, USA.

Ridgway, C 2011, *4th October 1536 – The Lincolnshire Rising and Trouble at Horncastle*, The Anne Boleyn Files, viewed 18 April, http://www.theanneboleynfiles.com/4th-october-1536-the-lincolnshire-rising-and-trouble-at-horncastle.

Ridgway, C 2012, *Martin Luther and Anne Boleyn*, The Anne Boleyn Files, viewed 20 June 2015, http://www.theanneboleynfiles.com/martin-luther-and-anne-boleyn.

Ridgway, C 2012, *Birth of Henry, Duke of Cornwall – New Year's Day 1511,* The Anne Boleyn Files, viewed 16 June 2015, http://www.theanneboleynfiles.com/birth-of-henry-duke-of-cornwall-new-years-day-1511.

Ridgway, C 2012, *On This Day in History,* MadeGlobal Publishing, UK.

Ridgway, C 2012, *The Birth of Margaret of Austria – 10 January 1480,* viewed 30 May 2015, http://www.theanneboleynfiles.com/the-birth-of-margaret-of-austria-10-january-1480.

Ridgway, C 2012, *The Fall of Anne Boleyn,* MadeGlobal Publishing, UK.

Ridgway, C 2012, *The Anne Boleyn Collection,* MadeGlobal Publishing, UK.

Ridgway, C 2013, *October 1536 – The Pilgrimage of Grace,* The Anne Boleyn Files, viewed 18 April 2015, http://www.theanneboleynfiles.com/october-1536-pilgrimage-grace.

Ridgway, C 2014, *Sweating Sickness: In a Nutshell,* MadeGlobal Publishing, UK.

Ridgway, C 2015, *31 January 1510 Catherine of Aragon suffers a still-birth,* The Anne Boleyn Files, viewed 16 June 2015, http://www.theanneboleynfiles.com/31-january-1510-catherine-aragon-suffers-still-birth.

Roberts, S 2014, "Grimsthorpe Castle and Nancy Astor", *Lincolnshire Life,* viewed 30 May 2015, http://www.lincolnshirelife.co.uk/posts/view/grimsthorpe-castle-and-nancy-astor.

Ross, D *Grimsthorpe Castle History, tourist information, and nearby accommodation,* Britain Express, viewed 31 May 2015, http://www.britainexpress.com/attractions.htm?attraction=272.

Royal Collection Trust 2015, *The Knights of the Garter under Henry VIII,* viewed 7 January 2015, http://www.royalcollection.org.uk/microsites/knightsofthegarter/MicroSectionList.asp?type=More&exid=144.

Ryrie, A 2008, *The Sorcerer's Tale: Faith and Fraud in Tudor England,* Oxford University Press, Oxford.

Russell, G 2014, *An Illustrated Guide to the Tudors,* Amberley Publishing, Gloucestershire.

Sainty, J C 1999, *Officers of the Green Cloth: Lord Steward,* viewed 29 September 2015, http://www.history.ac.uk/publications/office/greencloth.html#1

Sadlack, E 2001, *The French Queen's Letters,* Palgrave Macmillan, New York.

Skidmore, C 2013, *The Rise of the Tudors: The Family That Changed English History,* St. Martin's Press, New York.

Starkey, D 2009, *Man & Monarch: Henry VIII,* The British Library, London.

Starkey, D 2004, *Six Wives: The Queens of Henry VIII,* Vintage, London.

Strickland, A 1868, *Lives of the Queens of England, From the Normal Conquest,* Bell and Daldy, London.

"Suffolk Place and the Mint", in *Survey of London: Volume 25, St George's Fields (The Parishes of St. George the Martyr Southwark and St. Mary Newington),* ed. Ida Darlington (London, 1955), pp. 22-25, viewed 2 June 2015, http://www.british-history.ac.uk/survey-london/vol25/pp22-25.

Surdhar, C 2013, *Bloody British History: York,* The History Press, UK.

Tattershall Castle 2015, National Trust, viewed 30 July 2015, http://www.nationaltrust.org.uk/tattershall-castle.

Taylor, M J *BRANDON, Sir Charles (by 1521-51), of Sigston, Yorks,* The History of Parliament Trust 1964-2015, viewed 5 October 2015, http://www.historyofparliamentonline.org/volume/1509-1558/member/brandon-sir-charles-1521-51 .

The Amicable Grant 1525, Staging the Henrician Court bringing early modern drama to life, 28 June 2015, http://stagingthehenriciancourt.brookes.ac.uk/historicalcontext/the_amicable_grant_1525.html.

The Battlefield Trust, *Battle of Tewkesbury 4th May 1471,* UK Battlefields Resource Centre, viewed 18 April 2015, http://www.battlefieldstrust.com/resource-centre/warsoftheroses/battleview.asp?BattleFieldId=45.

The Battle of Bosworth 2014, History Learning Site, viewed 16 January 2015, http://www.historylearningsite.co.uk/battle_of_bosworth.htm.

The Field of the Cloth of Gold 2015, Royal Collection Trust, viewed 11 May 2015, http://www.royalcollection.org.uk/collection/405794/the-field-of-the-cloth-of-gold

The Brandon Family, English Monarchs, viewed 26 April 2015, http://www.englishmonarchs.co.uk/tudor_31.html.

The Dean and Canons of Windsor 2008, *St George's Chapel Windsor Castle,* Scala Publishers Ltd, London.

The Dean and Chapter of Westminster 2011, *Westminster Abbey Founded 960,* viewed 25th July 2015 Available from Internet http://www.westminster-abbey.org.

The Grimsthorpe & Drummond Castle Trust 2015, *Grimsthorpe Castle,* viewed 23 May 2015, http://www.grimsthorpe.co.uk.

The Royal Household 2015, *Order of the Garter*, viewed 7 January 2015, Available from Internet http://www.royal.gov.uk/monarchUK/honours/Orderofthegarter/ orderofthegarter.aspx.

Thorbury, W, "Westminster Hall: Notable events," in *Old and New London: Volume 3 (London: Cassell, Petter & Galpin, 1878)*, 544-560, viewed 28 July 2015, http://www.british-history.ac.uk/old-new-london/vol3/pp544-560

Thorton, M n. d., *The Battle of Bosworth,* viewed 16 January 2015, http://battlefield-site.co.uk/bosworth.htm.

Time Team Digital S20 DIG5 DAY1 – Suzie Describes Charles Brandon, Duke of Suffolk, 2012, timeteamdigital, https://www.youtube.com/watch?v=ZVTs38d-x3s.

Trowels, T 2007, *Westminster Abbey A Short Tour,* Scala Publishers, Northburgh House, London. UK.

Trueman C 2008, *Foreign Policy 1549 to 1553*, viewed 29 September 2015, http://www.historylearningsite.co.uk/tudor-england/foreign-policy-1549-to-1553.

Urban, S 1803, *The Gentleman's Magazine and Historical Chronicle,* Nichols and Son, London.

Velde, F 2014, *List of the Knights of the Garter*, viewed 7 January 2015, Available from Internet http://www.heraldica.org/topics/orders/garterlist.htm.

"York House", in *Survey of London: Volume 18, St Martin-in-The-Fields II: the Strand*, ed. G H Gater and E P Wheeler (London, 1937), pp. 51-60, viewed 2 June 2015, http://www.british-history.ac.uk/survey-london/vol18/pt2/pp51-60.

Walford, E, "Southwark: High Street", in *Old and New London: Volume 6* (London, 1878), pp. 57-75, viewed 2 June 2015, http://www.british-history.ac.uk/old-new-london/vol6/pp57-75.

Weir, A 1991, *The Six Wives of Henry VIII,* Grove Press, New York.

Weir, A 2008, *Henry VIII: King & Court,* Vintage Books, London.

Weir, A 2009, *The Lady in the Tower: The Fall of Anne Boleyn,* Jonathan Cape, London.

Wilkinson, J 2010, *Mary Boleyn: The True Story of Henry VIII's Favourite Mistress,* Amberley Publishing, Gloucestershire.

Wilson, D. 2009, *A Brief History of Henry VIII*, Constable and Robinson Ltd. London.

Wodderspoon, J, 1839, *Historic Sites and Other Remarkable and Interesting Places in the County of Suffolk*, R Root, Cornhill.

Wooding, L, 2005, *Henry VIII*, Routledge, Oxfordshire.

Wriothesley, C, 1875, *A Chronicle of England During the Reigns of the Tudors, From A.D.1485 to 1559*, Camden Society.

Notes

Chapter 1 - The Beginning (1484 – 1485)

1. Oxford Dictionary of National Biography – Charles Brandon
2. Breverton 2014, p. 17
3. Ibid., p. 20
4. Ibid., p. 187
5. Bayani 2014, p. 173
6. Ibid., p. 175
7. Breverton 2014, p. 203
8. Penn 2011, p. 2
9. Breverton 2014, p. 42
10. Bayani 2014, p. 156
11. Ibid., p 183
12. Oxford Dictionary of National Biography – Charles Brandon
13. Richardson 2011, p. 297
14. Ibid., p. 368
15. Ibid., p. 369
16. Paston Letters, p. 512
17. Bayani 2014, p. 180
18. Skidmore 2013, p. 167
19. Richardson 2011 p. 369
20. World Public Library – Charles Brandon
21. Richardson 2011, p. 369
22. Gunn 2015, p. 55
23. Ibid., p. 55
24. Richardson 2011, p. 369
25. Gunn 2015, p. 16
26. Bayani 2014
27. Ibid., p. 182
28. Medieval Lives: Birth, Marriage and Death 2013
29. Licence 2012
30. Medieval Lives: Birth, Marriage and Death 2013

31. Ibid.
32. Breverton 2014, p. 220
33. Doran 2008, p. 13
34. Penn 2011, p. 1
35. Bayani 2014, p. 201
36. Ibid., p. 202
37. Ibid., p. 201
38. Ibid., p. 207
39. Breverton 2014, p. 231
40. Bayani 2014, p. 210
41. Ibid., p. 212
42. Ibid., p. 212
43. Ibid., p. 215
44. Skidmore 2013, p. 274
45. Meyer 2010, p. 9
46. Breverton 2014, p. 242
47. Bayani 2014, p. 215
48. Langley & Jones 2013
49. Merriam-Webster 2015
50. Bayani 2014, p. 216
51. Breverton 2014, p. 246
52. Ibid., p. 246
53. Bayani 2014, p. 217
54. Ibid., p. 217
55. Hutton 1813, p. 218
56. Bayani 2014, p 218
57. Meyer 2010, p. 12
58. Skidmore 2013, p. 322
59. Ibid., p. 320

Chapter 2 - The Early Years (1485 – 1509)

1. Oxford Dictionary of National Biography – Charles Brandon
2. Doran 2009, p. 84
3. Wilson 2009, p. 9
4. Baldwin 2015, 30
5. Breverton 2014, Chapter 28
6. Ibid., Chapter 22
7. Wilson 2009, p. 48
8. Loades 2012, p. 118
9. Oxford Dictionary of National Biography – Charles Brandon
10. Skidmore 2013, p. 187
11. Ibid., p. 197

12. Oxford Dictionary of National Biography – Thomas Brandon
13. Ibid.
14. Ibid.
15. The National Archives Currency Converter
16. Oxford Dictionary of National Biography – Thomas Brandon
17. Ibid.
18. Ibid.
19. Hall 1809, p. 41
20. Oxford Dictionary of National Biography – Charles Brandon
21. Loades 2012, p. 119
22. Oxford Dictionary of National Biography – Charles Brandon
23. Loades 2012, p. 119
24. Oxford Dictionary of National Biography – Charles Brandon
25. Penn 2011, p. 171
26. Hutchinson 2011, p. 95
27. Wilson 2009, p. 85
28. Richardson 2011 p. 369
29. The National Archives Currency Converter
30. Letters & Papers Vol. 4, 5859
31. Sadlack 2011, 396
32. Oxford Dictionary of National Biography – Charles Brandon
33. Ibid.
34. Taylor

Chapter 3 - Life at Court and a War with France (1509 – 1513)

1.   Penn 2011, p. 341
2.   Ibid., p. 341 - 345
3.   Letters & Papers Vol. 1, 20
4.   Weir 2008, p. 11
5.   Penn 2011
6.   Hutchinson 2011, p. 135
7.   Wilson 2009, p. 47
8.   Letters & Papers Vol. 1, 888, 1144
9.   Ibid., 1123 (65)
10. Baldwin 2015, p. 29
11. Ridgway 2015 - Catherine of Aragon suffers a still-birth
12. Letters & Papers Vol. 1, 353
13. Gunn 2015, p. 17
14. The National Archives Currency Converter
15. Oxford Dictionary of National Biography – Thomas Brandon

16. Ibid.
17. Ridgway 2012 - Birth of Henry, Duke of Cornwall
18. Hutchinson 2011, p. 153
19. Hall 1904, p. 24
20. Ibid., p. 25
21. Ibid., p. 25
22. Ridgway 2015 - Catherine of Aragon suffers a still-birth
23. Johnson 1969, p. 70
24. Loades 2012, p. 122
25. The National Archives Currency Converter
26. Ibid.
27. Gunn 2015, p. 30
28. Loades 2012, p. 122
29. Wilson 2009, p. 62
30. Ibid., p. 63
31. Ibid., p. 668
32. Loades 2012, p. 120
33. Hutchinson 2011, p. 160
34. Wilson 2009, p. 69
35. Ibid., p. 670 - 71
36. Doran 2008, p. 94
37. Gunn 2015, p. 28
38. Oxford Dictionary of National Biography – Charles Brandon
39. Ridgway 2012 - The Birth of Margaret of Austria
40. Letters & Papers Vol. 1, 2941
41. Ibid., 2941
42. Hutchinson 2011, p. 181
43. Letters & Papers Vol. 1, 2941
44. Wilson 2009, p. 85
45. Letters & Papers Vol. 1, 2701
46. Wilson 2009, p. 85
47. Velde 2014
48. Royal Collection Trust 2015
49. The Royal Household 2015
50. Ibid.
51. A copy of Brandon's plate can be seen at the Royal Collection online. http://www.royalcollection.org.uk/microsites/knightsofthegarter/MicroObject.asp?row=8&themeid=456&item=9
52. Oxford Dictionary of National Biography – Charles Brandon
53. Perry 2002, p. 122
54. Gunn 2015, p. 31
55. The National Archives Currency Converter

56. Ibid.
57. Letters & Papers Vol. 1, 25370
58. Ibid., 1947
59. Nichols 1846, p. 71

Chapter 4 - The Duke and the French Queen (1514 – 1515)

1. Letters & Papers Vol. 1, 2620
2. Hutchinson 2009, p. 2
3. Ibid., p. 6
4. Ibid., p. 7
5. Ibid., p. 13
6. Oxford Dictionary of National Biography – Charles Brandon
7. The National Archives Currency Converter
8. Weir 2008, p. 103
9. Ibid., p.98
10. Letters & Papers Vol. 1, 2617
11. The National Archives Currency Converter
12. Letters & Papers Vol. 1, 2684
13. The National Archives Currency Converter
14. Letters & Papers Vol. 1, 2679
15. Loades 2012, p. 45
16. Ibid., p. 46
17. Ibid., p. 47
18. Sadlack 2011, p. 109
19. Perry 2002, p. 70
20. Ackroyd 2012, p. 1
21. Wilson 2009, p. 62
22. Loades 2012, p. 64
23. Hutchinson 2011, p. 186
24. Perry 2002, p. 123
25. Letters & Papers Vol. 1, 3101
26. Perry 2002, p 126
27. Letters & Papers Vol. 1, 3146
28. Hutchinson 2011, p. 187 - 189
29. The National Archives Currency Converter
30. Loades 2012, p. 76
31. Ibid., p. 77
32. Bunbury 1844, p. 16
33. Loades 2012, p. 78
34. Sadlack 2011, p. 208 - 209

35.   Loades 2012, p. 81 - 82
36.   Letters & Papers Vol. 1, 3376
37.   Hutchinson 2011, p. 190
38.   Ibid., p. 191
39.   Loades 2012, p. 85
40.   Ibid., p. 95
41.   Letters & Papers Vol. 1, 3580
42.   Loades 2012, p. 95
43.   Letters & Papers Vol. 1, 3387
44.   Norton 2013, p. 124
45.   Wilson 2009, p. 47
46.   Perry 2002, p. 147
47.   Letters & Papers Vol. 1, 3429
48.   Perry 2002, p. 149
49.   Letters & Papers Vol. 1, 3461
50.   Loades 2012, p. 92
51.   Ibid., p. 93
52.   Perry 2002, p. 149
53.   Ibid., p. 150
54.   Sadlack 2011, p. 245
55.   Ibid.
56.   Loades 2012, p. 96
57.   Hutchinson 2011, p. 192
58.   Perry 2002, p. 152
59.   Loades 2012, p. 101
60.   Licence 2014, p. 115
61.   Loades 2012, p. 102
62.   Ibid., p. 111
63.   Sadlack 2011, p. 237 - 238
64.   Loades 2012, p. 103
65.   Sadlack 2011, p. 263
66.   Loades 2012, p. 103 - 104
67.   Perry 2002, p. 155
68.   Ibid., p. 155 - 156
69.   Harris 1989, p. 77
70.   Loades 2012, p. 114
71.   Letters & Papers Vol. 2, 222
72.   Loades 2012, p. 114
73.   Letters & Papers Vol. 2, 224
74.   Ibid., 227
75.   Sadlack 2011, p. 288
76.   Letters & Papers Vol. 2, 225
77.   Ibid., 367

78.   Gunn 2015, p. 44
79.   Sadlack 2011, p. 302
80.   Loades 2012, p. 117
81.   The National Archives Currency Converter
82.   Ibid.
83.   Letters & Papers Vol. 2, 436
84.   Loades 2012, p. 117
85.   The National Archives Currency Converter
86.   Loades 2012, p. 117
87.   The National Archives Currency Converter
88.   Loades 2012, p. 127
89.   Letters & Papers Vol. 1, 134
90.   The National Archives Currency Converter
91.   Letters & Papers Vol. 3, 2856
92.   Gunn 2015, p. 85
93.   The National Archives Currency Converter
94.   Gunn 2015, p. 47
95.   Loades 2012, p. 128
96.   Ibid., p. 171
97.   Letters & Papers Vol. 4, 3760
98.   Loades 2012, p. 129

Chapter 5 - The King's Man (1516 – 1532)

1.   Sadlack 2011, p. 353
2.   Letters & Papers Vol. 2, 1652
3.   Loades 2012, p. 157
4.   Letters & Papers Vol. 4, 5859
5.   Letters & Papers Vol. 2, 1935
6.   Loades 2012, p. 158
7.   Letters & Papers Vol. 2, 1935
8.   Ibid., 2170
9.   Ibid., 2347
10.   Loades 2012, p. 135
11.   Oxford Dictionary of National Biography – Charles Brandon
12.   Sadlack 2011, p. 355
13.   Loades 2012, p. 163
14.   Sadlack 2011, p. 356
15.   Wilson 2009, p. 117
16.   Ibid., p.117
17.   Ibid., p. 121
18.   Ibid., p.108
19.   Doran 2008, p. 114

20.   Loades 2011, p. 112
21.   Wilson 2009, p. 122
22.   Sadlack 2011, p. 344
23.   Ibid., p. 344
24.   Letters & Papers Vol. 3, 869.
25.   Wilson 2009, p. 123
26.   Sadlack 2011, p. 350
27.   A design for the pavilion can be seen in David Starkey's "Man &
       Monarch Henry VIII" edited by Susan Doran.
28.   Starkey 2009, p. 94
29.   Loades 2011, p. 113
30.   Gunn 2015, p. 60
31.   Wilson 2009, p. 122
32.   Letters & Papers Vol. 3, 906
33.   Wilson 2009, p. 124
34.   Ibid., p. 124
35.   Loades 2012, p. 164
36.   Ibid., p. 164
37.   Oxford Dictionary of National Biography – Charles Brandon
38.   Loades 2012, p. 164
39.   The National Archives Currency Converter
40.   Letters & Papers Vol. 2, 529
41.   Richardson 2011, p. 372
42.   Emerson 2015
43.   The National Archives Currency Converter
44.   Ibid.
45.   Gunn 2015, p. 126
46.   Harris 2002, p 78
47.   Letters & Papers Vol. 7, 1187
48.   Oxford Dictionary of National Biography – Charles Brandon
49.   The National Archives Currency Converter
50.   Ridgway 2015 - Catherine of Aragon suffers a still-birth
51.   Licence 2014, p. 115
52.   Hart 2009, p. 45
53.   Letters & Papers Vol. 4, 1431
54.   Weir 2008, p. 103
55.   Hall 1809, 263 - 264
56.   Wriothesley 1875, p. 13
57.   Wilson 2009, p. 124
58.   The National Archives Currency Converter
59.   Loades 2012, p. 132
60.   Letters & Papers Vol. 1, 3429
61.   Gunn 2015, p. 67

62.   Letters & Papers Vol. 3 3281
63.   Wilson 2009, p. 141
64.   Letters & Papers Vol 3, 3288
65.   Loades 2011, p. 172
66.   Oxford Dictionary of National Biography – Charles Brandon, Gunn 2015
67.   Loades 2012, p. 150
68.   Oxford Dictionary of National Biography – Charles Brandon
69.   Wilson 2009, p. 141
70.   Ibid., p. 141
71.   Loades 2011, p. 172
72.   Ibid., p. 172 - 173
73.   Loades 2011, p. 173
74.   Wooding 2015, p. 121
75.   Ibid., p. 121
76.   MacCulloch 1995, p. 45
77.   The National Archives Currency Converter
78.   All Kinds of History 2014
79.   Kadouchkine 2014
80.   The National Archives Currency Converter
81.   Wooding 2015, p. 122
82.   The National Archives Currency Converter
83.   Ibid.
84.   MacCulloch 1995, p. 45
85.   The National Archives Currency Converter
86.   All Kinds of History 2014
87.   Wilson 2009, p 144
88.   MacCulloch 1995, p. 45
89.   Wilson 2009, p. 144
90.   All Kinds of History 2014
91.   Staging the Henrician Court 2015
92.   Ibid.
93.   Betteridge & Freeman 2012
94.   Kadouchkine 2014
95.   Wilson 2009, p. 145
96.   Hall 1809, p. 674
97.   Loades 2012, p. 168
98.   Ibid., p. 168 - 169
99.   Full name: *The Ninety-Five Theses on the Power and Efficacy of Indulgences or Disputatio pro declaratione virtutis indulgentiarum*
100. Ridgway 2012 - Martin Luther and Anne Boleyn
101. Wilson 2009, p. 112
102. Ridgway 2015 - Catherine of Aragon suffers a still-birth

103.   Loades 2011, p. 192
104.   Ives 2005, p. 96
105.   Fraser 2002, p. 181
106.   Letters & Papers Vol. 4, 4851, 4857
107.   Ives 2005, p. 96
108.   Weir 1991, p. 204.
109.   Ibid., p. 204
110.   Ives 2005, p. 114
111.   Calendar of State Papers Spain Vol 3 Part 2, 1527-1529, 621
112.   Letters & Papers Vol. 4, 5535, 5547
113.   Ibid., 5597, 5598
114.   Ibid., 5635
115.   Ibid., 5733
116.   Fraser 2002, p. 204
117.   Ibid., p. 204
118.   Du Bellay, i. 115
119.   Calendar of State Papers, Venice Vol. 4, 694
120.   Ridgway & Cherry 2014, p. 106
121.   The National Archives Currency Converter
122.   Ridgway & Cherry 2014, p. 107 - 108
123.   Letters & Papers Vol. 12, Part 2, 998
124.   World Heritage Encyclopaedia – Arthur Bulkeley
125.   Letters & Papers Vol. 8, 894
126.   Oxford Dictionary of National Biography – Charles Brandon
127.   Baldwin 2015, p. 67
128.   Weir 2008, p. 467.
129.   Loades 2012, p. 178
130.   Hume 1905, p. 137
131.   Letters & Papers, Vol. 5, 340
132.   Ibid., 287
133.   Calendar of State Papers, Venice, Vol. 4, 761
134.   Letters & Papers Vol. 7, 1498, 37
135.   Letters & Papers Vol. 6, 415
136.   Loades 2012, p. 182
137.   Ibid., p. 179 - 181
138.   The National Archives Currency Converter
139.   Ibid.
140.   Ibid.
141.   Ibid.
142.   Ibid.
143.   Loades 2012, p. 132
144.   Ibid., p. 137
145.   The National Archives Currency Converter

146. Ibid.
147. Loades 2012, p. 131 - 132
148. Gunn 2015, p. 90
149. The National Archives Currency Converter
150. Letters & Papers Vol. 2, 436
151. The National Archives Currency Converter
152. Gunn 2015, p. 68
153. The National Archives Currency Converter
154. Loades 2012, p. 138 - 139
155. Wodderspoon 1839, p. 61
156. The National Archives Currency Converter
157. Oxford Dictionary of National Biography – Charles Brandon
158. Wodderspoon 1839, p. 61 - 62
159. De Worde 1884, p. 15
160. Velde 2014

Chapter 6 - The Tempestuous Years (1533 – 1535)

1.   Chapman 1974, p. 122
2.   Letters & Papers Vol. 6, 324
3.   Ibid., 759
4.   Ibid., 780
5.   Ibid., 1541
6.   Weir 1991, p. 262 - 263
7.   Letters & Papers Vol. 6, 1541
8.   Weir 1991, p. 262 - 263
9.   Ibid., p. 263
10. Perry 2002, p. 267
11. Ridgway 2012, p. 181
12. Ibid., p. 249
13. Letters & Papers Vol. 6, 548
14. Ibid., 601
15. Ridgway 2012, p. 146 - 147
16. Letters & Papers Vol. 7, 391
17. Sadlack 2011, p. 403
18. Loades 2012, p. 187
19. Letters & Papers Vol. 6, 693
20. Loades 2012, p. 188
21. Sadlack 2011, p. 406
22. Loades 2012, p. 189
23. Ibid., p. 190
24. Sadlack 2011, p. 407 - 408
25. Loades 2012, p. 191

26.   Ibid., p. 191 - 192
27.   The National Archives Currency Converter
28.   Loades 2012, p. 192
29.   The National Archives Currency Converter
30.   Baldwin 2015, p. 23
31.   Oxford Dictionary of National Biography – Charles Brandon
32.   Ives 2005, p. 18
33.   Letters & Papers Vol. 2, 529
34.   Wilkinson 2010, p. 115
35.   Baldwin 2015, p. 40
36.   Ibid., p. 40
37.   Letters & Papers Vol. 6, 1069
38.   Ridgway 2012 p. 418 - 419
39.   Letters & Papers Vol. 6, 1111
40.   Baldwin 2015, p. 28 - 29
41.   Ibid., p. 45
42.   The National Archives Currency Converter
43.   Letters & Papers Vol. 15, 942, 52
44.   Letters & Papers Vol. 9, 1063
45.   The National Archives Currency Converter
46.   Ibid.
47.   Ibid.
48.   Ibid.
49.   Loades 2012, p. 193
50.   Letters & Papers Vol. 9, 437
51.   The National Archives Currency Converter
52.   Loades 2012, p. 194
53.   Letters & Papers Vol. 7, 281
54.   Weir 2008, p. 349
55.   Letters & Papers Vol. 9, 386
56.   Baldwin 2015, p. 42
57.   Ibid., p. 42
58.   The National Archives Currency Converter
59.   Letters & Papers Vol. 9, 217
60.   Letters & Papers Vol. 7, 882
61.   Letters & Papers Vol. 9, 178, 301

Chapter 7 - Rebellion (1536 – 1537)

1.   Fraser 2002, p. 281
2.   Mackay 2014, p. 153
3.   Ibid., p. 156
4.   Letters & Papers Vol. 10, 200

5.   Inside the Body of Henry VIII
6.   Ibid.
7.   Lipscomb 2009, p. 61
8.   Norton 2013, p. 184
9.   Letters & Papers Vol. 10, 282
10. Baldwin p. 46
11. Letters & Papers Vol. 10, 243
12. Chilvers 2010, p. 16
13. Suffolk Place and The Mint
14. York House
15. Ives 2005, p. 308 - 309
16. Fraser 2002, p. 287 – 291
17. Weir 2009, p. 89 – 92, Letters & Papers Vol. 10, 876
18. Weir 2009, p. 132 - 137
19. Letters & Papers Vol. 10, 876
20. Ibid., 848
21. Weir 2009, p. 196 - 197
22. Letters & Papers Vol. 10, 876
23. Weir 2009, p. 212 - 213
24. Ibid., p. 213
25. Ibid.
26. Ibid., p. 215
27. Ibid., p. 218
28. Ibid.
29. Ibid., p. 219 – 220
30. Ibid., p. 220
31. Fraser 2002, p. 309 - 311
32. Weir 2009, p. 241
33. Ibid., p. 241 - 245
34. Ibid., p. 234
35. Letters & Papers Vol. 10, 896
36. Weir 2009, p. 261
37. Ibid., p. 264
38. Ibid., p. 266
39. Ibid.
40. Ibid., p. 266 – 267
41. Ibid., pg 270
42. Ibid., p. 271
43. The National Archives Currency Converter
44. Gunn 2015, p. 135
45. Fraser 2002 p. 317
46. Ibid., p. 329
47. Oxford Dictionary of National Biography – Henry Fitzroy

48.   Ibid.
49.   Lipscomb 2009, p. 150
50.   Ridgway 2013 – The Pilgrimage of Grace
51.   Ridgway 2011 - The Lincolnshire Rising and Trouble at Horncastle
52.   Ridgway 2013 – The Pilgrimage of Grace
53.   Lipscomb 2009, p. 151
54.   Ridgway 2011 - The Lincolnshire Rising and Trouble at Horncastle
55.   Letters & Papers Vol. 11, 615
56.   Ibid., 656
57.   Ibid., 672
58.   Ridgway 2013 – The Pilgrimage of Grace
59.   Letters & Papers Vol. 11, 717
60.   Ibid., 721
61.   Ibid., 939
62.   Lipscomb 2009, p. 152
63.   Ibid., p. 153
64.   Letters & Papers Vol. 11, 759
65.   Ibid., 764
66.   Ibid., 780
67.   Ridgway 2013 – The Pilgrimage of Grace
68.   Lipscomb 2009, p. 153
69.   Letters & Papers Vol. 11, 780
70.   Ibid., 1103
71.   Ibid., 1155, 5
72.   Ibid., 764, 1103
73.   Ridgway 2013 – The Pilgrimage of Grace
74.   Letters & Papers Vol. 11. 1235
75.   Ibid., 1236
76.   Lipscomb 2009, p. 164
77.   Ibid., p. 165
78.   Kesselring 2002, p. 601
79.   Bernard 2007, p. 402
80.   Surdhar 2013
81.   Letters & Papers Vol. 12, Part 1, 424
82.   Letters & Papers Vol. 11, 1238
83.   Letters & Papers Vol. 14, 1103
84.   Letters & Papers Vol. 14, 1103
85.   Letters & Papers Vol. 12, Part 1, 1284
86.   Baldwin 2015, p. 52
87.   Ibid., p. 204
88.   Chilvers 2010, p. 35
89.   The National Archives Currency Converter
90.   Letters & Papers Vol. 13, Part 1, 1349, 1329

91.   Letters & Papers Vol. 13, Part 2, 1182, 18; Letters & Papers Vol. 14, Part 1, 651, 45
92.   Gunn 2015, p. 159
93.   Ibid., p. 157
94.   The National Archives Currency Converter
95.   Ibid.
96.   Gunn 2015, p. 159
97.   Ibid., p. 145
98.   Letters & Papers Vol. 12, Part 1, 364
99.   Ibid., 318
100.   Letters & Papers Vol 13, Part 2, 6, 57
101.   Richardson 2011, p 372
102.   Urban 1803, p. 528
103.   Burke 1833, p. 36
104.   Licence 2014, p. 288
105.   Letters & Papers Vol. 12, Part 2, 911
106.   Ibid., 911
107.   Licence 2014, p. 288 - 289
108.   Brigden 2001

Chapter 8 - Final Years (1538 – 1545)

1.   Brimacombe 2004, p. 81
2.   Brady 1876, p 493
3.   Letters & Papers Vol. 13, Part 1, 642; Part 2, 1118, 1119, 1182, 20, 21, 27; Vol. 14, Part 1, 191, 27, 28, 359, 651, 48, 1018
4.   The National Archives Currency Converter
5.   Letters & Papers Vol. 14, Part 1, 1018
6.   Ibid., 651, 38
7.   Binyon 1900, p. 335 - 336
8.   Chilvers 2010, p. 19
9.   House of Lords Precedence Act 1539
10.   Lehmberg 1977, p. 102
11.   Records of the Lord Steward, the Board of Green Cloth and other officers of the Royal Household
12.   Ibid.
13.   Gunn 2015, p. 167
14.   Weir 1991, p. 377
15.   Ibid., p. 381
16.   Licence 2014, p. 298
17.   Weir 1991, p. 384
18.   Weir 1994, p. 385
19.   Ibid., p. 389

20.   Ibid., p. 390
21.   Ibid., p. 392
22.   Letters and Papers Vol. 14, Part 2, 754
23.   Ibid.
24.   Licence 2014, p. 308
25.   Doran 2008, p. 180
26.   Starkey 2004, p. 630
27.   Ibid., p. 638.
28.   Letters & Papers Vol. 9, 386
29.   Letters & Papers Vol. 15, 860
30.   Loades 2010, p. 117
31.   Letters & Papers Vol. 15, 845
32.   Ibid., 872
33.   Ibid., 898, 908
34.   Ibid., 991
35.   Starkey 2004, p. 642
36.   Ibid., p. 644
37.   Ibid., p. 647
38.   Licence 2014, p. 318
39.   Ibid., p. 326
40.   Ibid., p. 327
41.   Ibid., p. 334
42.   Ibid., p. 335
43.   Letters & Papers Vol. 16, 961
44.   Gunn, 2015, p. 200
45.   Chilvers 2010, p. 19
46.   Licence 2014, p. 336
47.   Ibid., p. 337
48.   Baldwin, 2015 p. 61
49.   Letters & Papers Vol. 16, 1414, 1422, 1426
50.   Licence 2014, p. 339 - 340
51.   Calendar of State Papers, Spain, Vol. 6, 232
52.   Baldwin Smith 2008, p. 187
53.   Letters & Papers Vol. 17, 124
54.   Richardson 2011, p. 372
55.   Harbison 2014
56.   Hutchinson 2006, p. 104
57.   Letters & Papers Vol. 18, Part 1, 224
58.   Ibid., 814, 884,
59.   Ibid., 962
60.   Ibid., 96, 109, 152, 172, 186
61.   Wilson 2009, p. 315
62.   Letters & Papers Vol. 18, Part 1, 836

63. Ibid., 836
64. Wilson 2009, p. 315
65. Bain 1890, p. 64
66. Ibid., p. 266
67. Letters & Papers Vol. 19, Part 1, 314
68. Hutchinson 2006, p. 105
69. Wilson 2009, p. 318
70. Ibid., p. 324
71. Letters & Papers Vol. 19, Part 2, 222
72. Letters & Papers Vol. 19, Part 1, 694
73. Hutchinson 2006, p. 110
74. Nichols & Bruce 1863, p. 28
75. Ibid.
76. Ibid.
77. Ibid.
78. Ibid.
79. Ibid., p. 29
80. Ibid., p. 34
81. Ibid., p. 29
82. Ibid., p. 33
83. Ibid., p. 29
84. Ibid., p. 30
85. Ibid.
86. Ibid., p. 31
87. Emerson 2015
88. Nichols & Bruce 1863, p. 33
89. Ibid., p. 34
90. Ibid., p. 37
91. Ibid., p. 38
92. Ibid., p. 39
93. Ibid., p. 41
94. Wilson 2009, p. 325
95. Letters & Papers Vol. 19, Part 1, 835
96. Hutchinson 2006, p. 111
97. Letters & Papers Vol. 19, Part 1, 949
98. Gunn 2015, p. 178
99. Letters & Papers Vol. 19, Part 2, 222
100. Hutchinson 2006, p. 112
101. Letters & Papers Vol. 19, Part 2, 424
102. Ibid., 378
103. Ibid., 483
104. Gunn 2015, p. 179
105. The National Archives Currency Converter

106.   Gunn 2015, p. 180
107.   Letters & Papers Vol. 20, Part 1, 846, 92
108.   Oxford Dictionary of National Biography Katherine [Kateryn, Catherine; née Katherine Parr]
109.   Baldwin 2015, p. 61
110.   Ibid., p. 75
111.   Letters & Papers Vol. 13, Part 1, 583
112.   Calendar of State Papers, Spain Vol. 8, 204
113.   Letters & Papers Vol. 17, 957
114.   Letters & Papers Vol. 21, Part 2, 417
115.   Ryrie 2008, pp. 21 - 22
116.   Letters & Papers Vol. 20, Part 2, 134, 140, 147, 156, 176
117.   Calander of State Papers, Spain, Vol. 8, 126
118.   Letters & Papers Vol, 20, Part 2, 176
119.   Ibid., 176
120.   Ibid., 197
121.   Wriothesley 1875, p. 160
122.   Hall 1809, p. 863
123.   Bodleian Library, MS Ashmole 1109, fo. 142v, 143r
124.   Ibid., fo. 143r, 143v, 144r
125.   Ibid., fo. 143r
126.   Ibid., fo. 143v
127.   Ibid., fo. 143v, 144r
128.   Ibid., fo. 144v, 145r
129.   Ibid., fo. 145r
130.   Ibid., fo. 145v
131.   Gunn 2015, p. 174
132.   Letters & Papers Vol. 18, Part 1, 536
133.   Ibid., 809, 957, 964
134.   Bodleian Library, MS Ashmole 1109, fo. 145v, 146r
135.   Hutchinson 2006, p. 119 and Weir 2008, p. 485
136.   Pote & Leake 1749, p. 367 - 368
137.   Hume 2013

Chapter 9 - Legacy

1.   Letters & Papers Vol. 20, Part 2, 598
2.   The National Archives Currency Converter
3.   Ibid.
4.   Ibid.
5.   Ibid.
6.   Gunn 2015, p. 191
7.   Oxford Dictionary of National Biography – Charles Brandon

8. The National Archives Currency Converter
9. Baldwin 2015, p. 63
10. Oxford Dictionary of National Biography – Charles Brandon
11. Ibid.
12. Trueman 2008
13. Baldwin 2015, p. 97
14. Ibid., p. 37
15. Oxford Dictionary of National Biography – Charles Brandon
16. Ridgway 2014
17. Baldwin p. 99
18. Wilson p 104 - 105
19. Oxford Dictionary of National Biography – Charles Brandon
20. Wilson 2009, p. 58 - 59
21. Letters & Papers Vol. 12, Part 2, 171
22. The National Archives Currency Converter
23. Richardson 2011, p. 371
24. Gunn 2015, p. 163
25. Emerson 2015
26. Richardson 2011, p. 371
27. Ibid., p. 372
28. Emerson 2015
29. Richardson 2011, p. 372
30. Perry 2002, p. 267
31. Oxford Dictionary of National Biography – Frances Brandon
32. Ibid.
33. The National Archives Currency Converter
34. Oxford Dictionary of National Biography – Frances Brandon
35. Richardson 2011, p. 168
36. de Lisle 2013, p. 259
37. Ibid., p. 273
38. Ibid., p 276
39. Oxford Dictionary of National Biography – Frances Brandon
40. de Lisle 2013, p. 283 - 284
41. Ibid., p.286
42. Oxford Dictionary of National Biography – Frances Brandon
43. Richardson 2011, p. 168;
    Oxford Dictionary of National Biography – Frances Brandon
44. Emmerson 2015
45. Weir 2008, p. 98
46. Merriam-Webster 2015
47. Medieval Lives: Birth, Marriage and Death
48. Licence 2014, p. 84
49. Wilson 2009, p. 157

50.   Letters and Papers Vol. 1 2941
51.   Merriam-Webster 2015
52.   Wilson 2009, p. 120
53.   Hutchinson 2006, p. 119
54.   Bernard 2007, p. 200

Chapter 10 - Appearance

1.   Fisher 2002, p. 20
2.   Encyclopaedia Britannica – Jean Perreal & Jean Clouet
3.   Fisher 2002, p 24
4.   Ibid., p. 24
5.   Ibid., p. 23
6.   Ibid., p. 23
7.   Hui 2013
8.   Ibid.
9.   Master of the Brandon Portrait
10.   Ibid.
11.   Christie & Masson 1838, p. 18
12.   National Portrait Gallery London
13.   Pennington 1982, p. xix & xxiv
14.   Velde 2014
15.   Hans, the Younger Holbein The Complete Works 2015
16.   The Art Institute of Chicago
17.   The National Archives Currency Converter
18.   Holbein: Eye of the Tudors 2015
19.   Doran 2008, p.118
20.   Davey 1911, p.43 – 44
21.   Ibid., p. 44
22.   Letter & Papers Vol. 1, 2171
23.   Benger 1822, p. 53
24.   Weir 2008, p. 98
25.   Letters & Papers Vol. 3, 402

Chapter 11 - Why was Charles Brandon so Successful?

1.   Loades 2012, p. 121
2.   Letters & Papers Vol. 1, 2171
3.   Ibid., Preface
4.   Ibid.
5.   Benger 1822, p. 53

6.   History of Jousting
7.   Medieval Jousting Tournaments
8.   Medieval Rules for Jousting
9.   Hall 1809, p. 674
10.   Perry 2002, p. 150
11.   Levitt 2014
12.   Knapton 2014
13.   Wilson 2009, p. 49
14.   Levitt 2014
15.   Ibid.
16.   Ibid.
17.   Hutchinson 2009, p. 13
18.   Weir 2008, p. 103
19.   Loades 2012, p. 128 & 200
20.   Letters & Papers Vol. 2, 367
21.   Letters & Papers Vol. 1, 2620
22.   Knight 1840, p. 232
23.   Letters & Papers Vol. 9, 386
24.   Loades 2012, p. 180
25.   Weir 2008, p. 485
26.   Hutchinson 2006, p. 119
27.   Bayani 2014, p. 217
28.   Knight 1840, p.231
29.   Granger 1824, p. 104

Index

A

C

D

E

F

Meet Sarah Bryson

Sarah Bryson is a researcher, writer and educator who has a Bachelor of Early Childhood Education with Honours. She currently works with children with disabilities. She is passionate about Tudor history and has a deep interest in Mary Boleyn, Charles Brandon, the reign of Henry VIII and the people of his court. She is the author of *Mary Boleyn in a Nutshell* and *Charles Brandon: The King's Man*.

Visiting England in 2009 furthered her passion and when she returned home she started a website, queentohistory.com, and a Facebook page about Tudor history. Sarah lives in Australia, enjoys reading, writing and Tudor costume enactment, and wishes to return to England one day.

ISBN: 978-84-943721-1-7

Mary
Boleyn
in a nutshell

History
"In a Nutshell"
Series

SARAH BRYSON

In **Mary Boleyn in a Nutshell**, **Sarah Bryson** discusses the controversies surrounding Mary Boleyn's birth, her alleged relationships with two kings, her portraiture and appearance, and her life and death. Mary survived the brutal events of 1536 and was able to make her own choices, defying the social rules of her times by marrying for love. It is from Mary that the Boleyn bloodline extends to the present day.

Thomas Cranmer
in a nutshell

History
"In a Nutshell"
Series

BETH VON STAATS

ISBN: 978-84-943721-3-1

In **Thomas Cranmer in a Nutshell**, **Beth von Staats** discusses the fascinating life of **Thomas Cranmer**, from his early education, through his appointment to Archbishop of Canterbury, his growth in confidence as a reformer, the writing of two versions of the English Book of Common Prayer and eventually to his imprisonment, recantations and execution.

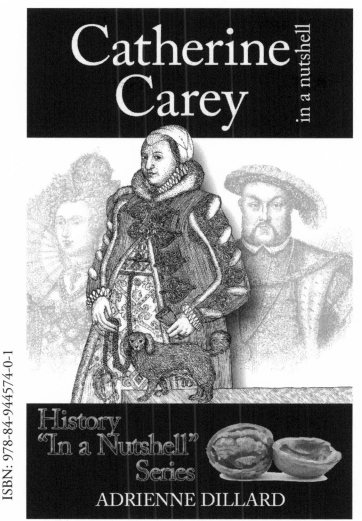

Catherine Carey
in a nutshell

History
"In a Nutshell"
Series

ADRIENNE DILLARD

ISBN: 978-84-944574-0-1

Catherine Carey in a Nutshell examines the life of Catherine Carey, daughter of Mary Boleyn, from the controversy surrounding her paternity through her service to Henry VIII's queens, the trials of life in Protestant exile during the Tudor era, and the triumphant return of the Knollys family to the glittering court of the Virgin Queen. This book brings together what is known about one of Queen Elizabeth I's most trusted and devoted ladies for the first time in one concise, easy-to-read book.

Sweating Sickness
in a nutshell

ISBN: 978-15-009962-2-2

History
"In a Nutshell"
Series

CLAIRE RIDGWAY

In **Sweating Sickness in a Nutshell**, **Claire Ridgway** examines what the historical sources say about the five epidemics of the mystery disease which hit England between 1485 and 1551, and considers the symptoms, who it affected, the treatments, theories regarding its cause and why it only affected English people.

ISBN: 978-84-944574-2-5

Henry VIII's Health
in a nutshell

History "In a Nutshell" Series

KYRA KRAMER

Tudor histories are rife with "facts" about Henry VIII's life and health, but as a medical anthropologist, Kyra Kramer, author of Blood Will Tell, has learned one should never take those "facts" at face value. In **Henry VIII's Health in a Nutshell**, Kramer highlights the various health issues that Henry suffered throughout his life and proposes a few new theories for their causes, based on modern medical findings.

Known for her readability and excellent grasp of the intricacies of modern medical diagnostics, Kyra Kramer gives the reader a new understanding of Henry VIII's health difficulties, and provides new insights into their possible causes.

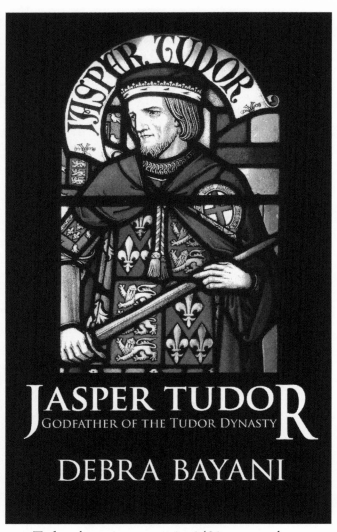

ISBN: 978-84-943721-0-0

Jasper Tudor, born in secrecy in 1431, rose to become one of the key supporters of King Henry VI during the difficult period of English history known as the Wars of the Roses. Devoted to the Lancastrian cause and to his nephew Henry Tudor, Jasper's loyalty led him through a life full of adventure.

In this detailed biography, Debra Bayani clearly shows that Jasper Tudor was a key figure in the tumultuous history of England, detailing his life from his birth in 1431 to his death in 1495. He can rightly be called the "Godfather of the Tudor Dynasty".

GEORGE BOLEYN

TUDOR POET, COURTIER & DIPLOMAT

CLARE CHERRY & CLAIRE RIDGWAY

ISBN: 978-84-937464-5-2

George Boleyn has gone down in history as being the brother of the ill-fated Queen Anne Boleyn (second wife of Henry VIII) and for being executed for treason, after being found guilty of incest and of conspiring to kill the King.

This balanced biography allows George to step out of the shadows and brings him to life as a court poet, royal favourite, keen sportsman, talented diplomat and loyal brother. Clare Cherry and Claire Ridgway chart his life from his spectacular rise in the 1520s to his dramatic fall and tragic end in 1536.

Non Fiction History

Anne Boleyn's Letter from the Tower - **Sandra Vasoli**
Jasper Tudor - **Debra Bayani**
Tudor Places of Great Britain - **Claire Ridgway**
Illustrated Kings and Queens of England - **Claire Ridgway**
A History of the English Monarchy - **Gareth Russell**
The Fall of Anne Boleyn - **Claire Ridgway**
George Boleyn: Tudor Poet, Courtier & Diplomat - **Ridgway & Cherry**
The Anne Boleyn Collection - **Claire Ridgway**
The Anne Boleyn Collection II - **Claire Ridgway**
Two Gentleman Poets at the Court of Henry VIII - **Edmond Bapst**
A Mountain Road - **Douglas Weddell Thompson**

"History in a Nutshell Series"

Sweating Sickness in a Nutshell - **Claire Ridgway**
Mary Boleyn in a Nutshell - **Sarah Bryson**
Thomas Cranmer in a Nutshell - **Beth von Staats**
Henry VIII's Health in a Nutshell - **Kyra Kramer**
Catherine Carey in a Nutshell - **Adrienne Dillard**
The Pyramids in a Nutshell - **Charlotte Booth**

Historical Fiction

Struck with the Dart of Love: Je Anne Boleyn 1 - **Sandra Vasoli**
Truth Endures: Je Anne Boleyn 2 - **Sandra Vasoli**
The Colour of Poison - **Toni Mount**
Between Two Kings: A Novel of Anne Boleyn - **Olivia Longueville**
Phoenix Rising - **Hunter S. Jones**
Cor Rotto - **Adrienne Dillard**
The Claimant - **Simon Anderson**
The Truth of the Line - **Melanie V. Taylor**

Children's Books

All about Richard III - **Amy Licence**
All about Henry VII - **Amy Licence**
All about Henry VIII - **Amy Licence**
Tudor Tales William at Hampton Court - **Alan Wybrow**

PLEASE LEAVE A REVIEW

If you enjoyed this book, *please* leave a review at the book seller where
you purchased it. There is no better way to thank the author and it
really does make a huge difference!
Thank you in advance.

Printed in Great Britain
by Amazon